MY BOOK :- Robin Fabel 1995

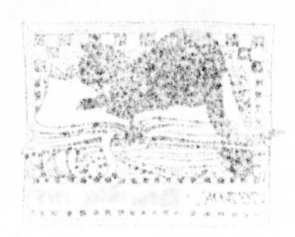

SPAIN: FORGOTTEN ALLY OF THE

AMERICAN REVOLUTION

SPAIN: FORGOTTEN ALLY
OF
THE AMERICAN REVOLUTION

By

BUCHANAN PARKER THOMSON

THE CHRISTOPHER PUBLISHING HOUSE
NORTH QUINCY, MASSACHUSETTS

PRINTED IN
THE UNITED STATES OF AMERICA

Dedicated to

My Daughter

Geraldine Buchanan Parker Deas

and My Son

Captain Austin Smith Parker

United States Marine Corps (Ret.)

(who grew up with this book)

PREFACE

Ask any American, with the exception of the trained historian, "What do you know of the aid given by Spain to the United States in its struggle for independence during the Revolutionary War?" The answer will be short and instantaneous: "Nothing! I never knew that Spain gave us any assistance during our Revolutionary War." Ask the same question of many students of American history and the answer will be the same.

Having asked this question of hundreds of Americans over the past fifteen years, the correct answer to it became a personal quest, first to be pursued through the published and unpublished records available in the Great Valley of the Mississippi, all the way from the Great Lakes to New Orleans; the materials to be found in the Carolinas, Georgia, Florida and Virginia; the collections of the Ohio Valley and the Illinois; the files of documents in Philadelphia and New York; and, at last, through that mother-lode of research, the Library of Congress.

On the premise that the whole story of any military and diplomatic struggle cannot be found in the archives and libraries of one country alone, the quest led directly to the magnificent Archivos and Bibliotecas of Spain. It is in the reading salons of the ancient Archivo de Indias in Seville, the Biblioteca Nacional and the Biblioteca del Consejo Superior de Investigaciones Cientificas of Madrid, in the Alcazar de Segovia, depository of the multitude of military records, and in the isolated quiet of the great Archivo General de Simancas that the story of Spanish aid to the American Colonists finds its completion.

A compelling sense of the continuity of Spain's long history is brought home to the investigator in that great Castillo, the Archivo General de Simancas, once the home of Isabel and Ferdinand, "Los Reyes Catolicos," situated in lonely grandeur high above the river Pisuerga on the plateau of Castile, midway between the distinguished Universities of Valladolid and Salamanca. From the thousands of military reports, personal letters and official documents to be found there, the story of aid to the Colonists may be reconstructed.

In the long quest, two years were spent in a painstaking search, not only for the diplomatic and governmental documents which would recreate the impersonal record, but also for those which would reveal

5

the more human and personal part played by youthful commanders on the field of action in North America.

On the further premise that the story of a war should be recorded, not only by means of the documents of Kings and Diplomats, but also by those of the forgotten young men who spent their blood and courage on the soil of America, this book attempts, in a small way, to take the reader from Europe to Louisiana and the Frontier of the South and West.

It is impossible to acknowledge the great debt owed to the hundreds of Spaniards and Americans who have graciously and freely given of their time and knowledge to the subject matter of this book. Throughout the long search one thing has been proven without question; there are no frontiers among Scholars; there are no frontiers in kindness and courtesy.

Added to recognition of the generosity of the erudite staffs invariably to be found in the Archivos and Bibliotecas of Spain there must also be paid a tribute to their humor and spontaneous wit, qualities not usually associated with the austerity customarily found within the purlieus of such cloistered walls of learning.

An especial acknowledgment must be made to Don Ricardo Magdaleno, Director of the Archivo General de Simancas and coauthor of the "*Catálogo de los Documentos de Inglaterra,*" and to Senorita Concepcion Alvarez Feran, Archivist, who, for six months painstakingly followed the process of these investigations; to the kindly advice of Don Luis de la Paz, assistant Director of the Archivo at Simancas; to Don José de la Peña, Director of the Archivo General de Indias, who inducted the author into the mysteries of the American Story from his austerely beautiful office in Seville; to the distinguished historian, Don Miguel Gomez del Campillo, author of the tremendous *Relaciones Diplomaticas Entre España y los Estados Unidos*, compiled from the documents of the "Archivo Historico Nacional" for the Biblioteca del Consejo Superior de Investigaciones Cientificas of Madrid; to Doña Mercedes Gaibrois de Ballesteros, Real Academia de la Historia, and to her son, Professor Manuel Ballesteros Gaibrois, whose Doctoral Thesis on Gardoqui has not yet been published; to J. Navarro Latorre, coauthor with F. Solano Costa of *Conspiracion Espanola?* for his excellent advice and concise collation of Spanish Authors; to Professor J. Ramon Barcelo, director of a division of the Consejo Superior of Madrid, whose courtesy resulted in a valuable sojourn in the University of Valladolid; to the Marques de Villa Alcazar, through whose personal interest the author received a Grant-in-Aid from the Del Amo Foundation of California, and the generous support of Señor Don Jaime del Amo, President of the Foundation set up by his family for aid in Spanish-American Studies; to the Honorable

James Dunn, United States Ambassador to Spain, whose personal interest opened the door to the completion of the research in Spain; to Professor John Reid, Cultural Attaché to the United States Embassy in Madrid and to Professor Max Savelle, Head of the Department of History at the University of Washington, whose encouragement through the long investigation was of great value.

To the innumerable Spanish friends who opened the doors of their homes to a stranger and fulfilled the ancient saying, "My house is Yours" to the letter; Rafael and Felisa de Sanchez Moreno, from their old house in the Calle Mayor; Doctor José and Manola Aznarez, from their quarters in the Avenida Borbolla across from the beautiful park of Maria Louisa in Seville; to the brilliant Matilde Medina, of "Radio España"; to the Staff of the University of Valladolid, from Professor Luis Suarez, its youthful Director of Studies for Strangers, and his gifted assistant, Federico Wattenberg; the genial Professor Alfredo Malo, down to the venerable "Crier of Classes," "La Hora"; to the "Botones," thirteen-year-old "Manuel"; and to "Sebastiana of Simancas" who looked after the well-being of her charges in the Residencia with a rod of iron and a tongue of honey.

Through all these, and hundreds of others, the spirit of Spain shines out in the full radiance of its courtesy and kindness.

To make acknowledgement, by name, to all those who, here in the United States, have been of great value to this study is impossible since it would run into many pages, but the work of three men must be mentioned with deep gratitude; John Walton Caughey, author of the definitive book *Bernardo de Galvez in Louisiana;* James Alton James, author of the splendid works, *Oliver Pollock* and *George Rogers Clark;* and to that great and distinguished Historian, Samuel Flagg Bemis, whose *Pinckney's Treaty* and *The Diplomacy of the American Revolution* are known throughout the world.

The author's final tribute must be paid to the detailed labor and meticulous editing of Robert Stanley Thomson, author of *Fondation de L'État Indépendant du Congo,* without whose limitless patience and astute criticism, this volume might never have been completed.

To all these, and many more, is due the deep gratitude of a searcher for the truth in this forgotten chapter of United States history.

For any mistakes that may be found the author pleads guilty, asking only that the reader generously remember that the only documents included within this book were selected from thousands with the express purpose of telling as concise a story as possible of the assistance rendered to the United States by Spain, our forgotten Ally, in the time of our greatest need.

B. P. T.

CONTENTS

SPAIN: FORGOTTEN ALLY OF THE

AMERICAN REVOLUTION

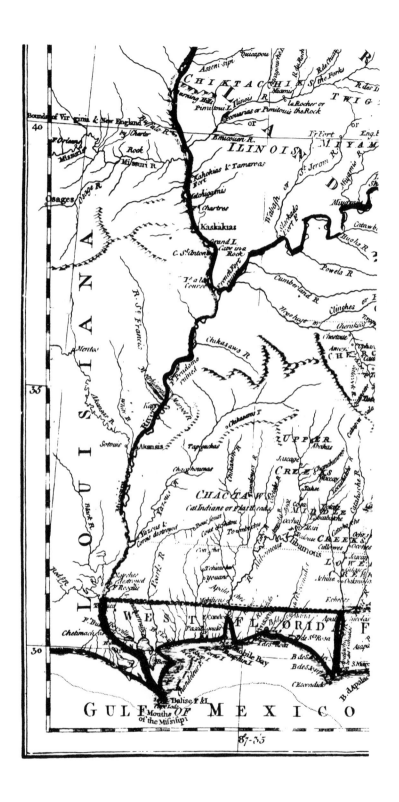

INTRODUCTION

Until the last quarter of the eighteenth century, Europe was very much the same old world it had been in the seventeenth. In 1775, the Hanoverian, George III, sat upon the throne of England; Carlos III, strongest of the Bourbon kings to occupy the throne of Spain, held court at San Ildefonso just outside Madrid; his nephew, Louis XVI, ruled in France from his palace at Versailles; Maria Theresa, shrewd daughter of Charles VI, was Empress of Austria; a onetime German princess reigned as Catherine II, Czarina of all the Russias. The theory of the divine right of kings was paramount throughout the world in the year 1775.

Internecine wars in which religious differences played an important part were, to be sure, a thing of the past, but wars in which the masses of the people were pawns in the game of power politics and dynastic ambition were still all too frequent. The economic factor, though present and at work beneath the surface, as in all ages of history, was not clearly recognized as a potent force in human destiny, as it has come to be today; overseas possessions existed for the glory and well-being of the mother countries. The Old World was still the center of gravity. So it came about that the British Colonies in North America became involved in wars with their colonial neighbors as they were drawn into quarrels originating in Europe.

Between the close of the Seven Years War, better known to Americans as the French and Indian War, in 1763, and the year 1775, something happened. The situation became reversed and England found herself engaged in a war that soon involved both Spain and France, which originated not in Europe but in the New World.

This is not the place to discuss the causes of the American Revolution. They were many and complex. Let it be recognized frankly that neither France nor Spain entered the struggle for the Independence of the American Colonies from pure altruism. Nations have always acted for reasons-of-state as they do to this day. But this is not to say that the participation of these two countries did not substantially contribute to the winning of Independence.

The story of the contribution of France has often been told. But what of the contribution of Spain? That story has been sadly and inexplicably neglected. It is the purpose of the present work to reveal that story dispassionately and objectively as it was unrolled in Spain itself and on the continent of North America. It is a story revealed in the actions and the testimony of Americans and Spaniards — traders, soldiers, diplomats, as well as simple citizens, both Spanish and American, who played their heroic roles and who are until this day forgotten heroes of a forgotten ally.

The complex forces which united to bring about an open break between the American Colonies and England were rising rapidly to a crescendo in the final quarter of the eighteenth century. By 1775, the rising wind of revolt reached hurricane velocity. As early as 1771, the Colonists along the Eastern seaboard were being irresistibly drawn closer to the vortex of the approaching storm. Their loyalties were being strained to the breaking point by the system of taxation foisted upon them by England to pay for the costly late war against the French.

The hated stamp tax on tea had already brought about the famous "Tea Parties" in Boston and Charleston Harbors. But in 1771, the "Regulators" made up of the men of the frontier in North Carolina, rose up in open angry rebellion against the oppressive measures of Governor William Tryon and there followed a pitched battle between the "Tidewater Men" led by the Governor and the frontiersmen. The "Regulators" were defeated but the widespread and deep-seated feeling of resentment, of which the rebellion was symptomatic, remained.

The men of the Colonies had fought side by side with the English troops in the French and Indian War. They had undergone the bitter and humiliating experience of taking orders from British commanders who knew nothing of frontier warfare. They had paid in their own blood while learning the tactics that were to stand them in good stead in the turbulent years ahead. The long and dreadful marches through forests, over rivers, and into the snows of Canada, had bred a confidence in the men of the Colonies along with a scornful distrust of British leadership. A certain young Major of Virginia, George Washington, had won his spurs as a leader in the frontier fighting.

The stormy petrel of Massachusetts, Samuel Adams, found his eloquence well-matched by the hothead, Patrick Henry, a future Governor of the Dominion; the canny wisdom of the great Benjamin Franklin was aligned in the same cause with the Pamphleteer Thomas Paine; the Rutledges, Laurenses and Pinckneys, of South Carolina were supping their madeira in the clubs and taverns along the harborfront of Charleston while anxiously discussing the news brought in by the latest "Packet" from Plymouth.

Women throughout the length and breadth of the Colonies, timidly or hotly, according to their station or inclination, discussed the terrible taxes over heavy mugs of tea in frontier cabins, or from delicate bone china in the Adam drawing rooms of the seaboard.

The wind of revolt was sweeping through the land from North to South, from the sea to the blue mountains and wide rivers of the frontier, and no man could see the end of it.

Across the water, in France, the Intellectuals, Rationalists and Romantics alike, were busy writing and discussing; sometimes in witty, sometimes in bitterly biting fashion, and coining for their own narrow circle, slogans which were later to become the slogans of a people. In the Salons of Paris these leaders set the tone and dominated the talk among the Intellectuals around the tables of the Coffeehouses of Paris as well as in the drawing rooms of the fashionable hostesses of the day.

Representing the more advanced press and theatre of the day was that remarkably clever and agile-minded playwright, author of the much discussed "Barber of Seville," onetime resident of Spain, nobleman by right of a purchased title, swashbuckling and colorful, possessor of many talents that were equalled only by flamboyant weaknesses, son of the watchmaker of Paris, Pierre Augustin Caron de Beaumarchais.

South of the barricade of the Pyrenees, the isolated provinces of Spain knew little of the news of the outside world. There were not so many papers and pamphlets to be read and discussed. Those of the cities were more interested at this time in printing what was happening in trade out of Bilbao, Cadiz and Barcelona. Although the loss of the French Colonies in North America was of much concern to the Court and to those who foregathered in the smart Tertulias, and Coffeehouses in the great Plaza Mayor of Madrid, the trend of international affairs did not filter down through all strata of society as in France, nor were the independent and insular people of Spain interested in activities outside their own provincial capitals and pueblos.

The loss of the French Empire in North America did not cause a ripple of anxiety in the remote regions of Extremadura or in Badajoz. The news did not disturb the distinguished quiet of the great Universities of Salamanca, Valladolid or Seville, although the talk might have taken the form of academic speculation as to the influence of the disaster upon the future politics of the French Court.

In a matter of a few short years, these same quiet speculations were to be replaced by a surprising fury of activity. Events in North America were to turn the pastoral province of Palencia into one vast weaving center to supply blankets for a fighting people across the seas. Burgos, ancient city of Castile, dreamed beside the quiet river Arlanzon, little knowing what part it was to play in the North-American drama.

In the purlieu of the Intellectuals of Madrid the fact that a colony called Louisiana had been ceded to Spain as compensation for her participation in the Seven Years War on the side of France created a feeling of righteous justification; Spain had faithfully lived up to the terms of the Bourbon Family Pact. There was mild speculation as to just how important that far-off colony might be in adding to the vast holdings of New Spain. It would form a barrier against further British expansion on the Gulf of Mexico and constitute a claim to equal control of the great Mississippi waterway.

It was bruited about among those who knew about such things that the American Colonists along the seaboard had proved themselves to be tough fighters against the French. They had proved themselves at Quebec and in the forests east of the Mississippi during battles with the savages of that region.

At San Ildefonso, King Carlos III looked upon the new colony of Louisiana as no great prize for all the money he had expended in behalf of the Family Pact. The cost of maintaining a government over so vast a territory, populated by Frenchmen, Mulattos, Negros and Indians would not be small; added to that would be the price of defending it.

The acquisition of New Orleans gave Spain a base from which she could protect the lines of communication between Cuba and Mexico, but this task would not be easy now that England was entrenched in both East and West Florida and the strategic gain would not offset the loss of the fur trade from Canada, formerly monopolized by the French. The information from the Indies, that there was a rising spirit of revolt among the British colonists to the north and east of Spain's holdings, was therefore eagerly received. Perhaps it might be wise to encourage such a revolt; a buffer state between Louisiana and Canada would be a welcome solution to Spain's problem.

The Americans, like the Spanish, understood the great rivers and forests. They had men who knew the country as far west and south as the Mexican border. They knew the ways of the Tribes. They were as accustomed to the trade along the Great River as the French. It might be a good plan to have the Minister of the Indies, José de Gálvez, Count of Sonora, (so named because of his fine work as Official Visitor for the Crown to New Spain) begin a close investigation of the state of the British Colonies. His nephew, young Bernardo de Gálvez, was known to have done excellent work in Northern Mexico against the troublesome Apaches. He, and others like him, might be able to get the information. Havana, where the trading vessels of the colonists were doing a vast business, could be made the intelligence center and become a listening post of great value.

Carlos III was keenly alive to the necessity of maintaining the Family Pact with Louis XVI although, up to this time, it had cost Spain dearly. On the other hand, the bitter blow to France in the loss of her American colonies made it even more necessary for her to work closely with Spain for the freedom of the seas in the interest of her commerce.

Carlos had chosen his Ambassador to Paris carefully, both for his experience as a suave man of the world, well able to hold his own in any social capacity amidst the highly volatile and explosive situations continually arising at the French Court, and for his ability and astuteness in handling delicate diplomatic affairs. His training from birth and his education made the Count de Aranda one of the most acute observers of the international political scene in the fast-changing kaleidoscope of European politics as well as a much sought-after gentleman of the drawing rooms and salons where the affairs of the world were often more freely discussed than in the chancelleries of the nations involved.

The Prime Minister at the Spanish Court, the Count de Grimaldi, had a keen knowledge of the dangers to Spain since the fall of France in North America, and feared the rising power of England on the high seas. His cautiousness in action on any matter that might bring down the wrath of the English navy and thus endanger the trade with the West Indies, was equal to that of the King. He was slow to act openly but, when the need arose, he could act discreetly and efficiently — a fact the Americans were later to learn when their need of help was great indeed.

José de Gálvez, Count of Sonora, was a man of another breed. As Minister of the Indies, he chafed under the caution of Grimaldi. Head of the famous family of Macharaviaya, near Malaga, long seated in Andalusia, a family of the oldest and purest blood in Spain, he had probably the widest knowledge of any man in the country concerning affairs in North America and the West Indies.

Together with Aranda and Grimaldi, later to be joined by Floridablanca and the quietly efficient merchant, Hidalgo, Diego de Gardoqui of Bilbao, he was to become one of a group of powerful men close to the throne of Spain who controlled the difficult business of supplying aid to the desperate American colonists and eventually influenced the decision to go to war with England at the most important hour of their struggle.

Sympathy for the Americans, when they began open hostilities against the mother country, ran high throughout Spain. At this time

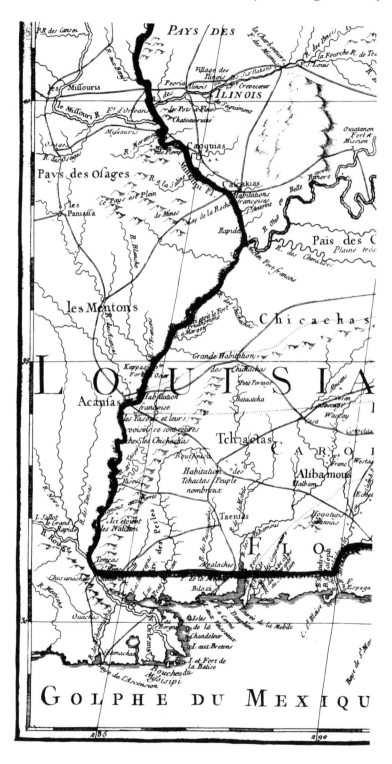

Spain was not in a position to make her sympathy openly known. She was engaged in a war with Portugal over possessions in South America that was costing her vast amounts in money and many men and ships. England, the open ally of Portugal, held the dangerous points of Minorca, Mahon and Gibraltar. Her navy was the most powerful on the seas, second in numbers only to the Spanish fleet.

Carlos III was, at this time, diplomatically involved in peace negotiations with Portugal and could ill afford to enter into any alliance that might endanger the successful conclusion of these negotiations. To become openly engaged in the struggle of the American colonists against the mother country would certainly lead to a declaration of war against England and invite an immediate blockade of all Spanish ports, thus ending all possibility of signing the desired treaty with Portugal and effectively closing the door to any aid for the Americans. The close alliance with France would be of no help because the navy of France would be completely impotent against the powerful combination of the navies of England and Portugal, should they decide to close her channel ports. Such was the position of Spain when the Americans began hostilities against England.

Part One

AID FOR THE AMERICAN COLONIES

ORIGINATING IN AND

CARRIED FORWARD IN SPAIN

CHAPTER I

1.

Early in the year 1776, two powerful and astute men make their first appearance upon the American scene. Any story of aid to the United States during the Revolution might well begin with the activities of Charles Gravier, Count de Vergennes, Minister of Foreign Affairs at the court of Carlos III's nephew, Louis XVI, the new Bourbon King of France, and the brilliant and farsighted Spanish Ambassador, the Count de Aranda. The Spanish diplomat at the French Court was, from the beginning of the American struggle, personally in wholehearted sympathy with the Colonists and in favor of any plan to get immediate aid to them. However, it was Aranda, who, in an almost clairvoyant moment, made the observation that, should the Colonies win their battle for independence from the mother country, it might well mark the beginning of a new pattern for all the peoples of the great colonial empires and become the opening wedge for splitting-off their colonial possessions from all the imperial thrones of Europe.

Early in the spring of 1776, these two men, the Count de Vergennes and the Count de Aranda, became close allies in working out the first plan for getting assistance secretly to the revolting Colonies. It was agreed between them that in order to insure the secrecy required for the all important business, since neither Court was to appear openly as an ally of the insurgents, all monies and supplies should be handled by a third party and his activities should have the character of open-business transactions.

Their first move was to obtain a fund for the setting up of such an undertaking. Accordingly it was arranged that the two Bourbon Courts would unite in making an outright gift of two million livres tournoises, one million to come from each Court. These two million livres would be the capital fund to launch the enterprise. Vergennes was to be responsible for the dispensing of the fund. The plan having thus been perfected, Aranda wrote a secret despatch in his own hand to the Marquis de Grimaldi, Prime Minister of Spain on June 7, 1776.

23

"Sir,

I am writing you this reserved [secret] despatch in my own writing because the Count de Vergennes has recommended that I communicate directly with you, privately, so that no one either here or there be informed of it, only ourselves in order that you may inform His Majesty and the secret may not become known. The point is that, we have agreed that the time has come for supplying the American Rebels with those services which may be accomplished without revealing either the source or the channels; and he has obtained from this Sovereign a million livres tournoises of which he will send half a million in hard money since Canada has a shortage of coins, there being no paper-money in use there as in the rest of the Colonies; and portuguese gold coin used to be bought in England for use there, since gold is most esteemed in those countries. They were to be sent to Cap Francoise in the Island of Santo Domingo where an absolutely reliable person would advance them to the Colonies as though they came from a business Company and as a loan that could be balanced by articles of the Country at usual prices when the Colonies should be able to start free trading.

And in the same fashion the second half of the million should be transferred and invested in articles useful for the maintenance of the war. Moreover they [the French] were closing their eyes to many more remittances of arms and munitions collected by some agents of the Colonies and even those made by French dealers who aided in smuggling them from the Islands either alone or by favouring those Americans who arrived, personally, in search of them.

Recently they [the Colonists] were favoured when they bought 15.000 guns and the Contractor of Armament was not required to pass them into his Majesty's service. It is known that they are making Campaign Artillery at Liège and elsewhere for the Americans; and being already engaged with tenacity it is necessary to offer the means by which they [English and Colonials] weaken each other; as much for destroying the English, as for bringing the Colonists to reason at the beginning of their Independence.

I have promised the Count de Vergennes not to reveal the slightest bit of his confidence, and I beg your Excellency, once this is communicated to the King, to keep it quite reserved and I have been told that it is not necessary to inform the French Ambassador since, through me, the King and your Excellency are now informed."[1]

On the twenty-seventh of June 1776, in an autographed, private document, Grimaldi acknowledged this personal message from his Ambassador and conveyed to him the agreement of King Carlos to enter into the foregoing arrangement. Grimaldi stated clearly that the government of Spain was in sympathy with the cause of the Americans and hoped for their success. He approved the advisability of working to aid them in concert with France and stressed the importance of secrecy. The pertinent passage of this despatch read:

". . . The King orders me [to send] to your Excellency the adjoining credit of a million livres tournoises in order to be spent for that purpose. We cannot do it directly and maintain the indispensable secrecy, but your Excellency will settle the matter with the Count de Vergennes as to the sort of assistance on which this amount is better to be invested and the best way to send it to its destination, either by well-known means in France, or by shorter means if such may be discovered, as you and the Count de Vergennes shall agree upon. In order to avoid talk and suspicion, the finance minister has been told by myself [Grimaldi] that this amount was for you to buy something at His Majesty's request, and I write this letter in my own writing so that no one else need be informed of this secret.

God preserve your Excellency for many years. . . ."[2]

2.

Thus, in June 1776, when the American Revolution had just begun, we find both Spain and France acting officially, though under the seal of secrecy, as allies of the English Colonies against their mother country. Even before this date, however, supplies had been going out on a haphazard basis through the ports of Spain, France and also Holland, as ship captains from America picked up arms and ammunition in personal trading ventures. Moreover, much important trade of this nature had been going on through the Spanish ports in the West Indies as well as through the famous port of St. Eustatius in the Dutch West Indies. With the connivance of Spanish, French and Dutch traders in the Islands, American smuggling and privateering operations had been keeping the Colonial forces supplied with the sinews of war. From these same ports as bases, American captains had been able to prey upon British merchant vessels during the first months of the war to an appalling extent. They had captured some seven-hundred British ships carrying valuable cargoes destined for England. The goods thus captured were traded in the Islands for war materials or for any goods badly needed in the Colonies. From St. Eustatius alone, a tiny, rocky spot of land in the Dutch West Indies, the merry game of eluding the British navy went on with incalculable benefit to the Colonial cause.

But it remained for Vergennes and Aranda, in Paris, to put the first official program of assistance from their respective nations into operation. First, the necessary money must be in hand, and it was speedily forthcoming. We find Aranda, in a private despatch dated July 12, 1776, acknowledging to Grimaldi the receipt of Spain's initial contribution which was to be expended with the like amount donated by France:

"Excellency,
Sir,

I have an autographed letter from your Excellency enclosing therewith another to be forwarded to this [French] Royal Exchange Treasurer, in which His Majesty draws a million livres tournoises to be invested in accord with this Court, on suitable assistance to the American Colonies now resisting English rule.

I have spoken to the Count de Vergennes and told him I have that amount disposable; but that it were better that it go the way France uses [sic] for sending an equal amount of money to the help of those Colonies, without mentioning Spain. We reached an accord on that matter and we arranged to discuss the investment of it at a later date. I acknowledge the receipt and later I shall communicate what has been done. God preserve you, . . ."[3]

(Spanish translation from original Spanish.)

During their conversations on the subject of aid to the Americans, Vergennes and Aranda had discussed at length the question as to whom they should entrust the very delicate matter of handling the two million livres tournoises; whoever their chosen agent might be, he would have the responsibility for purchasing an enormous quantity of war supplies, for arranging the vast details for their shipment and, above all, for maintaining absolute secrecy over all operations. The man who was selected by Vergennes for this vital post was recommended to Aranda in a letter dated July 24, 1776. Vergennes wrote:

"Mr. Beaumarchais, who will have the honor of presenting to you this letter, is the reliable man I had the honor to talk to you about. He will expound for you the matter of our talks and he will take your orders about what is still necessary to be done. I beg your Excellency to accept and favour him and ask the same favour that you accept my testimony of his perfect loyalty of which I am proud. . . . I remain his Excellency's most obedient servant. . . ."[4]

3.

In these words was introduced one of the most controversial characters ever to play a part in the saga of the American Revolution, none other than that chameleon of Parisian society, the watchmaker's son, Pierre Augustin Caron de Beaumarchais. Before going into further detail relative to the story of the remarkable Beaumarchais it is well to have before us additional official correspondence over the transfer to France of the million livres donated by the Court of Spain to the cause of the Americans because there has been much obscurity surrounding the fact of Spanish aid. There can be no question whatever that the million livres, constituting one-half of the joint contribution of the two governments was turned over. Aranda wrote Grimaldi, August 5, 1776:

". . . enclosed is a copy of the receipt given to me by M. du Vergier, appointed by the Minister of State, M. de Vergennes, for receiving . . . 'I have received from His Excellency the Count d'Aranda, Extraordinary Embassador of His Catholic Majesty, the amount of one million pounds cash that I shall pass in the same way to the bearer of this present voucher. . . . Paris, August 5, 1776,

Du Vergier' "

Aranda also enclosed with his letter his personal receipt for the money received from Spain and which he had turned over to Du Vergier:

"I have received four million reales de vellon (equal to one million pounds or Livres Tournoises) from Mr. Francisco de Llovera in virtue of order [the order from Grimaldi authorizing the payment — this authorization in full is in the King's secret papers] on the back of this sheet. . . . Aranda."

On the back of the sheet were these words:

". . . that is to say, a million tournoises pounds, for purposes that the Marquis of Grimaldi advised me upon the part of His Majesty. Paris, August 5th, 1776. Yo, M. Francisco de I. Lovera."[5]

Du Vergier was not alone in acknowledging receipt of the money on the part of France. On August 2, Vergennes sent Aranda his own receipt in these words:

"I have received from the hands of His Excellency the Count d'Aranda, Extraordinary Ambassador of His Catholic Majesty, the discharge given to him by M. du Vergier, Chief Commissary of the Royal Treasury, to the amount of a million tournoises pounds that His Excellency has had computed according to the agreement between our respective Courts, as an evidence that I have given [sic] the present declaration at Versailles, 2 August, 1776."[6]
(Archive copies in French and Spanish. Translation from the Spanish.)

Aranda promptly forwarded all letters relative to his secret transactions to Grimaldi and the latter in turn brought them to the attention of the King. August 26, he wrote his Ambassador a secret despatch in his own hand, saying:

"Excellency,
I have brought your two letters of the 8th and 12th inst. referring to the million pounds destined, as our part, to help the Americans in the English Colonies, to the notice of His Majesty and the King approves whatever has been done in accordance with the Count de Vergennes. That Minister's receipt for the aforementioned sum and sent by you will remain in the State Secretary's office and guarded with appropriate reserve and secrecy. God preserve you etc. Ildefonso, August 26th 1776."[7]

Just twelve days from the date of this despatch, Aranda wrote Grimaldi in eloquent terms of the assiduousness and speed with which he and Vergennes had implemented their plan for giving material aid to the American Colonies. It is a welcome surprise to find that the far-flung activities which the plan entailed could go forward with such speed in a time of generally slow communication.

"Excellency,
My Dear Sir,
From the two million tournoises pounds assigned by the two Courts to help the English Colonies of America, there has now been sent to them:
    216 - brass cannons
    209 - gun-carriages
    27 - mortars

```
     29 - couplings
 12.826 - shells
 51.134 - bullets
    300 - thousands of gun-powder
 30.000 - guns, with their bayonets
  4.000 - tents
 30.000 - suits
```

Two high, Graduate officers of distinction are also sent, able to command as Generals, one of the Ordnance, M. du Coudrai by name; the other is a Brigadier of Infantry, born in America, Mr. Hopkins; a relative of whom is now acting Admiral in the Colonies.

38 officers of all ranks are now going there with the purpose of forming and training two Regiments of Artillery.

Many engineers

Many workmen

Lead to make gun-bullets

All these are now being embarked from different harbors and in small vessels purposely spread out in case of being lost or of falling into English hands; All is being done as though it is being bought or arranged by their emissaries or Agents.

All these boats go the route to the Bermuda Islands since it is known to be the shorter route and less harassed by the English. The population in those Islands is free so far, made up a lot of Filibusters that England has been anxious to take. The American Colonists are frequent visitors to these Islands and their Inhabitants are inclined to join with those Colonies should they become independent.

The man supposed to be the Head of the Company handling these matters and who is in charge of forwarding assistance to the Colonies writes to them often on political matters, and he takes a part in all dealings, protected by the Correspondent they have up here, M. de Dienne; but Your Excellency must not forget all this happens under the Count de Vergennes, with his approval and his supervision. I enclose herewith a copy of the last letter sent to the Colonies in August, and the Commander of the Ship entrusted with the full confidence of the Congress, has learned it well, and has orders to throw it overboard, well ballasted to be sunk in the sea in case of capture by the English. And in case some men might escape capture, the Captain will try to teach them the message by heart.

Your Excellency may see this letter *with a report* I am sending by another communication with this envoy, *given to me by the Count de Vergennes himself, asking me to advise you that his Embassador knows nothing of this. Your Excellency must remember to think of this when talking with him, because the Very Christian King says it is sufficient for the King, his Uncle, to know the thinking of this Court by means of myself.* God preserve you etc. Paris, September 7th, 1776 [underlining by the author].

P.S. I was told by M. de Vergennes yesterday at Versailles that he would introduce me to Hopkins and today, after writing this letter, he has called with a paper that the Minister gave him, of which I am enclosing a copy. He told me he was the one of whom I knew and that he hopes to sail next month.

Among other subjects about which we talked, he asked me if Spain would allow the Americans to take refuge in her ports, both in Europe and in America, while·conveying English and Portuguèse preys. I replied that I would not be able to answer that. Any answer of mine would be a reckless one. He insisted upon asking my personal opinion on that at least because he was in a hurry to have contact with the Colonies. I told him to question this Court [France], as it is usual to confirm such opinions in both Courts, and when I have word from the Cabinet here I shall explain all to the Catholic King."[8]

4.

Grimaldi's response to the question asked by Hopkins, an American ship captain, was forthcoming in October. He wrote Aranda that because Spain was at war with Portugal, captured prizes taken by the Colonists in American waters might be taken into ports in Spain's West Indies for sale or for trade but that, so far as the ports of Spain herself were concerned, the Law of the Indies forbade such use.

To return to the details of the program for aiding the American Colonies, for which Vergennes and Aranda had become responsible for their respective governments, and to the career of Caron de Beaumarchais, who had been chosen as their agent: It was in February of 1776, that this brilliant and versatile personality, enthusiastic partisan of the Colonial Cause, met an American, then residing in London, Arthur Lee.

The first meeting between the two men took place at a dinner given by John Wilkes, Lord Mayor of London, who had long and openly espoused the cause of the revolting Colonies. Around the dinner table the spellbinder of the salons of Paris, famous playwright and pamphleteer, associated on occasion with secret activities of the French Court, brilliant and persuasive conversationalist made a profound impression upon the American. He spoke eloquently of his hope of enlisting help for the Colonies in France. He was likewise hopeful that Spain would be persuaded to come to their aid for he had resided for a time in that country. Because of the existing Family Pact, he believed that the Courts of Spain and France could be induced to act in concert in giving the Colonies all the supplies of which they were in need in order to prosecute the war against England to a successful conclusion. He saw himself in the guise of their self-chosen champion and mouthpiece. He felt that his own Court would act forcefully if the King could be prodded into action.

Immediately after his return to France he assigned himself this task. He prepared a Memorial to the Court urging, with all the power of a facile pen, that France should come to the aid of the Colonies, not failing to bolster his plea with a recital of the advantages that would accrue to France for so acting. Beaumarchais had a witty tongue and an engaging effrontery, the lack of which would have deterred almost any other man from thus importuning the Court. These qualities, and the fact that he had hopes and plans for aiding the Americans caught the attention of Vergennes at the very moment when he and Aranda were searching for a modus operandi to implement their own plan for lending succor to America.

Beaumarchais became their sole agent to direct the program. His first move was to set up a fictitious company bearing the name "Hortalez et Cie" by means of which he could make purchases of supplies, arrange for their shipment to the Colonies, contact American agents living in France and account for the monies spent. It was a company that was under no circumstances to be known as a representative of the governments of Spain or France. It was arranged that Beaumarchais should submit reports of the use of the money given by the two courts to Vergennes and Aranda who would in turn pass them on.

Beaumarchais maintained a correspondence with secret agents of the Colonies in North America and throughout the islands of the West Indies. He established contact in the first instance through an old merchant friend, M. de Dienne who had done business with the Americans for many years.

Hortalez et Cie set up headquarters in Paris. Branch centers were located in the port cities so that it could keep in direct touch with American sea captains who were constantly slipping into French harbors. To the merchants of France the business of Hortalez et Cie was a matter of the greatest importance; the supplies it purchased with the funds donated by the Bourbon Courts were purchased from these merchants. The profits they made from transactions with Hortalez et Cie were just as much due to a Spanish investment in American aid as to a French investment. In other words, the business of Hortalez et Cie was doubly valuable to the economy of France.

But France, and the King, benefited in quite another way from the activities of this dummy company. Ironically, the King had returned to him, indirectly, not only a part of the initial secret grant, but also, pro rata, a part of the grant made by the Court of Spain. It came about in this way: speed was very important if aid to the Americans was to be effective; during the long and costly war with England, resulting in the loss of the French colonial empire in America, great stores of arms and ammunition had poured from the factories of Europe to supply the military needs of France. The need of these stores ceased with the signature of the peace treaty of 1763. A vast surplus was left in the arsenals. Now, in 1776, the guns were fast becoming obsolete, the powder was deteriorating.

Beaumarchais considered himself fortunate to be able to purchase these supplies quietly at a reduced rate and forward them to the Americans. Beaumarchais paid twenty-five francs per musket and so much per pound-weight for mortars. Before removing gunpowder from the arsenals he was obliged to deposit security.[9] Some of the guns proved, on delivery, to be of little or no use and Washington's Inspector-General was forced to declare that, for safety's sake, all such shipments should be carefully inspected upon arrival before being issued to soldiers in the field.

The French Court had done well for France in securing the million livres tournoises from Spain, considering that the entire amount given by both Courts would be returned to French merchants and to the King. In so far as Spain was concerned, her advantage lay solely in the hope that the speedy supplying of arms to the Americans would enable them to keep the British so fully occupied that Carlos III would be left free to bring the war with Portugal to an end without the interference of England in the peace negotiations.

5.

Beaumarchais learned very soon that American captains were subjected to many hazards before the goods consigned by Hortalez et Cie were safely in the hands of the Colonists. By late summer 1776, he was searching desperately for a safer method of shipping his purchases. He entered into negotiations with the representative of the Continental Congress in France, Silas Deane and, as a result, on October 15, he made an agreement with Silas Deane as Agent for the United Colonies of North America. Hortalez et Cie were thenceforth to be protected against the loss of vessels bearing goods purchased for the account of the Colonies. The agreement is one of the first official contracts to be found wherein Beaumarchais and Deane entered into the ownership of a fleet to be used exclusively for the supplying of men and arms to the United Colonies:

> "JOHN JOSEPH DE MONTHIEU AND HORTALEZ AND COMPANY agreed with SILAS DEANE to furnish a certain number of vessels on account of the UNITED COLONIES OF NORTH AMERICA. These vessels to be held at the ports of HAVRE, NANTES, AND MARSEILLES at the disposal of HORTALEZ AND COMPANY. If captured or lost they are to be paid for by the COLONIES, according to amount of bill of sale agreed to by HORTALEZ AND COMPANY. [the agreement also lists the costs of transporting passengers, officers, sailors, soldiers, and servants] . . .
>
> Signed at Paris, October 15th 1776 by
> MONTHIEU
> RODRIQUEZ HORTALEZ & CO.
> SILAS DEANE, AGENT FOR THE
> UNITED COLONIES OF NORTH AMERICA."[10]

While Beaumarchais was enthusiastically at work purchasing supplies, contacting sea captains and securing ships in which to forward his purchases the furious activity in the ports aroused the attention of an increasing number of British secret agents and stirred up such a storm of rumor and loose talk that the secrecy of the enterprise soon vanished. Paris became rife with open discussion of the aid being shipped to the Colonies. Officers and men scheduled to sail had been sworn to secrecy, but an unfortunate incident occurred that dealt a blow to Washington anxiously awaiting the arrival of artillery and engineer officers whose training could be put to use in instructing his green recruits.

When the *Amphitrite*, one of a group of three ships scheduled for North America with a most valuable cargo of arms and many men enlisted in the service of the Colonies, sailed, she carried aboard a highly-trained officer of engineers, one Du Coudrai, for whom a brilliant future was enthusiastically envisioned by Beaumarchais. The vessel was delayed at Nantes and Du Coudrai returned to shore while awaiting the time for her departure. It is not known just how his mission became known but he was afterward suspected of having talked too freely of his destination. The *Amphitrite* sailed without him and he returned to Paris discomfited and downcast.[11]

Beaumarchais himself became the victim of a most unhappy accident which soon revealed him to the world as the real head of the fictitious company, Hortalez et Cie; he had written a letter to a friend of the Americans in London and had outlined to him the whole plan of his operations; he had confided this letter into the hands of a trusted messenger with instructions to deliver it in person to the addressee. The messenger, not knowing the man to whom he was to deliver the letter by sight, delivered it secretly by night into the hands of a man of the same name, but a man who was neither a friend of Beaumarchais nor a friend of the Colonial Cause. By the next morning the letter was in the hands of the minister for overseas affairs, and the unfortunate messenger, learning his mistake when the damage had been done beyond repair, fled back to France by the first means available. Beaumarchais now stood forth as the director of the operations covered by the name of Hortalez et Cie and the whole plan of aid to the revolting Colonies became known all over England.

There was nothing the discomfited Beaumarchais could do to remedy a bad situation. The result of his indiscretion was that the British government took immediate steps to intercept all vessels sailing from French ports and to double their efforts to seize and search all vessels entering those ports with American goods intended for trade for war supplies. The English Ambassador protested bitterly to the Court of France over the activities of Hortalez et Cie and the prestige of the colorful and witty author of "The Barber of Seville" suffered an eclipse. It was not long before the Bourbon Courts came to the conclusion that he could no longer be usefully employed and severed all ties with him.[12]

According to the original plan for dispensing the two million livres tournoises given by Carlos III and Louis XVI, purchases for the initial outlay of arms and supplies were to be paid for in commodities shipped to Europe by the Colonies as soon as normal trade relations could be established. All goods which reached France safely during the war were to be sold in the open market and the proceeds of such sales would then be applied to further purchases of war supplies. Thus, there would be set up a revolving fund which would serve Hortalez et Cie as the basis for credit for the account of the Colonies. Now that the British had been alerted and were tightening their patrols along the coast of France, it became rapidly apparent to Beaumarchais that the idea of Vergennes and Aranda would not work. He began sending urgent pleas to Vergennes, and through him to Aranda, for additional funds to sustain his rapidly expanding activities.

Confidence in his sagacity was meanwhile beginning to ebb. The Spanish Ambassador reported to his court that some new method of aiding the Americans would have to be found soon, now that the secrecy so vital to Madrid was no longer possible. He had a second grave reason for concern; it was becoming apparent to him that the funds which had been given equally by the two nations were being credited by the Americans *solely* to the Court of France while the reluctance of his own government openly to announce the giving of this substantial aid was putting Carlos III in the unenviable position of having given none. Aranda's correspondence with the Prime Minister, Grimaldi shows him to be anxious to set in motion a new modus operandi which would give Spain a more direct control over such funds and supplies as she was sending to the Colonies.[13]

FOOTNOTES

[1]Aranda to Grimaldi, June 7, 1776, Archivo Historico Nacional, Madrid, Papeles de Estado (cited hereafter as A.H.N.); Legajo 4072, reservada no. 1, minuta autógrafa.

[2]Grimaldi to Aranda, June 27, 1776, A.H.N.; Legajo 4072.

[3]Aranda to Grimaldi, July 12, 1776, A.H.N.; Legajo 4072, reservada no. 4., autógrafa.

[4]Vergennes to Aranda, July 24,1776, A.H.N.; Legajo 4072, reservada autógrafa, copia.

[5]Aranda to Grimaldi, August 5, 1776, A.H.N.; Legajo 4072. Enclosed with the despatch are copies of du Vergier's receipt for one million pounds tournoises, one in French and one in Spanish, also the record of payment of one million pounds tournoises to Aranda, signed by Ventura de Llovera and receipt for this sum signed by Aranda.

[6]Vergennes to Aranda, August 11, 1776, A.H.N.; Legajo 4072. Copy in French and Spanish.

[7]Grimaldi to Aranda, August 26, 1776, A.H.N.;Legajo 4072, reservada no. 7, autógrafa, original.

[8]Aranda to Grimaldi, September 7, 1776, A.H.N.; Legajo 4072, reservada no. 8, autógrafa, copia.

[9]René Dalsème, *Beaumarchais*, translated by Hannaford Bennett (New York, 1929), p. 262.

[10]Silas Deane to the Committee of Secret Correspondence, October 15, 1776, cited in *The Diplomatic Correspondence of the American Revolution*, Jared Sparks, ed. (12 vols., Boston, 1829-30), 1: 53-54.

[11]Silas Deane to the Committee of Secret Correspondence, January 20, 1777, *ibid.*, 1: 102.

[12]Juan J. Yela Utrillo, *España ante la Independencia de los Estados Unidos*, Graficas Academia Mariana (Tomos 2, Lerida, 1925), Tomo 1: 239-246. A doctoral thesis.

[13]A.H.N.; Legajo 4072.

CHAPTER II

1.

About this time, the American Congress set up a Commission with headquarters in Paris to act as the official representative of the United Colonies in their dealings with the states of Europe. It was headed by that man of many talents, Benjamin Franklin. Silas Deane and Arthur Lee, who was sent over from London, were assigned to the Commission as his colleagues. Franklin's experience in England and his knowledge of men and affairs soon made him a respected and popular figure. He quickly became the toast of Paris. It is interesting to note that the headquarters of the Commission, although located in the quiet suburb of Passy and therefore outside the limits of Paris and its gay and gossipy salons, speedily became an open secret everywhere on the continent.

Franklin became the rage and was pursued with invitations to all the salons in the city. His quiet wisdom and biting wit, coupled with his extraordinary simplicity of manner and sober dress exerted a strange fascination in a center where sprightly conversation was an art and where both men and women went to extremes in elegance of attire. He was no less a marked man in the streets. Aranda wrote to his Prime Minister that Franklin was without doubt one of the most astute and brilliant men in Europe, both as a diplomat and as a philosopher.

Soon after the Commission began to function, rifts developed over the question as to who was to act for them in the handling of such supplies as should go forward to the Colonies. Franklin had great confidence in his old friend, Dr. Dubourg, and had quietly engaged to make use of the Doctor's loyalty to the American Cause for this service. But Vergennes and Aranda, having already arranged through Hortalez et Cie for the same purpose, were now too deeply involved to change the agent of a venture which their governments had underwritten to the extent of two million livres. Both Silas Deane and Arthur Lee had known and assisted in working out of the plan now in operation so Franklin was prevailed upon to let the arrangements stand. His good friend Dr. Dubourg, however, was considerably disgruntled over the whole affair.[1]

During October 1776, Beaumarchais found himself in dire difficulties: the funds of his company were exhausted; his private sources
of help were likewise dried up; the cost of his contracts for supplies
was rising astronomically. He reached a decision; he prepared a
Memorial which he submitted to both the Courts of France and
Madrid. Vergennes sent the Memorial to Aranda, enclosing also with
his covering letter a long despatch for Grimaldi which the latter was to
place under the eyes of the King of Spain. Aranda passed the information on to Grimaldi, as requested, saying:

"Excellency
Sir,
    A few days after my anterior letter the Count de Vergennes gave me a
memorial to read, a copy of which he obtained for me to enclose herewith explaining the meaning of this petition. Of course I replied that he was aware that
my Court was not bound to contribute in equal parts with his Court in
everything connected with the English Colonies but we had given the one
million tournoises pounds to match the million given by France to be invested
and forwarded to them in the matter of the urgent support about which we had
talked in the beginning. That presently [there are] the expenses of the Buenos
Aires Expedition, plus others that might occur at any time, [and] according to
the present aspect of affairs with Portugal, I did not think it a wise thing to
engage my Court to share indefinite risks. He thought my ideas on the matter
were prudent and limited himself to requesting that I send you a copy, not to
imply a petition but for the information of the King.
    The so-called Banker of both Courts, is the celebrated Caron de
Beaumarchais, author of the enclosed memorial, and this Cabinet is using him
as a go-between for the dealings and sending of assistance, which he has done
with speed and agility. He has been clever enough to create a Company able to
foresightedly discover what must be found and despatched.
    I think he has succeeded in all that he proposed to France and I have no
doubt he thinks he can rely upon us, due to the French Minister's influence in
presenting the possibility of our eventual help; but, as I tell you, M. de
Vergennes is just suggesting and not demanding, I believe you may answer
favorably according to the circumstances and the urgency, so that they do not
refrain entirely from their assistance.
                                                    God preserve you."[2]

The Memorial which went along with the foregoing despatch reads:

"Memorial to the Courts of Spain and France by their Common Banker.
    Both Courts after having correctly considered how important it is to quickly
help the Americans, know that these [Colonists] are not wanting in courage or
soldiers but they only need ammunition and clothing.
    The Ministers of both Courts have thought best to proceed in this matter,
without alarming the English, to begin trade with this new Power, and this
Trade has been established under the supervision and the protection of the two
Ministers.
    Each Court has supplied their Common Banker with one million of Tour-

noises pounds, to begin with, and both desire to continue accordingly. And accounts on this affair have been made, are, and will be submitted at once, either to the French Cabinet or to the Spanish Ambassador.

As of Now, since the first purchases, have been made, boats are loaded with military stores and ready to sail, it will be noted that, in this first step, expenses have been much higher than funds provided by both Courts for their Banker.

Due to this it would be convenient that both Courts share equally the additional costs to repay this Banker's advances and it would be well if each Court contributed in equal extent to enlarge this business by that providing the steady credit that will be needed.

Now if we wish to put this machinery [plan] into operation, by the time articles are returned by the Americans to cancel our remittances, it would be best to sell those articles and spend their value received on new remittances. Otherwise this machinery [plan] must run on the Banker's credit.

Now, if this Mechanism [program] stops, we shall ruin the fruit of our first efforts. New Orders will allow purveyors to go on supplying the Americans, according to their need, just as ships are arriving.

Since we have now emphasized this need for tenacity, I must now explain the course of the operation, and invite each of the Courts to stand behind the other, to be equal in this, not only in monetary help but in supplying Credit.

The first consignment consists of:

     300 thousands of Gun-powder [Pounds?]
      30 thousand guns
       3 thousand tents
     200 cannons, gun-carriages, fore-trains, and all mountings
      27 mortars, gun-carriages etc.
100,000 bullets
 13,000 bombs

And the suspended purchase of 8 transport vessels: tools for about 30 officers and those anticipated for three months. Complete clothing for 30,000 men requires:

  95,000 ells of stuff for soldiers uniforms
150,000 ells satin de chalons for lining
 42,000 ells fabric for shorts and pocket-lining
 60,000 pairs of wool stockings
120,000 dozen buttons for soldiers
 30,000 blankets
 30,000 ells stuff for officers
 24,000 ells satin de chalons
 18,000 ells fabric for soldier-shirts
 15,000 pounds thread in different colours
  1,000 pound silk
100,000 common needles
100,000 little awls
 30,000 pocket-knives
 30,000 woolen-caps
 30,000 neckerchiefs
 30,000 pair shoes
 30,000 pair garter-buckles
   600 tinplate boxes

This remittance of clothing amounts nearly to .... 2,500,000 Pounds
War ammunition and vessels amount more or less 2,500,000   ''
Advance money to the Officers and Seamen   600,000   ''
                                      Total 5,600,000   ''
Of this Amount Spain and France have given each 1,000,000   ''
Given by both Courts 2,000,000   ''
Residue for the Banker to be paid by both Courts 3,600,000   ''
Each of them to furnish 1,800,000   ''
The French Court has exceeded its quota as the Banker has received in advance all War Munitions leaving today; all of these have been taken from French Stores and Dock-yards by official permission.

And the advance payment from France has been so high that when Spain equals her, not only will this shipment be paid for, but there will be enough to go on trading with the remittance that will be available.

French Court has supplied in ready money 1,000,000
In ammunition, more or less, ... 2,500,000
                         Total 3,500,000
She adds to this, the benefit of over-paying, but helps her Banker also by giving all her business to him in order to establish his credit all over Europe.

It should appear only fair that Spain, which helps in no way toward the supplying of goods, give to the Banker of both Courts the sum of 2,500,000 to equalize her with France, and to compensate for profits gained by over-paying and the credit inherent to the management of banking in France, it is convenient that Spain grant the Common Banker the 4 percent of gold-mining [sic] that Spain retains.

This balance of assistance from both Courts is enough to insure the success of this great affair and any further aid to America would not be necessary, as America would then be supplied with all necessary means to be free of English rule and, greater than this, be able to take over the Bermuda Islands this next winter since these are essential to the trade between America and the European Nations.

Spain is asked to answer as soon as possible concerning the afore-mentioned matters.

The Americans have requested the Banker to ask permission from both Courts to carry all preys taken by American ships from the Portuguese into the ports of Spanish and French Colonies. As soon as that permission be granted the Americans will send a Fleet to seek out and attack all Portuguese Fleets coming from Brazil and they promise to well avenge all insults from the Portuguese toward both themselves and Spain. A quick answer is begged equally on this important question."[3]

In this remarkable Memorial it is plain that Beaumarchais regarded Spain as solely the source of money which was to be given, even to the point of granting four percent to the "Common Banker" for his services. What does not appear in the Memorial is the fact that none of the common fund was to accrue in trade or by other means to the Spanish Court or to the Spanish people but that all possible purchases were to be made in France unless it became impossible to supply them in that country.

Beaumarchais either chose to ignore, or was not informed of the supplies being shipped in American vessels that were sailing in and out of Bilbao, Barcelona and Cadiz. He can scarcely have been totally ignorant of the complaints being made by the English Ambassador at Madrid against the shipments of arms coming out of Barcelona, particularly when British merchants of Plymouth, long accustomed to trading with those Spanish ports were known to be quietly buying arms in Barcelona for resale to American captains, thus making tidy fortunes at the expense of British arms in America.

2.

It is not surprising that the Spanish Ambassador in Paris should begin to look upon the operations of Beaumarchais and Hortalez et Cie with suspicious eyes. At every opportunity he questioned Vergennes as to the state of supplies going to America. The very interesting summary of one of these conversations with Vergennes was the subject of a despatch he addressed to Grimaldi, October 10, 1776. It covered not only the affairs of the Americans but also the plans which Louis XVI entertained with respect to Canada:

"Sir,

Thursday, the 3rd, on the eve of the journey of the Court from Choisy to Fontainbleau, I went to Versailles to pay my respects to His Majesty and I had an opportunity for an informal talk with the Count de Vergennes.

While speaking of the English Colonies I mentioned that I was surprised that we did not know of any important event taking place in New York as late as this October, the journey from there being only 25 to 30 days at the longest. I was shown a letter from Quebec, just arrived on August, 12th, confirming the time necessary for a letter to come directly. From its meaning I gathered that it was from an Agent who had been sent to explore the dispositions and inclinations of the people of that country toward returning to French rule.

By the letter I noticed that not only the inhabitants but the Indians along that border were longing to return to the rule of France. Without disclosing that I knew the writer was an Emissary to the Canadians, I wondered aloud, that should the Rebels win in the Colonies, they would not stop until they threw the English entirely off the Continent. And then I asked him if France might be thinking of returning to Canada, and trying now to influence the natives to again be under French control, instead of maintaining a union with the English Colonies.

He answered that that was the idea, but on much better terms for everybody. He had no doubt that the country was ready for that, but it would be better for France to take only the mouth of the St. Laurence River and its Islands, leaving the rest of the land for a Free State of Farmers and Merchants to govern themselves as they chose, under the sole protection of France, allowing them to become naturalized citizens of that country or France, with mutual free trade with France.

He added that the land would be populated by the French themselves and by anyone else wishing to go there. That national sentiment, usual intercourse with Europeans, their habitude, customs and temperament were so similar to the mother country that they would be useful to France, without being her subjects. France would be free of the burden of cost for troops formerly maintained there as well as for civil servants to carry on the government, to the natural vexation of the inhabitants. By keeping the Islands and the mouth of the River the land would be conveniently subordinated, as well as protect the valuable Fisheries of this section and in the Banks of New Foundland. With the Crown's Posts and the rest of the land, although independent, attached by ties of trade and sentiment to the Crown, the French could restrain the new Colonial State from offending France. That with Canada converted into a kind of Republic. . . . all this should mean better regulations, much better than restoring the Province to its former state of total submission to France.

To tell your Excellency my opinion, I should be very glad to see that happen, for two reasons: If France joins with our Party as a result of our dispute with Portugal, she will make stronger efforts having specific aims of her own; secondly, if to the north of the new Anglo-American State the Rebels will build, there is another Franco-American State adjoining, it would afford some relief to Spain and would not entail any annoying consequences, because from Canada, Our King's Dominions will never suffer due to the interposing English Colonies, and only these will be our rivals in time to come, owing to their position and their growing population.

I am sure that if France decides to break out she is thinking of using force against the English in the East Indies, for it is presumed that England gains great wealth from there and that they will gain much more in time, so France could take advantage of succeeding England there, and the latter could be destroyed there.

From these reports and rumors the King will surmise that should France carry out such ideas as I stated in my memorial of the 7th of last month, she will then have definite aims and not only will she damage England seriously in general, but by distracting and compelling her to expand her energies, France will also use more vigour.

I think this Cabinet is well aware that if England retrieves her fortunes, not only will they fail to show any gratitude to France for not intervening, but they will take as a pretext the assistance and aids given by permission of this Kingdom, and they would tolerate a masked intervention with indirect help, to render difficult the reconquest [of Canada].

God preserve you. . . ."4

From this long letter from Aranda, it is easy to see with what urgency the Spanish Ambassador was hoping for more active help from France. Above all, he wanted to see the Americans succeed and to have England kept so well occupied that she would not in the future be in any position to challenge Spain in North America.

Grimaldi's answer to Beaumarchais' plea for more money was that Carlos III, in view of commitments already made, could not make a flat amount available to bolster the plan of Hortalez et Cie but that the Court would continue to give all possible aid in goods and ammunition through her American posts. With reference to the request that American Corsairs and Privateers might bring their Portuguese prizes into the ports of Spain, he pointed out that Spain could not alter her "Indian Law" in this regard. Foreign vessels escorting prizes could not be permitted entrance except in case of "casualties." However, if it were a question of prizes taken from the Portuguese, then such vessels might be admitted to Spain's American ports, the Marquis of Casa Tilli, commanding the Spanish squadron in American waters, having been given orders to capture any Portuguese ship he encountered there by way of compensation and retaliation for their behavior toward Spanish shipping in the same waters. Americans entering these ports with Portuguese prizes would meet with little or no difficulty. Captain Hopkins had raised this same point before Beaumarchais. Grimaldi authorized Aranda to make this information known to the Americans.

Hortalez et Cie had covered itself against ships' losses by the agreement with Silas Deane but this agreement did not benefit the Americans. Their primary concern was badly-needed supplies and the only supplies that could help them were those actually delivered. The routes which were followed during the early months of aid were proving increasingly hazardous. Consequently Vergennes and Aranda had, by November, worked out an ingenious scheme by means of which they believed they could circumvent future captures by the British. It consisted simply of routing ships direct to the French Island of Santo Domingo. England could not touch the commerce between a friendly nation and one of its possessions. The new plan appears in Aranda's despatch of November 22 to Grimaldi:

"Excellency,
Sir,
    A few days ago I asked the Count de Vergennes for the state of private assistance that you had sent to the American Colonists and he replied that some ships were ready to sail in a few days with goods, war ammunition, and officers who are going to instruct the troops. That all these vessels had their papers as directed to Santo Domingo, in case they should meet with a stronger English Force, for on this route and in this way, we shall be able to avoid interception on the way, since it is permitted to send from this Continent to the French Isles as much as is necessary. . . ."[5]

3.

As the fateful year of 1776 was drawing to its close, the affairs of the Colonies took on a darker hue. The information reaching Madrid was black with news of disasters affecting Washington and his hard-pressed troops. The "Gaceta de Madrid" was publishing all the news that arrived from America, France and England. The stories in the public press of England were so distorted that little reliance could be placed in them. It was known that German troops had been sent over to America but the truth about their desertions was not broadcast through the papers. Carlos III kept closely informed of matters and his concern over the weakness of the Colonies, was expressed in a despatch which Grimaldi sent to Aranda on the ninth of December:

"Excellency,
  I have informed the King about the tenor of your letter of the 22nd of last month and His Majesty is glad to know the succours are on the way. Those will now be more urgent and necessary after the advantages taken by the English Forces and will help to stimulate the Rebels in their efforts. The King and his Cabinet think it so important to prolong that war that they are considering new means of supplying direct aid from us to the revolting Colonies. As soon as this is settled and the method decided upon, you will be informed."[6]

With feeling running high in favor of the Americans, the fear now began to arise that England might force the Colonies to surrender before aid sufficient to enable them to continue the struggle could reach them. Both in Spain and France as well as among the group of ardent supporters of the American Cause in England it was believed that the troops of Washington would be decisively beaten before arms and ammunition could get to them and that the Tories throughout the Colonies would be able to bring about a treaty of peace which would be in effect a complete surrender. It was during the dreadful month of December that the American Commissioners in Paris addressed their first letter to Aranda. They wrote December twenty-eight:

"Sir,
  We wish to inform you, we are addressed or sent by the United Provinces of America in order to advance the friendship with the Spanish and French Courts. For this purpose and to show you our personal devotion, we respectfully hope to visit you tomorrow or on any day most suitable to you, if you will please to make it known to us.
          We are proud of being — your most obedient and humble Servants-
  B. Franklin — Silas Deane — Arthur Lee — Plenipotentiaries of the
                  Congress of the United States of America."[7]

But all the news reaching Madrid during these months was not bad. The Count de Aranda was making good use of the sounding-board of Paris and his despatches to the Court carried a vivid picture of the troubles of the English at the Court of their own King, George III. The Spanish Ambassador in London, the Prince de Masserano was sending despatches almost daily recounting the gossip he had gathered at the great "Assemblies" or over the dinner tables of the King's Ministers.[8] The situation in London is portrayed to Grimaldi in a despatch of February 24, 1777, from Aranda:

"Excellency
Sir,
  England has contracted with the Duke of Wittenberg for a body of 2,500 men of his army to be sent to America. It appears certain that these troops were

offered last year when the Prince visited London; but the information is that
the offer was not accepted, that the Court preferred the soldiers of other Prin-
cipalities, because most of the German Colonists of Pennsylvania, and those in
other Colonies, were natives of the Palatinate and Swabia, neighboring
Provinces to Wittenberg, and they were afraid of their deserting because of the
patriotism of their friends.

It is well-known that the Margrave of Bareith [Bayreuth] has supplied a regiment of 1000 soldiers, together with more than a hundred Chasseurs; another
regiment of 1200 is supplied by Baden Durlac. These reinforcements and the
recruits for replacement that Hesse Casel, Hanan [Hanau] and Brunzveih
[Brunswick] have sent with their troops also, will not be enough — it is believed
— to fill the gaps so badly needed and that will exist there by the end of the
winter and at the beginning of the next Campaign; owing to the spread of
deseases [sic] that the English are under-going, as it is reported from New York;
because of desertions of soldiers which is much higher than they admit; and
from losses in battle that are so great that even in England it is known to be
higher than the Government admits, and it is known that the Court is taking
great care to conceal from the people.

It is supposed to be true that General Lee was taken prisoner by a body of
Partisans (English), and being considered one of the best American Leaders, his
loss means a considerable damage to them.

It is incredible what a lot of dealing is done with Americans at Nantes and
Bordeaux. They bring their own articles, according to their circumstances, and
they take as much as they can, paying very well for it.

Mr. Lee, one of the American Representatives who was here, who was to
leave, as I told you, has gone with a difference of three or four days from the
date I wrote you.

That Brigadier of the Ordnance, M. de Coudrai, who went out to command
the American Artillery, on board the AMPHITRITE when it sailed the first
time from Le Havre but having suffered bad weather and a shortage of food,
was forced to land at Lorient, he came to Paris, where he inconsiderately made
public some of the circumstances among them, the information that he was
only waiting for the ship's sailing after completing her reparations. They say
that for that reason a countermand was given and the AMPHITRITE has since
sailed leaving him ashore."[9]

The chagrin of M. du Coudrai was not his alone. Beaumarchais had
deep reasons for regretting this officer's inability to hold his tongue.
In every despatch from the Colonies, the petition for material aid was
accompanied by a desperate plea for experienced officers who could
train and command Continental troops at staff level. Washington, as
well as his command, was woefully lacking technicians for the handling of engineering problems and using artillery. As Beaumarchais was
to learn, the search for such men was not easily made. Hundreds of
young, enthusiastic partisans of the American Cause were flocking to
him to buy passage to America. Many of them, like the young Marquis
de Lafayette, were well able to pay their own costs, but there were few
experienced officers with the training of a von Steuben to take some of
the responsibility of command from the worried Washington.

Beaumarchais was unfortunate to have had many of his most valuable men prove of weak caliber after he had trusted them with important missions. Throughout the period of the war, costly papers were to disclose secrets of incalculable value to the English due to carelessness or the excitement of a moment of action. Captain Hopkins had early emphasized the importance of destroying all papers or sinking them in the sea rather than to allow them to reach the hands of the enemy. Franklin was constantly alert to the danger of such leakage. Arthur Lee mentions in one of his despatches the case of a captain who failed to properly ballast his papers, with the result that they were picked up after floating on the water and relayed to London, disclosing valuable secrets of the Continental Congress which had been written for the private perusal of the Commissioners in Paris.

4.

Some of the vicissitudes of correspondence at this time are illustrated by the history of a document written in the cover of a dictionary by Arthur Lee in London on June 3, 1776. It was addressed to the Committee of Secret Correspondence of the American Congress. The message was later found and delivered, September 4, 1778, to the Secretary of the Congress by Robert Morris. On December 7, 1778, it was placed in the hands of the Committee of Foreign Affairs by James Lovell, Secretary of the Congress, meanwhile having been copied from the dictionary and attested to by Lovell. This important document reads:

"Gentlemen,
    The desire of the Court of France to assist may be depended upon; but they are yet timid and the Ministry unsettled. Turgot, lately removed, was the most averse to a rupture with England; his removal is of consequence. The contention for the lead now is between Count de Vergennes and the Duke de Choiseul; both are friends to you and for vigorous measures. The disposition in France may for these reasons be relied on. Spain is more reserved, but surely when France moves Spain will cooperate. The clear revenue from the farm of tobacco is twenty four millions of livres to France. It has been hinted to me that she is likely to tell Great Britain, that if England cannot furnish it, she will send for it herself. You may judge, therefore, what an important instrument that is in your hands. A scotch banker, Sir Robert Herries, proposed to the Farmers in France to supply them at the home price here, that is, with the duty, to which they agreed. He then applied to this government for leave to import it, upon paying the duties, which was refused.
    In the last debate, Lord George Germaine, who is undoubtedly Minister, affirmed that no treaty would be held with you till you laid down your arms. My opinion is, that independence is essential to your dignity, essential to your present safety, and essential to your future prosperity and peace. Some of the Congress correspond with Mr. Jackson, of the Board of Trade, and Mr. Molleson, a scotch Merchant; the Intelligence they give goes directly to the Minister. . . ."[10]

In the Journal of the Committee of Secret Correspondence of the Congress we have the substance of a report made verbally to the Committee by a Mr. Thomas Story, who had been sent to Europe as early as 1775 to sound out the feeling in Holland, France and England. The report, never made public, was made October 6, 1776. It is interesting for many reasons: it shows that France had no thought of war with England, that Arthur Lee was aware of the real character of Hortalez et Cie before he left London to work with Franklin and Silas Deane in Paris, and, certainly by strong inference, that Vergennes gave the impression that the Court of France was the sole benefactor of the Colonies. Story is represented as having told the Committee:

> "On my leaving London, Arthur Lee requested me to inform the Committee of Correspondence, that he had several conferences with the French Ambassador who had communicated the same to the French Court; that, in consequence thereof, the Duke de Vergennes had sent a gentleman to Arthur Lee, who informed him that the French Court could not think of entering into war with England; but that they would assist America, by sending from Holland this Fall two hundred thousand pounds sterling worth of arms and ammunition to St. Eustatia, Martinique or Cape Francois; that application was to be made to the Governors or Commanders of those places, by inquiring for MONSIEUR HORTALEZ, and that, on persons properly authorized applying, the above articles would be delivered to them."

The Committee chose to keep the report secret from the fellow members of their own Congress. This was a most realistic attitude, human nature being what it is. They could not afford to offend France — which would certainly be the case if the news leaked out — nor run the risk of losing the promised supplies to British warships alerted to the sea lanes being used. On the other hand, they were willing to risk publicity if revelation of the report to the Congress might serve to lift the spirits of its members in a dark hour in the fortunes of the Colonial Cause. To their journal they confided these comments:

> "The above intelligence was communicated to the subscribers this day, being the only two members of the Committee of Secret Correspondence, now in this city; and on our considering the nature and importance of it, we agree in opinion that it is our indispensable duty to keep it a secret, even from Congress, for the following reasons.
>
> First — Should it get to the ears of our enemies in New York, they would undoubtedly take measures to intercept the supplies, and thereby deprive us, not only of those succors, but of others expected by the same route.
>
> Secondly — As the Court of France have taken measures to negotiate this loan and succor in the most cautious and most secret manner, should we divulge it immediately, we may not only lose the present benefit, but also render that Court cautious of any further connexion with such unguarded people, and prevent their making other loans and assistance that we stand in need of, and have directed Mr. Deane to ask of them; for it appears, that for all our intelligence that they

are not disposed to enter into any immediate war with Great Britain, though disposed to support us in our contest with them; we, therefore, think it our duty to cultivate their favorable disposition towards us, and draw from them all the support we can; and in the end their private aid must assist us to establish peace, or inevitably draw them in as parties to the war.

Thirdly — We find, by fatal experience, that the Congress consists of too many members to keep secrets, as none could be more strongly enjoined than the present Embassy to France, notwithstanding which, Mr. Morris was this day asked by Mr. Reese Meredith, whether, Dr. Franklin and others were really going as ambassadors to France; which plainly proves, that this Committee ought to keep this secret, if secrecy is required.

Fourthly — We are of the opinion that it is unnecessary to inform Congress of this intelligence at present, because Mr. Morris belongs to all the Committees that can properly be employed in receiving and importing the expected supplies from Martinique, and will influence the necessary measures for that purpose; indeed we have already authorized William Bingham to apply at Martinique and St. Eustatia for what comes there, and remit part by the armed sloop INDEPENDENCE, Captain Young, promising to send others for the rest.

Mr. Morris will apply to the Marine Committee to send other armed vessels after her, and also to Cape Francoise, (without communicating this advice), in consequence of private intelligence lately received that arms, ammunition and clothing can now be procured at those places.

But should any unexampled misfortune befall the States of America so as to depress the spirits of Congress, it is our opinion, that, on any event of that kind, Mr. Morris, (If Dr. Franklin should be absent) should communicate this important matter to Congress, otherwise keep it until part of the supplies arrive, unless other events happen, to render the communication of it more proper than it appears to be at present.

ROBERT MORRIS
B. FRANKLIN."[11]

It can never be charged that the two great Patriots, Franklin and Morris, were indiscreet in the keeping of valuable information secret though it was one of the most difficult and dangerous problems to be faced day and night during the war. This secret seems to have been well kept as to the second party to the gift of money and supplies by means of Hortalez and Company; even the Committee of Secret Correspondence makes no mention of Spain's partnership with France in this transaction!

Beaumarchais, through his own indiscretion, was the first to lay this operation open to the English through the stupidity of his personal messenger to London, as mentioned heretofore.

It was on October 23rd, 1776, that the Committee for Secret Correspondence wrote to Arthur Lee from Philadelphia:

"Sir,

By this conveyance we transmit to Silas Deane, a resolve of the Honorable, The Continental Congress of Delegates from the Thirteen United States of America, whereby you are appointed one of their Commissioners for negotiating a treaty of alliance, amity, and commerce with the Court of France, and also for negotiating treaties with other nations, agreeable to certain plans and instructions of Congress, which we have transmitted by various conveyances to Mr. Deane, another of the Commissioners. We flatter ourselves, from the assurances of your friends here, that you will cheerfully undertake this important business, and that our country will greatly benefit of those abilities and that attachment, which you have already manifested in sundry important services, which at a proper period will be made known to those you would wish. . . .

ROBERT MORRIS
B. FRANKLIN"[12]

FOOTNOTES

[1]Dalsème, *op. cit.*, p. 252.

[2]Aranda to Grimaldi, October 10, 1776, Archivo General de Simancas (cited hereafter as A.G.S.); Papeles de Estado, Legajo 1736, resevada no. 9, autógrafa original. A draft XIX, with variations is found in A.H.N.; Legajo 4072.

[3]Memorial of Beaumarchais, October 10, 1776, A.H.N.; Legajo 4072, secreta, no. 9.

[4]Aranda to Grimaldi, October 10, 1776, A.G.S. Estado; Legajo 1736, formerly A.H.N. 4506, no. 853, original. An autógrafa copia is found in A.H.N.; Legajo 4072.

[5]Aranda to Grimaldi, November 22, 1776, A.H.N.; Legajo 3884, reservada no. 12, original.

[6]Grimaldi to Aranda, December 9, 1776, A.H.N.; Legajo 4072, reservada no. 60, original. A copy is found in A.H.N.; Legajo 3884.

[7]The American Commissioners to Aranda, December 28, 1776, A.H.N.; Legajo 3884.

[8]Prince Masserano to Grimaldi, 1776, A.G.S., Papeles de Inglaterra; Legajo 6993, no. 236.

[9]Aranda to Grimaldi, February 21, 1777, A.H.N.; Legajo 4072, no. 971, autógrafa, copia.

[10]Arthur Lee to the Committee of Secret Correspondence, June 3, 1776, in *Diplomatic Correspondence, op. cit.*, 2: 14-16.

[11]Records of the Committee of Secret Correspondence, October 1, 1776, in *ibid.*, 2: 16-18.

[12]The Committee of Secret Correspondence to Arthur Lee, October 23, 1776, in *ibid.*, 2: 18-19.

CHAPTER III

1.

After Arthur Lee joined the Commission in Paris, it did not take him long to form the opinion that the promises of aid which had been made to him in London were far from being fulfilled and that the Court of France was showing little enthusiasm for the whole undertaking. To the Committee of Secret Correspondence he observed, in a despatch of January 3, 1777:

"Gentlemen,
    . . . I have had the happiness of joining Dr. Franklin and Mr. Deane, the day after the arrival of the former at this place. We have employed every moment in preparing the way for fulfilling the purposes of our mission. It is impossible to say yet in what degree we shall be able to accomplish our instructions and our wishes. The politics of this Court are in a kind of trembling hesitation. It is in consequence of this, that the promises made to me by the French Agent in London, and which I stated to you by Mr. Story, and others, have not been entirely fulfilled. The changing of the mode of conveying what they have promised was settled with Mr. Deane, whom Mons. HORTALEZ, or BEAUMARCHAIS, found here upon his return from London, and with whom, therefore, all the arrangements were afterwards made.
    I hope you will have received some of the supplies long before this reaches you; infinitely short as they are of what was promised in quantity, quality, and time, I trust they will be of very material service in the operations of the next campaign. It is that, to use the words of our arch enemy, to which we must look forward, and no exertions in preparing for it can be too great, because the events of it must be very decisive. I have the honor to be . . ."[1]

While the Commissioners were finding their way through the multifarious secrecies and circumlocutions of the famous Beaumarchais and his Company, the hard-pressed Americans were already being placed in possession of sorely-needed supplies along the western frontier through the Spanish Governor of Louisiana at New Orleans. The orders of Carlos III to his commanders in the West Indies were being implemented in the form of powder for guns of Fort Wheeling and Fort Pitt and along the far-flung posts of the Ohio.

The Commissioners in Paris were becoming extremely anxious to have a direct representative in Madrid so that they might urge upon the Court of Spain a closer liaison with the Colonies, even, if possible, to the point of an open declaration on their side. Franklin had hoped to make the long and arduous journey himself but the state of his health, together with his advanced age, made such a mission dangerous in the extreme. Thus it came about that Arthur Lee was chosen to go to Spain, in his stead.

Aranda had previously advised against the sending of any American agent to Madrid and had explained at length that the arrival of such an agent would at once become known to the British Ambassador. The result would be disastrous to the system already set up and in operation for getting aid secretly to the Colonies. The Agent's presence would soon be noised about Madrid because the city was smaller than Paris and therefore more easily covered by the spies of the British Ambassador, Lord Grantham. If the knowledge got into his hands surveillance over the ports of Bilbao, Barcelona and Cadiz would be doubled, while these ports had hitherto been able to accept American Corsairs and Privateers as "Casualties" or ordinary traders without the difficulty that existed in the ports of France.

When word reached Madrid early in 1777, that an American Envoy was on his way thither, the Court decided that such a contretemps must be avoided at all costs. It so happened that just one month before Lee arrived on the soil of Spain, Grimaldi had been replaced as Prime Minister by the Count de Floridablanca. Because Grimaldi was familiar with all previous dealings with the Americans, he was chosen to go to Burgos, in the province of Castilla la Vieja and, intercepting Lee, to confer with him there. In this way the chance of a meeting becoming known in the capital would be reduced, if not obviated.

The important meeting took place at Burgos, March 4, 1777. To it came also, as interpreter and adviser, Don Diego de Gardoqui, an outstanding merchant of Bilbao. He had been asked to attend because he spoke English fluently, was thoroughly conversant with the commercial affairs of England and was well-known throughout Europe for his personal integrity as well as for his business acumen. Like Grimaldi, he was well informed on all matters concerning the secret aid previously sent to the Americans; his great mercantile establishment at Bilbao had participated in much of the activity. Gardoqui introduced himself to Lee in a letter from Madrid, dated February 17,1777, and tactfully outlined the idea of their meeting away from the capital:

"Sir,
    My person and House, in the commercial way, are well-known in the American Colonies, not only on account of our long-standing correspondence of thirty to forty years, but also on account of the true affection with which we have endeavored to serve them. I am lately arrived at Madrid, on some par-

ticular affairs, which have occasioned my treating with the Ministers of State, who have honored me with their especial favors and trust, and of course this has led me into the bottom of the principal affairs of Europe, among which I have talked about your coming from Paris to Spain, undoubtedly with the design of treating on the subject of the Colonies, as I judge they have already done, and continue doing at Paris. But I have heard that in such a small place as Madrid, it would be absolutely impossible to remain incognito, either by your own or any other name, and you would of course be spied upon by the gentlemen here who have a real interest therein, and consequently you could not treat with the ministers without hurting the Colonies in the highest degree by your own doings; and, besides, you would set this Court at variance without success. I judge you will improve the opportunity which offers by chance and I think is an excellent one, and have, therefore, no objections to hint it to you; being fully assured that it will cause no displeasure here.

The Marquis de Grimaldi intends to set out soon for Biscay, and I propose to do the same for my house in Bilbao, all which we shall so manage as to meet, one with the other, at Vitoria, where we shall tarry under some good disguise until our mutual arrival; and as this noble Minister has had to this day the entire direction of all affairs, and is of course fully acquainted with His Majesty's intentions, I believe he is the most proper person with whom you may treat either in said place, or in some country house that might be picked for that purpose, and thereby avoid the inconveniences which must inevitably follow by your coming to Madrid.

By the aforesaid belief I have given you further proof of my attachment to the Colonies, and I must also add with all truth that the principal persons here are of the same opinion, although the present state of affairs obliges them to make no show thereof. In short, Sir, I hope you will approve of my proposed method being the safest and most natural to carry on the views of both parties. I beg you will give me an answer through the same hands, as will deliver the present to you, not doubting that you will tarry at Vitoria until we get there, and you will also observe that you will be at full liberty to proceed to Madrid if you should judge proper, after you have talked over the matter with the nobleman.

I have the honor to subscribe myself,

                                                            JAMES GARDOQUI
P.S. Having considered upon the properest place for our meeting, we have decided it on that of BURGOS instead of VITORIA, which pray note accordingly, and I hope to meet you there."

Lee replied to the wise suggestion of holding the meeting in Burgos and wrote to Gardoqui from that place on the 28th of February, 1777:

"I have the honor of yours of the 17th and, agreeable to your request will wait for you at this place."[2]

2.

Thus, early in 1777, the strong, quiet figure of Gardoqui is introduced on the stage of American affairs. During the conference between these three men Lee, Grimaldi and Gardoqui who probably more than all but a few others knew the needs of the Colonies, a very clear understanding was reached. Future aid from Spain was promised as a continuing policy of the Court. In the atmosphere of a small provincial town and in the simple, unspectacular fashion of principals who need only a thorough understanding of one another and their respective points of view, they set up the plan for administering the delicate but necessary machinery of supply. The wonder is that so little of the work of these men has been given a proper appraisal in the history of the times.

Grimaldi made the situation of his government perfectly clear to Lee; going into the situation with Portugal in detail; explaining the time necessary for the regular Treasure Ships, so vital a part of Spain's economic stability, to arrive home from their annual voyage; making clear that the Spanish navy had been alerted for special duty in the guarding of these convoys; clarifying the position of England toward Portugal and adding the significant comment that, should there be an open declaration of war between England and Spain, all supplies then leaving Spanish ports and all supplies in future would be cut off from the Colonies, the result of the inevitable blockade of Barcelona, Bilbao and Cadiz; these ports were presently engaged in sending quantities of secret war supplies to the Americans, such trade being a legitimate business.

Grimaldi also informed Lee that only a short time before this conference at Burgos, Vergennes had suggested an open policy of aid in common, that to this suggestion the Ministers of Spain had replied with proposals for a more effective alliance for military action; that France and Spain arm as rapidly as possible, organize a special combined squadron of twelve ships, take on a few French troops from the island of Santo Domingo and from that base and Cape Francoise take joint action after effecting a juncture with the Spanish troops in the Indies. To this plan Vergennes had objected, fearing to arouse the suspicions of the English and bring on reprisals along the channel ports.

Lee was told that an open declaration of war could not be made at that time but that stores of ammunition, guns, powder and clothing would be deposited at Havana and New Orleans where they could be safely delivered to the Americans, either in their own ships or in Spanish ships plying those waters. Supplies would be collected at Barcelona, Bilbao and Cadiz for shipment in Spanish vessels to those ports. Lee pleaded vainly for the open interposition of Spain and France. Grimaldi answered him in words which have since become famous for, though his words summed up succinctly the position of Spain at the moment, they contained a promise which was soon to be fulfilled to the letter in the battles for Mobile and Pensacola:

"You have considered your situation and not ours. The moment has not yet come for us. The war with Portugal — France being unprepared, and our treasure ships from South America not being arrived makes it improper for us to

declare immediately. These reasons will probably *cease within the year* and
then will be the moment."[3]   [underlining by the author]

Lee felt constrained by his instructions to send a Memorial to Carlos
III, but, as for the planned visit to Madrid, he deemed it unwise and
unnecessary after having listened to the Marquis de Grimaldi's clear
statement of Spain's position. He decided, however, to continue conferences with Gardoqui who, for his part, set to work at once on the
organization of aid which had been agreed upon.

Gardoqui's emergence upon the diplomatic stage brought an end to
the official operations of the famous Beaumarchais as a representative
of the Court of Spain. The change gave great relief to Aranda in Paris
and deep satisfaction to those Americans who were to do business with
Spain and look to her for help for their Cause. Gardoqui arranged immediately to sever his personal connections with the family firm in
Bilbao in order that there could be no taint of speculation against
himself or his family over the transaction he would be engaged in on
behalf of the King. It would have been impossible to dispense with the
House of Gardoqui which had such wide ramifications in the world of
European trade and was skilled and long experienced in commercial
dealings with North America. Gardoqui's plan for dealing both in
money and supplies proved to be so well conceived and so efficiently
carried out that neither Lord Grantham, the British Ambassador in
Madrid, nor any of his network of spies could discover any connection
between the funds being expended and the Court of Carlos III
although they were well aware that help was going out to the
Americans.

3.

Lee's first report to the Committee of Secret Correspondence after
the Burgos conference was sent from that place March 8, 1777:

"Gentlemen,
    A person of high rank having been sent to confer with me here, I am
authorized to assure you, that supplies for the army will be sent to you by every
opportunity from Bilbao. I can say to you with certainty, that a merchant there
has orders for that purpose; he is now here with me to have a list from me, and
to contract for blankets, which are manufactured in this part of the country. I
am also desired to inform you of ammunition and clothing being deposited at
New Orleans and the Havanna, with directions to *LEND* [author's italics] them
to such American vessels as may call there for that purpose.
    I am trying to get a sum of money put into our hands immediately, that we
may the more assuredly answer your bills, should you find it necessary to draw,
and perhaps pay for some ships in Europe. It will also be my endeavor to
procure some able Veteran Officers from the Irish Brigades in this service. . . .
                              I have the Honor to be . . ."[4]

In the Memorial which Lee addressed to Carlos III, referred to above, he had asked that the Spanish Ambassador at the Hague be instructed to authorize Sir George Grand of Amsterdam to pay-over sums for the use of the Commissioners, either Franklin, Deane or Lee, when the need for purchasing supplies in Holland should arise. Sir George had already been trusted with such transactions by the Court of France and was known to be of the highest personal integrity.

The plan of operations which Lee had agreed upon with Gardoqui in the conferences at Burgos, and later at Vitoria, was developing with great smoothness and rapidity. It was, therefore, in a happy frame of mind that Lee sent the Committee of Secret Correspondence a report of progress, dated Vitoria, March 18, 1777:

"Vitoria, March, 18th, 1777

Gentlemen,

I had the honor of writing you on the 8th from Burgos, since which I have had another conference at this place for greater secrecy and despatch. In addition to the supplies, which I informed you were to be furnished through the House of Gardoqui by every opportunity, and the powder and clothing which are at New Orleans, and will be advanced to your order, I am assured of having credit from time to time on Holland, and that orders will be given to receive your vessels at the Havanna, as those of the Most Favored Nation, the French, are received. They are to examine whether there are any Veteran Irish Officers fit for your service, and if there are, to send them. I have avoided stipulating any return on our part.

In conformity with the above arrangement, I have settled with M. Gardoqui, who now is with me, and from whom I have received every possible assistance, to despatch a vessel with all possible expedition, laden with salt, sail and tent cloth, cordage, blankets, and war-like stores, as he can immediately procure, and an assortment of drugs as I think will be necessary for the three prevailing camp deseases [sic]. Those who furnish these supplies are very desirous of an expedition being ordered against Pensacola, in order that the possession of that place may render the communication between the Southern Colonies and New Orleans, from which they would wish to succor you, more sure and more secret. The Captain has my directions to make for Philadelphia, or any port to the Southward, and wait your orders. At M. Gardoqui's desire, I have given him a recommendation to all the American Captains, who may sail from Bilbao, whether in Public or Private service, to receive such stores as he shall send them for your use.

When this is arranged, I shall return to Paris, where the business of the credit upon Holland is to be settled, and of which you shall have notice by the first opportunity. In my former letters from Bordeaux and Nantes, I took the liberty of remarking upon the deranged state of your Commerce. I find here that you have not sent any vessels to Bilbao, though as being the most convenient, it is most frequented by private vessels. It is a free port, has no Custom-House, and therefore business is despatched with more secrecy and expedition. Rice, indigo, tar, pitch, and turpentine, bear a good price there, and fish in Lent. By the Provincial laws of Biscay, tobacco is prohibited, but it may be landed at the port of San Sebastian, some fourteen leagues distant; and it sells well in Spain; but it must be strong Virginia tobacco for this market. The House of Gardoqui has promised to collect from other places, such things as I have informed them will be proper for your service.

As M. Montandauine, and Mon. Schwieghauser at Nantes, and the Messrs. Delapys at Bordeau, are the best and most respectable merchants, so the Gardoquis are at Bilbao. Their zeal and activity in our Cause were greatly manifested in the affair of the privateer; they are besides in the special confidence of the Court, and one of them has been employed as interpreter in all our business. . . .

ARTHUR LEE"[5]

James Gardoqui was a man of action. Once his word had been given and a plan of action decided upon he proceeded at once to its execution. Lee later mentioned this quality and paid sincere tribute to his forthright activities on behalf of the Cause. Shortly after Gardoqui's return to Madrid from his last meeting with Lee at Vitoria he wrote the latter a reassuring letter. He had acted upon the promised financial credit with such promptness that his letter was in Paris almost before the American Agent had had time to make the return journey to that city.

"Madrid, April, 28th, 1777

Dear Sir,

The 24th instant, I had the pleasure to pay my last Compliments to you, enclosing twenty second bills, amounting to 81,000 livres, French money, as per duplicates herein to serve in case of need; and I being still without your favors, I have only to forward to you a further sum of 106,500 livres, in sixteen bills, as per memorandum at foot hereof, to my credit, advising me of it in due time, by which you will oblige him who longs for the pleasure of hearing from you, and is with very unfeigned esteem and respect . . . .

JAMES GARDOQUI"[6]

In a letter of May 8, 1777, from Paris, Lee thanked Gardoqui and assured him that the amounts received would be used for the purposes settled at Vitoria, at the same time begging him to extend his [Lee's] thanks to his *unknown friend*.[7] [underlining by the author]

What these purposes were, that is, what were the items most urgently needed by the Colonies, are revealed in detail in the files of Gardoqui. He placed immediate orders for 11,000 pairs of shoes, 41,-000 pairs of stockings, 18,000 blankets in addition to large shipments of tentings, shirtings and medicines. Here is Gardoqui's original list and statement of goods purchased or ordered by means of letters of credit given to the American Commissioners:

"Complete Memorial of supplies and costs before September, 1777. Amounts, Estimates and Balance rendered:

Balance of Mr. Grand; rendered June 10, 1777 . . . . 664,178.II.
Payments to August, 14, 1777 . . . . 170,196.II.I
Drafts since that time by the Commissioner,
Mr. Williams 30,000. 0.0

Agreements have been made for 30,000 suits of
  clothing, approximate cost, each 35 libres,
. . . . 1050,000. 0.0
Ditto . . . for 1,000 fusees 18,000. 0.0
Ditto . . . for 100,000 pds. of copper and tin for
                          casting cannon 150,000. 0.0
Ditto . . . 100 tons of Salt Petre 110,000. 0.0
Ditto-For shoes and pistols ordered by Mr.
  Williams, also including the ships for
  carrying out the Goods 250,000. 0.0
Repairs for vessels (several), supposed cost 50,000. 0.0
Paid Mr. DeLap of Amsterdam 40,000. 0.0
Cordage, Anchors, and for a 64 (?) gun ship 200,000. 0.0
To compleat and load the ship in Holland the
  least sum will be 550,000. 0.0
Mr. Grand received July, 10 . . . . 500,000. 0.0
Balance against the Commissioners by their
  estimate 1454,018. 0.0
Balance as above 1.454.018.10.0
To be received in October 500,000. 0.0
Balance against the Commissioners after receiving
  the sum of -500,000 will be 954,018,10.0
Balance as above . . . 954,018.10 . . . . Total-
                                                    1,454,018.10.0
Blankets, shirts, cloathes [sic] brass cannon and many other articles soon will be
necessary are not reckoned but they will amount to a very considerable sum.
For Instance —
80,000 blankets at 7 libres 560,000.0.0
800,000 shirts at 4 libres 320,000.0.0
20,000 shoes at 3.10 . . . . 70,000.0.0
10,000 sterkings-(already bought) 15,000.0.0
70,000 ditto (not bought) 105,000.0.0
100 tons of Powder (wanted) 200,000.0.0
Brass cannon cannot be estimated at present.
The sum which the Commissioners will be indebted
  by October 2,244,018.0.0
The Commissioners orders are for 80,000 suits of cloaths, compleat, but only
30,000 are ordered, to compleat this order they will want . . 1,750,000.0.0
To give each soldier two shirts 320,000.0.0
60,000 pairs of shoes 210,000.0.0
Furniture for 3,000 Horse 450,000.0.0
Brass cannon already ordered will at least
  amount 2,000,000.0.0
Adding the charge of transportation and expenses of every kind these goods
must be sent in armed vessels, the Congress has ordered eight ships of the
Line 3,000,000.0.0
to be purchased which will altogether amount
  to 7.730,000.0.0
The ships of war may now be purchased and probably for the money at which
they are estimated at: They are absolutely necessary as well for carrying goods
as to engage in open commerce and bring back the products of America for
payment of the sum wanted.

The estimate does not include many necessary articles, as the Congress would like if their trade were protected by eight ships of the line, they would be able to procure them in exchange for their production."[8]

Gardoqui gave the order for the weaving, collection and baling of the blankets and other woolen articles to the weaving centers of the Province of Palencia of which Vitoria is the capital. Palencia was at this time the center of the finest of the wool-weaving industries in the country. Gardoqui's orders threw this peaceful province into a fever of activity; in every pueblo men, women and children worked furiously in order to complete the work. The plazas in the small towns were piled high with the product of their hands while being baled for shipment to the city of Palencia. Excitement spread throughout the province when it became known that the blankets were destined for the army of Washington in America.

The influx of Gardoqui's orders brought feverish activity to the ports of Barcelona, Bilbao and Cadiz. In the matter of arms and ammunition, absolute secrecy was required since Spanish arsenals, like the arsenals of France, were under the direct ownership of the Crown. Gardoqui made arrangements with De La Riva, a banker of Madrid, to handle the release of such material by the government and in this way effected its transferal without arousing undue suspicion. By September, 1777, Spain had given Lee directly 187,500 livres for expenditures made *outside of Spain* besides having contributed a priceless amount in goods not listed in value, all this without any qualification whatever as to repayment.

FOOTNOTES

[1]Arthur Lee to the Committee of Secret Correspondence, January 3, 1777, in *Diplomatic Correspondence, op. cit.*, 2: 20-21.

[2]Gardoqui to Lee, February 17, 1777, in *ibid.*, 2: 33-35.

[3]Don Miguel G. del Campillo, Nota Preliminar y Catálogo in *Relaciones Diplomaticas entre España y los Estados del Norte America* (Archive Nacional, Madrid, July, 1944).

[4]Lee to Committee of Secret Correspondence, March 8, 1777, in *Diplomatic Correspondence, op. cit.*, 2: 40 (letter); 2: 41-44 (Memorial).

[5]Lee to Committee of Secret Correspondence, March 18, 1777, in *ibid.*, 2: 47-53.

[6]Gardoqui to Lee, April 28, 1777, in *ibid.*, 2: 59.

[7]Lee to Gardoqui, May 8, 1777, in *ibid.*, 2: 60-61.

[8]Gardoqui to the American Commissioners, A.H.N.; Legajo 3884. Also, in Yela, *op. cit.*, Tomo 1: 130-135.

CHAPTER IV

1.

During this same September of 1777, the Court was besieged with Memorials and pleas for aid to the Colonies. Beaumarchais's account has been mentioned previously. The Spanish Crown had responded readily to the plea for succor made by Lee at Burgos. Now, the American Commissioners sent Carlos III a Memorial in which, at length and in detail, they lay the basis for their request for a loan or a subsidy. Signed at Passy by the full Commission, the Memorial constitutes the first direct request for funds.

"Memorial presented by the American Deputies to the Spanish and French Courts — Sept. 1777 — (Original)

To his Excellency the Count de Vergennes, Minister for the Foreign Affairs of France, . . . and to his Excellency the Count d'Aranda Embassador of Spain. . . .

A Memorial from the Commissioners of the United States of America; The Congress some months since acquainted us, that 80,000 suits of clothes will be wanted for their army next winter: also a number of brass cannon, fusils, pistols, etc. and a large quantity of naval stores.

To pay for these, they informed us that they had purchased great quantities of tobacco, rice, indigo, potash, and other produce of the country, which they would forward to us as soon as the great difficulty of procuring ships and mariners for the Merchant-Service, with Convoys of force sufficient, could be surmounted.

They also directed us to borrow two millions sterling in Europe on the credit of the United States; which sum, if the loan can be effected here, would have been most profitable in the factories of these Kingdoms, been greatly to the advantage of their people, not only in encouraging and increasing their present industries, but, by introducing the knowledge of these manufactures and products, as well as the taste for them, would have become the source of great future commerce.

The Loan was found to be, in our present circumstances, difficult and without the Aid of some credit from France and Spain, seems impossible. Also the ships bringing such products of America to us have been intercepted, some by the treachery of the seamen, but chiefly by the Enemy's ships of war, which, together with the difficulty mentioned above, of finding ships, and the blocading of our Ports, has left us hitherto disappointed in the expected remittances.

But France, having furnished us with some money in regular payments, and kindly promised us a continuance of them: and Spain, having given us Expectations of considerable Aids, though without specifying the quantity, the Commissioners conceiving that it would not be less than what France is giving, and impressed with the urgent necessity for clothing, etc., ventured to order 30,000 suits of clothing: and have also ordered and contracted for considerable quantities of Arms and other Necessaries for which they are now indebted.

Spain after furnishing us with 1,870,500 livres in money, and some Naval Stores, sent directly from her ports (the value not yet known to us) has desisted. And the Commissioners find themselves extremely embarrassed by their engagements, and likely to be discredited with their Constituents by the expectations they have anticipated of effectual aids from France and Spain, if not a Diversion that might be favorable to the States: but the worst of this is the prejudice to their Cause that the Country must suffer through the disappointment in supplies.

The Commissioners received soon after their arrival, kind assurances of the amity of France and Spain and substantial proof of it which will ever be remembered with gratitude. They, by authority of the Congress, offered proposals for a Treaty of Commerce, and for uniting the force of the States with that of France and Spain, in conquering, for those Crowns, the English Sugar Islands, together with other advantages and stipulations, in case Britain should begin a war against them on account of the Aids granted to us: which proposals the Commissioners hope were not disagreeable and they have long expected, with anxiety, an answer to them.

Some late occurences in France related to our armed vessels and their prizes, and the cessation of exportation of war-like stores and supplies from Spain, might occasion a doubt about the disposition of those Courts towards the United States: might occasion a feeling that the attitude had changed, if the Commissioners had not the fullest confidence in their dispositions as being well-founded in the True Interest of those Kingdoms; and as it is believed that no cause has been given on the American side for their diminution.

They therefore ascribe the late Strictness in France to the circumstances of the Times; and the stoppage of supplies from Spain to the inattention occasioned by occupation with other great Affairs. And they hope that a little time will remedy both the one and the other.

In the meanwhile, they request a present supply proportioned to their needs which will appear by the accompanying Estimate. France and Spain, (as stated in a former memorial), will gain greatly by the American Commerce in the way of products and manufacturing of goods, by the growth of their shipping and service for seamen, by the furnishing of more employment to their people; and, of course, the increase of their Naval Power, while that of Britain is diminished and weakened in proportion, which will double the difference. But they [the Commissioners], offer these advantages not in a manner of putting them up for sale for a price, but as ties of Friendship they wish to cultivate with these Kingdoms.

Also, knowing, that after a Peace settlement in the States, a few years will enable them to repay the Aids that may be lent them, they feel more freedom in asking for greater assistance by way of a *LOAN* [author's italics] than they would presume to ask by way of a *SUBSIDY*. [author's italics.]

But if these Powers apprehend that the granting of such Aid may be the means of occasioning a War between them and Britain, and present circumstances render such a War not desirable; and if they should then decline the same, and advise the Americans to make PEACE; it is requested that these Courts, as friends of the United States, assist them with advice and influence in the negotiation, so that their liberties and Freedom of Commerce may be maintained.

And they further request to be explicitly informed as to the present intentions of these Courts respecting their promises, that they may communicate as much of the same to the Congress as may be necessary in the regulating of its conduct, and thus preventing any misapprehension that the above-mentioned proceedings might otherwise occasion.

They can assure your Excellencies that they have no word of any Treaty on foot in America for an accord, nor do they believe there is any, nor have any propositions been made by them to the Court of England: nor any smallest overture been received from there which they have not already communicated; the Congress having the fullest confidence in the good will and wisdom of these Courts and having, accordingly given us Orders to enter into no Treaty with any other Power inconsistant with propositions that are likely to be accepted; and to act with their advise and approbation. And the Commissioners are firmly of the opinion that nothing would induce the Congress to accept any terms involving exclusive commerce with Britain, except through despair of obtaining aid and support from Europe.

But, since it is probable that England is not yet weak enough or humbled enough to agree to any equitable terms of a truce; and, as the United States, through aid that would be much less than that required to be spent by France and Spain should they enter the war, would be able to continue the war with England as long as may be necessary; the Commissioners request that these powers resolve upon granting such Subsidy as may be sufficient for the purpose; or otherwise lend to the said States the sum they wish of two millions sterling (2) at the rate of six per cent interest; which they have every reason to believe the States will be well able to pay after a successful closing of the war, and which they mean to perform punctually.

Dated this day at Passy-of September, 1777 —

B. FRANKLIN
SILAS DEANE
ARTHUR LEE — (PUBRICADOS TODOS MENOS LEE)"[1]
[all signed in person except Lee]

2.

In this long and desperate Memorial it is very interesting to note again that the Commissioners fail to mention the cash gift to Hortalez et Cie or Beaumarchais by Spain when the receipts for the one million livres tournoises had long been in the hands of the French Minister Vergennes. While taking note of the interruptions in the flow of supplies from the ports of France, the Memorial fails to acknowledge that a stream of supplies was going out to the Colonies from the ports of Spain. The Commissioners suggest that the interruption, which was causing them so much concern, might be attributable to the action of American privateers who were preying indiscriminately upon the commerce of friendly countries. (This ticklish problem was to embarrass both Courts and the Commissioners at a later date when both Franklin and John Jay were to categorically deny any knowledge of such activities.) The "Strictness" at the Court of France to which they refer was the subject of long argument and friction over the actions of these American captains in bringing their prizes into French ports. The British Ambassador in Paris had lodged bitter complaints against the countenancing of such activity by a friendly state. Similar complaints had been lodged by Lord Grantham at Madrid. The latter had not met with the success of his colleague in Paris due to the astute intervention of Gardoqui in an incident affecting an American vessel. The vessel in question had been pursued directly into a Spanish port by a British warship and captured under the eyes of the inhabitants of the town. Gardoqui promptly secured the release of the ship and her crew, enraging the British Ambassador by the bland reminder that, once in Spanish waters, pursuit of the ships of friendly nations could not be tolerated. The point was a delicate one since many of these American captains were operating in such a reckless manner that they were also giving trouble to the commerce of Spain and France and without the knowledge of the American Congress. There were instances of captures of French and Spanish ships and the confiscation of cargoes of food and produce destined for the use of the population. This was an attack upon legitimate trade. This unrestrained privateering almost succeeded in bringing about a break between the two Courts and the struggling Colonies at the critical moment when the Commissioners were urgently pressing for more aid and supplies in order to continue the war. Gardoqui was an invaluable ally of the Americans in so many ways but in no way more than by acting quietly and astutely in their behalf to keep these privateering activities from the sensitive ears of the British in Madrid. His knowledge of English, his widespread contacts in the world of trade made him the ideal man for settling such troublesome affairs. The House of Gardoqui at Bilbao was in a position to make it abundantly plain to ship captains that they must not trifle with the Law of Nations if they hoped to use Spanish ports for speedy repairs and to sail away with full bottoms. When one of the Gardoqui family thus stated the case to them, both American and British captains were made to see reason. It was the unbridled privateering operations which made the French King more cautious in supplying the Commissioners with needed aid.

Perhaps the Memorial would have reached Madrid in a slightly altered form had Lee been present to sign it in person, for Lee knew what Franklin and Deane did not know (or at least as clearly as he knew it), that succor from Spain was continuing. However, the Memorial brought to a head the important matter of payment for supplies from Spain, heretofore taken as gifts from the Court to the Colonies. On this head Lee wrote to Gardoqui September 25, 1777:

"Sir,

I have now before me your favors of May, 5th, and 29th, together with the last, of the 4th of this month. By this time I expect that you have been apprized, or upon applying upon those who gave you orders you will be informed, that with regard to what has been remitted, both in money and effects, no return is expected, agreeably to what you know passed at Vitoria, and of which I informed both you and your Minister and my Constituents in the letters, which I had the honor of reading to you at that place. It gives me satisfaction that everything has been arranged and settled; and I am relieved of the embarrassment of appearing to have understood so ill what passed, or so greatly to have misrepresented it.

We are now to begin on a new footing, and I shall take care that my constituents be duly informed, that for all the aids they receive hereafter from your quarter, they are to make returns in pitch, tar, etc. to your house, agreeable to your letter. I beg to know by your next, whether the same arrangement is to take place for the future with regard to the deposits at the Havanna and New Orleans, or whether nothing further is to be transmitted through those channels, if that is so, the trouble of sending thither and the disappointment may be prevented.

I have the honor to be, ..."[2]

Lee followed this clear letter of agreement as to future aids through the House of Gardoqui with a long letter to the Congress, dated, Oct. 6, 1777, in which he states that he has urged Gardoqui to send on as many blankets as possible to prepare for the coming winter campaign and concedes that all articles bought through that house are to be paid for with products from America but also states that he *privately* hopes that they will actually be paid for by the King of Spain. This explains a matter that was in future to cause much confusion in estimating the cost of aid given by the Court, one item that was never satisfactorily cleared nor understood by the Congress; namely: the thirty-thousand blankets for which Gardoqui had contracted among the weavers of Palencia; and for which his house had paid in advance, in order to get this work done among the small weaving centers of that province in time for that winter's campaign. This order Lee had clearly contracted for after the written agreement between himself and Gardoqui for future payments on goods ordered through the House of Gardoqui.

In this same report to the Congress, Lee explains the position of his arrangements and understanding with the now troublesome Beaumarchais and the company of "Hortalez." In all his dealings with "Mons. Hortalez" he was assured that no return was expected since the Court of France had made funds available up to two million-pounds sterling, in specie, arms, and ammunition, for which there was to be no repayment made. He does not mention to Congress that one half of this sum had been given outright by the Court of Spain. He likewise makes no mention of the fact that the Company of "Hortalez et Cie" was actually financed by a joint gift of money from the Courts of Spain and France, as agreed upon by the Count of Aranda and Vergennes in Paris, and backed by the two Kings, Carlos III and Louis XVI. It is possible, but not probable, that Lee was unaware of the source of these funds; Beaumarchais had made Lee privy to his plans while expounding them in London and later in Paris. If so, this gift of one million livres from the Court at Madrid was certainly one of the few secrets actually kept in France at that time. Certainly Beaumarchais made reports of the expenditures of these funds both to the French Court and to Madrid, as has been noted in detail heretofore. Lee goes on to state in this same report to Congress that the goods bought with these funds had already sailed in the three ships, the *Amphitrite*, *Mercure* and the *Seine.* He goes on to state: "The Minister has repeatedly assured us, and that in the most explicit terms, that *no return is expected for these subsidies.*"[3] [underlining by the author]

As late as 1778, the Commissioners were still disturbed over the status of Beaumarchais and the funds expended in 1776. In a letter to the Committee of Foreign Affairs of the Congress, Lee reveals the truly remarkable version of these transactions which Vergennes chose to offer them:

> ". . . On the 16th of September 1778, Count de Vergennes wrote as follows to Mr. Gerard, at that time French Minister to the United States, 'Mr. Franklin and his Colleagues wish to know what articles have been furnished to them by the King, and what M. de Beaumarchais has furnished on his own account; and they have insinuated to me that Congress is in the belief that all the articles that have been sent, or at least a great part of them, were on His Majesty's account. I have just answered them that the King has furnished nothing; that he has simply permitted M. de Beaumarchais to be provided with articles from his arsenals, upon condition of replacing them'. . . ."[4]

In future adjustments of debts between the Congress and the Courts of Spain and France it is understandable that no recompense was asked or expected by the King of Spain for his outright gift. But it is puzzling that at no time does it appear in the private correspondence of the Commissioners that the gift was ever made. There can be no cause for surprise that the Count de Aranda became alarmed over the equivocal position in which his Court was placed nor that the aid given by Spain remains to this day almost unknown to Americans.

3.

The critical year, 1777, had scarcely ended when Lee was again in correspondence with the Committee of Foreign Affairs with concrete evidence of the success of his Spanish mission. He wrote from Paris:

"Gentlemen,

I have the pleasure to inform you, that our Friends in Spain have promised to supply to us with *three millions of Livres* [underlining of the author] in the course of this year. I should be happy that immediate and precise orders were sent from Congress for the appropriation of it; which will prevent it being expended in a manner, perhaps, less useful than the purpose they may wish to fulfill. My last advise from Bilbao, assured me that they were shipping the blankets and stockings I ordered. . . .

I have the honor to be. . . ."[5]

The bills for these supplies, ordered after the agreement entered into by Lee, for the Commissioners, and Gardoqui for his Commercial House in Bilbao, were rendered by letter from James Gardoqui to Lee as follows:

"Bilbao, April, 1st, 1778,

Invoice of 75 bales of merchandise shipped on board the GEORGE, Captain, JOB KNIGHT, for Cape Ann, consigned to ELBRIDGE GERRY, on account of ARTHUR LEE.

No. I to — 75, bales containing fine large Palencia blankets, at 27
Riales, ... 52,002,00
Charges to
413 vares of wrappers, at 2-Riales, ... 823
To packing, lighterage, etc. 750
_____
1,576,00
Commission, 3 percent, ... 1,607,11
Riales of V. 55,185,11
Placed to the debit of Arthur Lee.
Bilbao, the 28th of March, 1778,
(errors excepted)
J. GARDOQUI & CO."[6]

The total number of blankets sent from Bilbao for the Congress Jan. 1778 amounted to 8668.[7]

From the time of his first meeting with Gardoqui in Burgos, Lee lost no opportunity to press the pleas of the Congress for stores and supplies needed for the Continental army. He had reason to be grateful for the speed and dispatch with which such orders were carried out, fulfillment being limited only by the availability of such stores within Spain. When vital material was not at hand, it was promptly ordered through Holland and credited to Lee. Purchases from that country are the subject of Lee's letter of May 23, 1778, to the Committee of Foreign Affairs:

"Gentlemen,

In consequence of your despatches by my colleague, MR. ADAMS, [agent in Holland] I lost no moment to press the renewal of the order for the supplying you with such stores as you want, and as that country affords, with the Court of Spain. I have the satisfaction to inform you that such orders are given, and I am assured will be carried into execution as speedily as possible. . . .

I have the honor to be. . . ."[8]

In June he was able to transmit the good news of a further grant of funds by Carlos III for the furtherance of the Cause and, at the same time, asked for instructions to guide him in his negotiations with the Court on quite a different subject:

"Paris, June, 1st, 1778.

Gentlemen,

Our Friends in Spain have promised to remit me 150,000 Livres more, which I shall continue to vest in supplies that may be useful to you.

I hope, in consequence of what I formerly wrote, to have express order of Congress relative to the line they choose to fix, between the Territories of the United States and those of the Crown of Spain. . . ."[9]

He had pressed the Congress time after time for word on the frontier question without getting any advice on this all important point. This subject of the frontier was, years later, to be one of the most vexing problems calling for settlement between the two nations when they came together to reach a final reckoning. Much disgruntlement would have been avoided for the negotiators of a later date had the Congress made some effort at settlement when Spain was generously pouring out supplies for the American Cause and feeling between the two countries was warmly cordial.

Throughout the critical years of 1777 and 1778, there appears to have been perfect accord between the Agent for the American Commissioners at Paris, in the person of Lee, and the Agent of the Spanish Government, James Gardoqui. Due to Gardoqui's enterprise the activity in all the ports of Spain equalled that of the ports in France. Through the remarkably efficient liaison between the banker De La Riva and the Court of Spain, and Mr. Adams, the American Agent at the Hague, funds expended in Holland were kept from the general knowledge. The merchant of Bilbao managed so adroitly that very little was known of what actually went out of Spain to the fighting forces in America. American Corsairs and Privateers slipped into her ports as well as those of her islands, refitted, took on supplies and sailed with the maximum secrecy possible under the trying circumstances of the times.

Lee fervently hoped for an open declaration of war between Spain and England and we find him anxiously watching and reporting on any news of the expected arrival of the Spanish Treasure Ships from South America. Franklin also looked forward to the possibility of an open declaration as soon as these ships should arrive. Grimaldi's statement at Burgos, quoted earlier, had been interpreted as holding out the hope of such a declaration by the Americans. Perhaps the wish had been father to the thought, but the expectation remained that eventually Spain openly would declare for the American Cause.

4.

The Memorial, which had been presented to both the Courts of Spain and France in October 1777, was studied carefully in Madrid. In the opinion of the Court it called for a fresh understanding with Paris and, accordingly, a Memorial was drawn up and sent to the Court of France. It is a clear, frank statement of the policies which Spain believed the two countries should adopt in their future dealings with the Colonies. It reveals in many ways why Spain felt reluctant to give support openly to the Americans:

"Memorial made by Spain and sent to France
San Lorenzo, 17th, October, 1777

On last September, the American Deputies residing in Paris, presented themselves to His Most Christian Majesty's Ministry, [French] and to the Count of Aranda, to place in their hands a duplicate copy of the same memorial.

The aim of this paper was to depict in vivid colour, the critical position in which the Colonies find themselves now; exhausted by their continuous efforts and by waste, they are almost unable to go on, without immediate and sufficient assistance.

They skillfully suggest the many advantages the Spanish and French Crowns could draw to themselves if they openly were on the American side; but, as they recognize that our Sovereigns have very different views, owing to a number of reasons, the said Deputies have limited themselves to an exposition of their actual needs, and the most appropriate means of remedying these.

Having first calculated the cost of numerous articles they are asking for, to provide clothing and armaments for their troops; in addition to Ordance and many other needed articles; besides the indebtedness in which they now find themselves, owing to prior purchases they cannot repay; because the British Navy had prevented them from returning goods they had destined for that purpose: all this has caused the Commissioners to look for a Loan, of corresponding amount under normal security usual in such a case. But, since they are very doubtful of bringing this project to good terms; oppressed by so many duties and suspicions that many of their own countrymen are against them; and since many assistances promised them have not arrived, as they had hoped they resort to the generosity of spirit of the Monarchs of Spain and France, and hope, under the present circumstances, they will be supplied with those means which will enable them to prosecute the war; and thus rendering of little use the enormous expenditures in which England is involved because of them.

They cannot but help stating how disheartened the Americans should be, considering the absolute need they have, and knowing that the aid is not supplied. This could hasten them into an adjustment with their Mother-Country; above all since meeting with such difficulties as their ship-owners have found in Spanish and French harbours recently. The Deputies treat slightly concerning the profits of direct commerce with their provinces; that such commerce would easily pay for money advanced, soon after peace was declared and their independence established; and on these premises they ask new and powerful aid, to the amount of two millions sterling, even though the Crowns lend that at the interest rate they mention. They wish too, to be informed about the true intentions of His Catholic Majesty and His Most Christian Majesty, so that their influence and salutary counsel, as perfect Allies, may be conveyed to the Congress for further decision.

The Count of Vergennes in his despatch to the MARQUIS of OSSUN [French Ambassador at Madrid] takes account of everything in the Deputies' Memorial.

The said Minister is aware of the possibility for these Commissioners to take advantage of our refusal, and that they could, on that ground, try to come to terms with England. So, the Count thinks it would be very simple to decide that, if we are assured that any such negotiation could not be initiated by them, after we have supplied that aid for which they are asking; because these disbursements, greater or smaller, would be less important in comparison with our main object of expanding this civil war, thus lessening the power of England more and more.

However, we cannot rely on such security, and we may well fear that there will be, among the Colonists, many who are inclined to renew friendship with the Mother-Country, either through extreme fear or through affection for that government.

Then in the opinion of this Minister, there is a third course for us to consider and it is this:

No matter how the Colonists might think, if we openly refuse these secret assistances that we have promised, and that they need, they may at last, be forced to look for some other remedy, having been deprived of sufficient means to go forward. England, chastened by experience, either would be satisfied by laying down a milder rule over her Rebel Subjects, or would try to transform them into faithful Allies, with the idea of leaning upon that Continent and its resources, for further and greater enterprises.

All this can contribute to considerable damage for the Spanish and French Powers; and, in such a situation, the weakened Colonists, short of strength, will not be able to refuse some acceptable offer from the Mother-Country.

All these things taken into consideration, and many others have been mentioned to the King. Vergennes says, that His Majesty was reluctant to make a final decision on such a grave matter, without first consulting with the King, his Uncle. But to avoid disappointing the Deputies he had pointed out that they would get some monetary help; as much as present circumstances would permit the said Court.

As to their hint about obtaining some battleships for them, France's opinion is that it would be neither feasible nor decent for both Crowns; and after much consideration, the French Ministry prefer that the Americans be given 6,000,-000 tournoises pounds, (half a million by each Crown) *as a present* [author's underlining] and that against this gift several tight agreements be exacted. For instance, to keep inviolable the secret about this gift, even from the Congress, that these said Deputies be bound to require permission from both Courts to enter into any negotiation, finally, that the said six millions to be given in installments, and deliveries should be halted as soon as the Courts know of any negotiation being under way; this last condition is quite necessary, to dispel a good many difficulties.

That Court wishes to know His Catholic Majesty's opinion on all this in order to proceed accordingly. And the Count of Vergennes ends his despatch with the statement that the *covenant* with the Deputies must not be *written:* [author's underlining] That the loan for 2,000,000 sterling should not be allowed: and that a part from the aid France has hitherto supplied, we must see that this actual conjuncture be conclusive for both Courts; with perhaps more from Spain, due to her vicinity to the Colonies and the huge extent of her Dominions in America.

This is a substantial abridgement of what the American Deputies have stated, and the annotations of this French Court about the affair, in order to explain more accurately the idea that the Catholic King and his Ministry have reached on these demands.

That the continuance of the American War is extraordinarily useful to the Crowns of France and Spain need not be proven and no one can doubt that it is very profitable for them to join their force and means to keep that. Therefore the Colonists must get our support; as much with real monetary assistance and useful goods for the war, as also by means of direction about their suitable behavior; and it is as well, if here in Europe, these two Courts behave with such firmness as to insure respect from our common enemy.

The two Crowns, being convinced of this axiom, have already acted in such a way up to now; they have openly supported the Americans in the ports of the two countries, have sent every kind of supplies to that country, and have demonstrated and taken precautions that have partially limited the English power, and have hindered Britain from falling upon the Colonies with her entire force.

In this respect it is to be noted that the Deputies are committing some errors and they do not *know* the *full value of Spanish aid* [author's underlining] given in behalf of their country. The French Court made up its mind to help them in secret in the year 1776 and we, on our part supplied them with half and half, that is, 2 millions of pounds, using this method as a matter of precaution.

Several ships loaded with goods, successively left Bilbao for the Colonies; they were provided with several amounts in Bills of Exchange, and other remittances have been sent, via Spanish America; their total amount we, ourselves, are scarcely able to appraise owing to the variety of hands, and places, through which they passed making it impossible; and considering that this aid is a generous donation, this surely may be acknowledged to be already of great importance.

The said gifts are like real currency, because they consist of foreign products, instead of those afforded by France; though while these [of France] were useful, and perhaps even greater, these were favouring her own subjects, for the articles with which the Americans were helped were bought there, and, if we mention this difference now it is only to make clear that our gifts meant a heavier burden for Spain, and this is the reason we are not able to go on to the limit which we had wished. But there is yet another more important point of which these Deputies seem not to have thought: it is our great Naval Power, which for two years has been developing and, from day to day is growing larger. It is so effective and powerful a help to the Colonies that if used in an openly declared war could not be as free to be used in such a way because in such case we should have to disperse it according to our own defense, but today it ably threatens England and protects the Americans.

Let us honestly ask ourselves why the British Cabinet wastes such enormous sums on arming so many ships of the line, on so many expenses on the matters in which they are engaged, and why so many troops are kept in their ports, apparently useless. To be sure, they would answer, it is in order to be in condition to check any action by the Spanish and French fleets.

You will infer from this that these fleets then divert the English force, and if the Americans can be made to realize this, they will know that it is a stronger support than our sending two or three millions which would arrive late, or never.

By next November we shall have at Cadiz 20 Ships of the Line ready for any service. We have 9 at Vera-Cruz and the Windward Isles, with a great many Frigates. General Cevallos' forces are free and may be sent wherever we wish. So, while we enjoy full peace, Spain has presently 113 vessels, completely manned, and of all kinds, together with some others in good condition, to be armed at once. England, knowing this, has her best battle-ships unable to fight the Americans.

All this is indicated to show that Spain cannot spare, under such circumstances, the sums demanded by the Deputies, and they, honestly speaking must not exact so many sacrifices, especially when we are running the risk of becoming involved, in spite of ourselves, in a war on their behalf.

But we do not refuse absolutely to go on supplying them with our assistance, according to our circumstances. On the contrary, this shall be done as usual and they will be at once aware of it. Granting this, we must examine the remaining arguments of Count Vergennes' despatch, to make clear the manner in which this business is considered here.

The same cautiousness is maintained by His Most Catholic Majesty's Cabinet, in order to avoid any written compromise. It invites full confidence in them, and their Superiors, for any oral agreement to be accomplished according to all stipulations. Our gifts could become a waste if, they used them as a trick. We have begun with merely conjectural previsions, and are willing to risk gains against losses, because pacts are difficult to manage with such a people; Congress will deny what their Commissioners have promised at their own convenience, and the said Commissioners could always find a thousand expedients to do so. We must work secretly and cautiously in our own interest since they are more interested in displaying the support they get. We have had too many experiences in this.

Nevertheless, it is necessary to encourage and help them, and not to reveal our rightful distrust; But this policy must be followed, especially in Paris by His Catholic Majesty's Cabinet, which is both wise and clever enough to behave correctly.

The Catholic King is persuaded that, as long as the American Provinces remain united, they will not hear of any arrangement which is not based upon Independence, unless the British arms obtain so speedy a progress that they conquer the whole country. Fortunately, that is very far from a reality yet; and presently His Majesty and his Ministers think that both Courts must reduce their policy to these points:

1st — To first show the Deputies how enormous are the expenses we have contracted for their country and the fruits they are harvesting from them.

2nd — To encourage them with good hopes and immediate and real gifts, each Court in proportion to its responsibilities, but without fixing the amount. Nevertheless, if we are in time and agree that it is wiser to continue the war, between our two Crowns, we can easily make up the residue to the amount of 6 millions tournoises pounds.

3rd — To recommend them to be cautious and measured in their speeches and dealings, so that they may become aware that everything can be lost due to their own indiscretions, because they cannot understand the reasons by which our Courts work.

4th — To advise them that it is more important for their Colonies, than for us, not to admit any arrangement without the guarantee of these two Crowns, or without a subsequent Treaty of Alliance with them.

5th — To dispel any difference and to make them understand that their conduct must be such that we may trust them, for their treachery would compel us to create many disadvantages for them.

6th — We must add that the war they wish us to join could have results more hurtful to them, as we should then need our army for our own defense.

Otherwise, these two Courts must presently lull the British Cabinet to avoid any claims by them in everything of any particular difficulty; but we must proceed with dignity and resolution in any incident that might happen, because immoderate compliance toward that proud nation only renders her the more exacting and she is never grateful for whatever is done by reason of Friendship and Temperance.

Finally — It seems that we cannot fail to prepare military stocks and take other measures, which have already been settled, especially in order to protect our own dominions.

That is all the Spanish Ministry has to say, making use of the special confidence allowed by His Most Catholic King's Ministry.

San Lorenzo el REAL, October, 17th, 1777."[10]

FOOTNOTES

[1]Memorial of the American Commissioners, A.H.N.; Legajo 3884; also in Yela, *op. cit.*, Tomo 2:130-35.

[2]Lee to Gardoqui, September 25, 1777, in *Diplomatic Correspondence* (Sparks, ed.) 2:97-98.

[3]Lee to the Committee of Foreign Affairs, October 6, 1777, in *Diplomatic Correspondence* (Sparks, ed.) 2:98-101.

[4]Letter of Lee quoting Vergennes to Gérard, in *ibid.* 2:101, footnote.

[5]Lee to the Committee of Foreign Affairs, January 15, 1778, in *ibid.*, 2:125.

[6]Gardoqui & Co. to Lee, April 1, 1778, in *ibid.*, 2:142-143.

[7]Memorandum concerning blankets sent from Bilbao, April 1, 1778, *ibid.*, 2:144.

[8]Lee to the Committee of Foreign Affairs, May 23, 1778, in *ibid.*, 2:162.

[9]Lee to the American Congress, June 1, 1778, in *ibid.*, 2:167.

[10]Memorial of the Court of Spain to the Court of France, San Lorenze el Real, October 17, 1777, A.H.N., Legajo 3884. Cited also in Yela, *op. cit.*, Tomo 1: Memorial LXX, pp. 130-135.

CHAPTER V

1.

Thus, in the fall of 1777, both Courts were seriously considering the future of the Americans. The American Commissioners were trying to make an outright loan of six million pounds; Washington, his army short of clothing and war supplies, was facing the winter that might well decide the fate of his country. The Tories, along with many secret sympathizers of the English, were scattered throughout the government posts of the various Colonies, some being seated in the Congress itself. Desperate Agents of the Colonies were becoming more and more indiscreet, announcing openly the sources of aid to America. By giving the strong impression that Spain and France were actually their open allies they hoped to weaken England's will to continue the war. But this mistaken idea had, as shown previously, already caused both Courts to reconsider the value of continuing to give aid. It is no wonder that Carlos III pointed out in his Memorial the danger which both Courts faced from indiscretions made by the Americans in loose talk. Franklin and Morris, as members of the Committee of Secret Correspondence of the Congress had learned how risky it could be to make a disclosure of important affairs. It is important to bear in mind that before the Memorial of the Spanish Court had been prepared, M. Grand had sent a statement of his account to Gardoqui, and, that through Gardoqui the Court had become aware of the vast amounts of aid which Spain had given through purchases made in France. These purchases on behalf of the Colonies benefited the people of France as well. Carlos III could also remind his royal nephew, Louis XVI, that the navy of Spain, because of its great strength, was holding England in check without an open declaration of war, to the mutual benefit of both Bourbon Courts.

Nevertheless, Lee continued to hope for an open break that would bring the two Courts into the arena of war as openly-declared and fighting-allies. During the rest of his stay in Europe he maintained a close liaison with Gardoqui. To the Committee of Foreign Affairs he submitted a final expense account which is brought up to January

1779 and in which are shown, in brief, the amounts he had received from Spain by way of remittances. But his account presents an incomplete picture of the total succor being given to the Americans at this time since it does not take cognizance of the help which was being given continuously through other means in the West Indies and from Havana, New Orleans and Mexico. Even King Carlos III himself, as his Memorial reveals, was unable to know the full extent of the help that had been given due to the numerous ways in which it had been transferred from Spanish into American hands. Incomplete though it is, this is the information which Lee sent to the Committee of the Congress:

"Paris, January, 5th, 1779

Gentlemen,
Public money expended.
. . . . 1777
    Remitted to Gardoqui at Bilbao
      (For supplies sent to Congress)
    1777, Nov. 29th, - 60,790
      May, 29th, 1778, - 14,599;
      Sept. 25th, - 24,654;
      January, 3rd, 1779, - 19,905 119,848

1778 . . .
    30,000 blankets ordered from Bilbao — 210,000 which he wrote Gardoqui ruefully, he had no money to pay for when billed.
    Charges on them 18,000
    [Other charges listed bring the total expenses to]   464,567

    Public Money received . . . .
    1777, May, Remittance from Spain 187,500
    1778, Oct. Two do   "   do 187,500
Interest on last three months 2,000
      Total 377,000
      Debit 87.567

    Jan. 1st 1779 . . . . 464,567 "[1]

To understand why the agents of the Colonies in Europe were intentionally indiscreet about the aid being given and why the Commissioners in Paris were constantly importuning the Bourbon Courts for more and ever more aid, it is well to go back two years and view through the eyes of a competent observer the situation in which the Americans found themselves shortly after the Commission had been set up in Paris. Writing in December, less than six months after the Declaration of Independence, Robert Morris painted a dark background for the mission of the Commissioners. Clearly, gravely and concisely he outlined the terrible state of the Colonies in the midst of the first winter of war; there had been costly military defeats with concomitant losses of matériel; December marked the end of the enlistment period for Washington's army; the militia of New Jersey had failed to respond to appeals for filling up the gaps in the dwindling force, due to desertion, sickness and completion of enlistment; the value of Continental money had declined very rapidly. Morris went on to say:

> "I must add to this gloomy picture one circumstance, more distressing than all the rest, because it threatens instant and total ruin to the American Cause; unless some radical cure is applied, and that speedily, I mean the depreciation of the continental currency. . . . Many refuse to take it: . . . and you may judge of its value, even among those when I tell you that 250 Continental money, or 6662-3 dollars is given for a Bill of Exchange of 100 sterling. . . ."[2]

Silas Deane, one of the Commissioners in Paris adopted the rate of exchange of five livres to one dollar (Continental) in devising a program of aid by way of a loan.

The general picture was indeed black throughout the Colonies. Washington was nearing the end of his fighting strength. A lift of spirit was badly needed. This came suddenly, dramatically upon the eve of the bitter Christmas of 1776, when Washington crossed the freezing Delaware to defeat the drunken Hessian troops and marched triumphantly upon Trenton. From the beginning of 1777, when the war rose to a crescendo from the Atlantic coast to the banks of the Mississippi, to 1779, we find the Commissioners responding to constant calls for help with renewed appeals for aid from the Courts of France and Spain until circumstances brought both nations into action and open warfare at the side of the Americans.

2.

It was a happy man who wrote the following letter to the Congress:

(Lee to the President of Congress)

"Paris, June, 21st, 1779,

Sir,
    I have the honor to inform Congress, that Spain has declared against Great Britain, and that their respective Ambassadors are recalled. Part of the Spanish Fleet has joined the French. . . .

Arthur Lee"[3]

Just six days after sending this triumphant letter, Lee addressed a Memorial to the Prime Minister of Spain, Floridablanca, to inform him of the latest news received by the Commission in Paris:

> "Paris, June, 27th, 1779,
> The English have taken possession of Savannah in Georgia, and are extending themselves in that State so as to form a connexion with, and establish an influence over, the Indian Nations that border all that country. They design also to possess themselves of Port Royal in South Carolina, and, if possible, Charleston.
>
> These acquisitions, if they are suffered, with their contiguous possessions, will give them such a command upon the coast and in the Gulf, as well as such means of exciting the savages, and seconding their enterprises, against the neighboring territories of Spain, as may be difficult to resist if they are not prevented. . . ."[4]

During the summer of 1779 the Commissioners waited hopefully for word that the Spanish and French fleets had effected a juncture. This glad news could be forwarded at last. On August 10, Lee happily wrote the Committee of Foreign Affairs:

> "Gentlemen,
> After a long delay through unfavorable winds, the Spanish and French Fleets joined off Cape Finnesterre the 26th of last month. . . . The Spanish and French ships are mixed together, the former twenty, and the latter thirty. Don Cordova commands a separate Fleet of sixteen Spanish ships of the Line, which attend the grand combined Fleet as a corps de re'serve. Don Ulloa cruises off the Canaries with four of the Line, and six more, block up the Bay of Gibraltar, while a Spanish Army invests the town by land. . . ."[5]

With the declaration of war in June, the Spanish Government fulfilled the implied promise made by Grimaldi to Lee at Burgos in 1777. The doubts in the mind of the astute Franklin were now dispelled, once and for all. Once the Treasure Ships had arrived from America and the necessary time allowed for the preparation of the fleet and the troops for action, the Spanish had made their tentative promise good. The time had come for them. Now the plan they had long before suggested to the Court at Versailles was put into action at once; the fleets of the two countries joined to give assistance to the forces of the harassed Americans.

The Commissioners were encouraged to believe that henceforth despatches from the Congress could be sent to them with more assurance of arrival than heretofore. So many of the instructions and orders meant for their eyes alone had become the property of the British through accidents at sea that they had at times almost despaired of their standing with the Courts of Europe, for lack of vital facts to back up their urgent pleas for more and more aid. That the hazards, if lessened, were by no means over is revealed in a letter Lee wrote to the Committee of Foreign Affairs, within a month after the fleets joined:

"Gentlemen,
    . . . The English papers tell us that the COUNT D'ESTAING of ten guns and fourteen swivels, with despatches from the Congress, was taken on the 14th of July off Cape Finnesterre, and that the despatches fell into their hands. . . ."[6]

That the Court of Spain accurately forecast the action England would take following the declaration of war was very quickly proven to be true, namely, that the British navy would at once go into action against their powerful Spanish opponent. Intelligence of this soon reached the Commissioners and Lee lost no time in passing on the information to the Committee of Foreign Affairs:

"Paris, October, 13th, 1779.
Gentlemen,
    I have certain intelligence, that Admiral Rodney is to sail immediately from England, with five Sail of the Line, to take Command of the Fleet of the West Indies. . . . His abilities and activities are great. . . . Count D'ESTAING is expected here in the winter, with twelve ships, which will leave the enemy a decided and dangerous superiority. . . ."[7]

This was grave news indeed, since it was known throughout Paris that Count d'Estaing was the ablest among the French fleet commanders, and in spite of the fact that Admiral De Grasse would now be operating along the American coast and in the Indies, the weak condition of twelve French vessels of the Line, necessitating their removal from combat at this time when England was sending out her finest fleet commander, brought on a feeling of depression that fast permeated the diplomatic circles of Paris. Franklin reported hearing the subject frequently discussed in the salons of the city but discreetly refrained from offering publicly any comment which might reveal his inner feeling of dismay at this critical juncture. The Commissioners placed their hopes upon the power of the Spanish fleet in American waters and sent to Madrid all the information they could obtain. In December, Lee sent the following communication to the Count de Floridablanca:

"Paris, Dec. 16th, 1779.
Sir,
    Your Excellency will have the goodness to permit me recalling to your consideration what I have already had the honor of stating to you, relatively to the plan of the common enemy to establish themselves in Georgia and South Carolina, in order to carry on more effectively the war against the possessions of Spain in America, and against the United States. I have most undoubted intelligence, that they are more and more determined on pursuing the plan. The good intentions of Count d'Estaing to drive them from Georgia having unfortunately, failed, and the departure of the French Fleet having left them a decided superiority on our coast, must give them fresh encouragement to prosecute their enterprise, and will render the assistance of His Catholic Majesty's squadron at the Havanna absolutely necessary to prevent its succeeding.

Suffer me, therefore, to entreat most earnestly your Excellency's attention to this, if other more near and important objects of the war should have hitherto diverted it.

I have the honor to be, . . ."[8]

Now that Spain was openly engaged in war with the common enemy, it was recognized by the American Congress that there would be need of an accredited representative of the Colonies, on the spot, in Madrid. There is no doubt that Arthur Lee had hoped and expected that when the time arrived he would be this representative. He had long been active in affairs with that Court and particularly, in association with Gardoqui, in the management of financial and material aids from the Spanish Throne. His hope was not to be realized, however. Shortly after his impassioned plea to Floridablanca, quoted above, he was notified that the Congress had appointed John Jay to the post. It was, in fact, on Christmas Day, December 25, 1779, that Lee wrote his last letter to the Congress:

"Gentlemen,
I have this day had the honor of receiving yours of the 13th of October, notifying me, by the resolve of the Congress of the same date, of Mr. Jay's appointment and my recall. . . ."[9]

This marks the close of the association between Lee and the quiet merchant of Bilbao, James Gardoqui. In a letter to the new Envoy, Lee expressed his appreciation of the courtesy and help he had received from the Spanish Throne, through its capable agent, Gardoqui, and paid tribute to the Spanish people and to the King's Prime Minister.

"To John Jay Minister from the United States of America to Spain.
L'Orient, March, 17th, 1780.
Sir,
. . . There is no Court in Europe, at which secrecy will so much recommend a negotiator, as that to which you are destined. Inasmuch, that as far as you can keep the capital parts of your negotiation entirely to your own breast, you will have reason to think it prudent. You are to negotiate with a people of honor and a Minister of wisdom. They will propose fairly and perform faithfully. You will not be embarrassed by intrigue, at least, none of Spanish origin, nor will it be advantageous to employ any. . . . The House of Gardoqui has executed what was entrusted to them with diligence, and as far as I can judge, with fidelity. They deserve your confidence. . . .

I have the honor to be, . . ."[10]

3.

The Minister from the United States, John Jay, found himself from the outset in the midst of urgencies for the Congress that were to try his soul. He early learned that the advice Lee had proffered was indeed sound and that a collaborator like Gardoqui was his most important link with the Court. At the time of his mission to Madrid, there was no official representative of Spain assigned in a like position to the Congress of the New Nation. According to the protocol of the Spanish Court, he, Jay, could not be received by the King as a full-fledged Ambassador. His business must be conducted through the Minister, Floridablanca, and his secretary, Campo. His situation was embarrassing in the extreme to a man of Jay's standing in the United States. He did not, from the beginning of his mission, relish being in a subordinate position either diplomatically or socially in Madrid.

The correspondence of Jay with the Court of Spain is of the deepest interest to Americans as well as to Spaniards. During his mission he was in constant personal contact with two men, James Gardoqui and Don Pedro Ortiz de la Riva. The latter was at this time in the powerful and strategic position of "Collector of Taxes and all monies for the prosecution of the war" by private order of the King.

It was through Ortiz de la Riva that Jay received funds, following instructions given by Don Bernardo del Campo, secretary to the Minister, Floridablanca.

Jay, early in his mission, submitted a long Memorial to the Minister, for transmittal to the King, in which he mentioned many points, all to show the good faith of the Americans and to assure the Throne that the people of the United States were in no mood to come to a compromise with the mother country. A few of these points will illustrate the case he sought to present on behalf of the United States:

"Memorial of John Jay — [In part]
Point —

(9th) — Because of the doctrine widely propagated in America by the sympathizers of the King of Great Britain, that no faith was to be placed in Americans up in arms against him, and the uniformity with which they have constantly proclaimed it, in practice as well as by their open profession of such, they have destroyed all confidence, leaving no room for doubt among Americans, that, should they again become subjects of the King of Great Britain, on certain terms, that such terms would as little impede the progress of future oppression as the Capitulation of Limerick in 1691 did with respect to Ireland.

(10th) — Because the treaty with France and consequently, virtue, honor, and every obligation due to the reputation of a rising Nation, whose fame is unsullied by violated compacts, forbid it.

(11th) — Because it has been publicly made evident that the sole interest of North America is to remain independent.

(12th) — Because the history of mankind, from the earliest ages, proclaims with a loud voice, that those who draw their swords against a Prince, deaf to the supplications of his people, must throw away the Scabbard.

(13th) — Because they do not consider the defense of their independence as difficult. The country is easily defended and very fertile. The people are soldiers, who, with reason, consider their liberty and lives as the most valuable possessions left them, and which they are determined shall neither be wrested or purchased from them but with blood.

(14th) — Because, in support of their independence, they have expressly, by a most solemn act, pledged to each other their lives, their fortunes, and their sacred honor. So that the bond of union thus formed for this purpose, of all the ties of common interest, common safety, mutual affection, general resentments, and the great obligations of Virtue honor, patriotism, and faith, may with reason be deemed equal to the importance of that great objective.

As to Whether there is any powerful party in favor of England and what consequences are to be apprehended from it? Whether the heads of such a party suffer themselves to be seduced by the promises of the British Government?

What has already been said on the subject of the Union of the people in North America will, I imagine, in great measure answer these questions.

If, by a party in favor of England is meant, a party for the relinquishing of the Independence of the United States, and returning to the dominion of Britain on any terms whatever, I answer, there is no such party in North America. All the open adherents to the Crown of Great Britain having either voluntarily quitted, or been expelled from the country.

That Britain has emissaries and masqued adherents in America, industrious in their little spheres to perplex the public measures, and disturb the public tranquility, is a fact of which I have not the most distant doubt, and it is equally true that some of these wicked ones are thought, by a few weak ones, to be patriots. But they cannot, with any propriety be called a party or even a faction.

The chief mischief they do is collecting and transmitting intelligence, raising false reports, and spreading calumnies of public men and measures. Such characters will be found in every country so circumstanced and America has not been negligent in providing laws for their punishment."[11]

4.

Jay sent a long despatch to the Minister, Floridablanca, in June 1780, in which he went into great detail as to the impossibility of the United States furnishing the materials for, building or manning vessels that could be exchanged for the money loan he and the Commissioners still hoped to arrange through the Spanish Court.

In this letter he agreed that the lumber, naval stores and shipbuilding facilities existed in the States in abundance; and that the Congress would be only too happy to exchange such natural assets for the monetary help, as well as for the protection of Spanish ports of supply, but that, unfortunately, there was no money to pay for the labor of getting out the materials, nor the construction of ships at this time.

He emphasized that, should it be possible to build such vessels, it would be impossible to find the men to man them, since the Congress was itself in straits to find men to man its own ships of war due to the great attraction of booty and free operation existing in the service of the hundreds of privateers operating in the American seas. Since

America had been in the war for a number of years, her resources were now reduced to the final effort needed for winning the struggle against Britain, leaving little of immediate value to offer in return for the hoped for loan but the pledge of repayment with interest after her commerce should once again be engaged freely between North America and Europe.

Jay says:

"Nor will their disappointment be less than their regret, when they find their credit diminished by the failure of a measure, from the success of which they expected to raise it. The sort of proposition made by His Majesty, to become responsible at the expiration of two years for the amount of the bills in question, and that, even to be done with interest, is a proof of his goodness, by which I am confident, the United States will consider themselves greatly obliged. But when it is remembered that Bills of Exchange, immediately upon being drawn and sold, become a medium in commerce, and pass through various hands, in satisfaction of various transactions, that the Drawer and every Indorser becomes responsible for their credit at every transfer, and that the object of the merchant last holding the bills, as well as of all other merchants, is money in hand actively employed in trade, and not money lying idle at interest greatly inferior to the usual profits to be gained in commerce. . . . I say, on considering these things . . . that the last holders of the bills would prefer recovering the amount of them with the usual damages on protests, to a delay of payment for two years with interest. Should these bills meet with this fate, His Majesty will readily perceive its influence on the credit, operations, and feelings of the United States; on the common Cause; and on the hopes of the enemy.

The necessity of prudence which retains His Majesty's Treasure in his American Dominions is an unfortunate circumstance at a time when it might be usefully employed.

There is, nevertheless room to hope, that the great superiority of the Allied Fleets and armaments in the American Seas, will in the course of a year or eighteen months, render its transportation safe and easy; and that the greater part of it may arrive before the bills in question would become payable. This will appear more probable when the time necessary to sell these bills, and the time which will be employed in their journey from different parts of Europe to this place are all added to the half a year which is allowed for the payment of them after they have been presented.

I am authorized and ready to engage and pledge the faith of the United States for the punctual repayment with interest and within a reasonable term, of any sums of money which His Majesty may be so kind as to lend to them.

As to the Aids heretofore supplied to the United States, I am without information relative to the precise terms on which they were furnished as well as to their amount. When I left Congress they appeared to me not to possess full and positive intelligence. I ascribe this not to omissions on the part of their Commissioners, who then had direction of their affairs, but to those miscarriages and accidents to which the communication of intelligence to a distant country is liable in time of war.

If it should appear proper to Your Excellency to order that I be furnished with an accurate and full statement of these transactions, I will do myself the honor of transmitting them immediately to Congress, and, as they happened prior to my appointment, I shall request particular instructions on the subject.

With respect to the repayment of such sums as Spain may lend to the United States; (as follows); by the latter furnishing the former with Frigates, etc. I beg leave to submit the following remarks for Your Excellency's consideration: In the United States there are timber, iron, masts, shipwrights, pitch, tar and turpentine, and Spain can furnish the other requisites; but neither timber, the iron, the mast, or other articles can be procured without money. The Congress is in great want of money for the immediate purpose of self defense, for the maintenance of their armies, and vessels of war, and all the other expenses incident to military operations. The Congress pressed by their necessities, have emitted bills of credit, till the depreciation of them forbid further Emissions. They have made loans from their great and good Ally, and in aid of getting a system of supplies, by taxation and domestic loans, they have for reasons I had the honor of explaining to Your Excellency, drawn upon me the bills above mentioned. These bills will be sold in the United States for paper money; and that money will be immediately wanted for the purpose already mentioned.

If therefore this money was to be turned into Frigates, the obvious ends for drawing those bills would not be attained. . . .

I can assure Your Excellency that the United States will be happy in any opportunity which may occur during the war, of joining their arms to those of Spain and in cooperating with them in any expeditions which circumstances may render expedient against the Floridas or other objectives. The Americans would most cheerfully fight beside the Spaniards and by spilling their blood in the same cause and in the same occasions, convince them of their ardent desire to become their faithful friends and steadfast Allies.

I cannot prevail upon myself to conclude, without expressing to Your Excellency my apprehension of the anxiety and painful concern with which Congress would receive intelligence of the failure of their bills; especially after the expectations they have been induced to conceive of the successful issue of their affairs here. What conclusions the Enemy would draw from the inability of Spain to advance the sum in question, even for men in arms against Britain, I forbear to mention. . . .

I still flatter myself that some expedients may be devised to surmount the present difficulties, and the harvest of Laurels now ripening for His Majesty in America will not be permitted to wither for want of watering; influenced by this hope I shall delay transmitting any intelligence respecting this matter to Congress, till Your Excellency shall be pleased to communicate His Majesty's further pleasure on the subject.

I have the honor to be with very sincere respect, and esteem, Your Excellency's most obedient and humble servant.

JOHN JAY"[12]

In the foregoing flowery letter sent by Jay, in June, we find him already feeling deeply compromised by the bills for which he felt responsible. It is not difficult to understand the position of the Crown after reading such an urgent plea as this supplication. It does however appear strange that the first officially-accredited Minister from the Congress should be forced to admit that he had no knowledge of all prior assistance given by Spain to the United States, neither the amount nor the value of it since he had surely been in touch with Lee who handled the bulk of such aids with Gardoqui, the latter being in constant contact with Jay himself.

It seems likewise incredible that the equal amounts of money given by the two Courts, Spain and France, even before the entrance of Lee into the negotiations, should be unknown to the American Minister. Communication by sea was, as Jay stated, uncertain, but since other important intelligence was constantly getting into the hands of Congress regularly it is strange that Jay was not made fully aware of the enormous amount of financial and material succor that had been given the Colonies both in Spain and through the West Indies and New Orleans.

The amounts heretofore listed in Lee's report, together with his financial statement rendered as of January 1st, 1777, surely must have been brought to the attention of the new Minister, either by the Committee of Foreign Affairs, to whom these reports were made, or by Gardoqui when he began the Spanish Government's transactions with Jay.

It is small wonder that the King, in his Memorial to Louis of France, should have mentioned the fact that little dependence could be placed upon promises, notwithstanding the personal honor of the men who were charged with the numerous transactions.

In the all important matter of the fixing of boundaries between the two nations in North America, the Congress had either been reluctant to act or too deeply engaged in the task of fighting the British, to give so important a subject between friendly nations the attention and courtesy of reply. With reference to the request for ships, to be built in America and used in joint action with the Spanish and French in the destruction of the valuable East Indian trade of England, Jay was also unable to comply other than to reiterate the need of ships for the defense of the States, holding out the possibility of a juncture of forces in a joint attack against the Floridas.

Although the plight of Congress was desperate, it is not surprising to find the Spanish Court reluctant to make a large outright loan while she was already engaged in a war that was giving powerful support to the Americans, without some form of acknowledgement other than diplomatic compliments and promises.

On September 15th, 1780, Don Bernardo del Campo, secretary to the Minister, writing to Gardoqui, speaks of Jay being more avid for money than he is to negotiate on other matters of importance.[13] Along with his letter in which he made the above statement to Gardoqui he included his letter of instructions from Floridablanca. In emphatic terms Floridablanca wrote:

"My Friend and Sir,
    In order to answer Jay, it is better that Gardoqui call upon him and say to him that we will not default in giving our aid, in so far as it is possible to do it. We

cannot help with money because it is not possible for us to get it in Europe, and we do not have it ourselves because the money that should come from America for the whole year, has not arrived, and we do not know when it will; and the money we were to have through a negotiation that was nearly completed, is going to fail us, due to the maneuvers of some High French personalities; (this should be communicated to the Ambassador and could be very useful to him).

Since they [the Americans] have not advised us in time, and have not asked our consent, we were not able to arrange our part of the affair in advance, in order to secure the acceptance of the Bills of Exchange when they were presented.

That, due to this, and to the fact that the Congress does not seem to think of giving anything in recompense, the King has good reason to be displeased; but, nevertheless, he had not changed, and will not change his attitude, and will continue the benevolence, friendship, and sympathy that he has always entertained for the Colonies; that, in consequence, if Jay or his Principals find a source of credit, guaranteed by the King for three years, for Bills contracted for up to the amount of 100,000 or 150,000 pesos, there will be no difficulty in carrying out the business.

Then, also, we will do all we can to supply clothing and other things, and finally, to put the King in a better mood, it is necessary that they present more effective signs of mutual esteem, and propose reciprocal means of recompense that — will strengthen a solid friendship and confidence, and will not continue to be confined, as at present, solely to polite words and protestations of pure compliments.

Gardoqui must inquire into the ideas of these men and try to find out what may be gained from them. And, if they tell him that we have changed our minds, he can give these two answers: First, — that if this were true, we would not use the system of guaranteeing their Credit, a method which is more public than a secret delivery of money; and second; that it is they who seem to have changed their minds, because, until now, we have not seen them do anything for Spain nor propose anything for her in return for our gifts, and for the cost of a war that has been started to the benefit of the Colonies themselves: To whoever does not agree with this, tell him that we have received information that they themselves are planning an understanding with the English, but that, as of now, we do not believe this; (this is being said because of the friendship of Carmichael with Cumberland). [Carmichael, Sec'y to Jay and Cumberland, the British Ambassador]

With reference to Gardoqui, he must prepare to go to the Colonies, if the whole picture does not change, which does not seem likely."[14]

FOOTNOTES

[1]Lee to the Committee of Foreign Affairs, January 5, 1779, in *Diplomatic Correspondence, op. cit.*, 2: 219-220.

[2]Robert Morris to the American Commissioners in Paris, December 21, 1776, *ibid.*, 1: 238-239.

[3]Lee to the American Congress, June 21,1779, in *ibid.*, 2: 250.

[4]Memorial, Lee to Floridablanca, June 27, 1779, in *ibid.*, 2: 252-253.

[5]Lee to the Committee of Foreign Affairs, August 10, 1779, in *ibid.*, 2: 255-256.

[6]Lee to the Committee of Foreign Affairs, August 24, 1779, in *ibid.*, 2: 258.

[7]Lee to the Committee of Foreign Affairs, October 13, 1779, in *ibid.*, 2: 262-263.

[8]Lee to Floridablanca, December 16, 1779, in *ibid.*, 2: 273-274.

[9]Lee to the Committee of Foreign Affairs, December 25, 1779, in *ibid.*, 2: 274.

[10]Lee to Jay, March 17, 1780, in *ibid.*, 2: 277.

[11]Memorial of John Jay to Floridablanca, A.H.N.; Legajo 3884 bis.; exp. 8, doc. 10.

[12]Jay to Floridablanca, June 1780, A.H.N.; Legajo 3884.

[13]Campo to Gardoqui, September 15, 1780, A.H.N.; Legajo 3884, exp. 4, doc. 75.

[14]Floridablanca to Campo, cited in Campillo, *op. cit.*, Nota Preliminar y Catálogo.

CHAPTER VI

1.

Floridablanca's observation was correct. It was fast becoming apparent that Spain was badly in need of a representative on the spot in Philadelphia: a man such as Gardoqui who was conversant with all the affairs of America in Spain; a man who was intimately informed as to the needs of the Americans, as well as to the resources available in his own country. Aside from the great value of Gardoqui's services in Spain, he had a natural reluctance to leaving his home as well as the great family establishment at Bilbao. He wrote to his friend, Bernardo del Campo on October 17th, 1780, expressing his personal feelings:

"Sir,
   You may believe me that, if it were not urgent, I should have done nothing involving my parting from the Commercial Company, and my Honorable friend knows there would have been nothing more convenient to me than to remain in the security of it, if not for me, then surely for my son, who would then remain in opulent circumstances. But it happens in my Family, like in many others, endowed with ample fortune, that they are punished by having a CAIN in the family who deprives them of joy. The settlement of accounts has waited long and I feel that we cannot waste it after reading what you honored me with in your letter. I think it better to take the latter in hand and forget the rest, as I wrote you in my last letter and, whenever you please, we shall talk and decide, for I have left this business in your hands.
   On the 11th inst. the American Privateer, THE PILGRIM arrived at Bilbao consigned to my firm. She has 18 guns of -9-, Captain ROBINSON, proceeding from Salem from where she sailed 11 weeks ago. During her journey she has taken 7 prizes, three of them off the coast of England, where they had been driven by a storm and were a part of the SANTA LUCIA Convoy. One of these prizes he sent to America, as he had done with the first four, but the other two were addressed to Bilbao. One of these loaded with tobacco, cocoa, and indigo, took the port of Morlaix, and the other, loaded with spermaceti, is still awaited at Bilbao.
   I remain obedient to your Lordship and pray God to preserve you."[1]

The settlement of accounts mentioned above was necessary in order to clear his family connections in Bilbao before assuming the duties assigned him by Floridablanca. On the back of his letter he added the cryptic information that Carmichael and Jay had succeeded in con-

tacting a private banker who was proceeding upon the plan suggested
by the Prime Minister in his instructions to del Campo. With his usual
modesty, Gardoqui mentions in this postscript that they have paid him
the honor of suggesting that his writing in behalf of this plan might
add some weight, while at the same time disclaiming any idea of trying to force the matter through any prior knowledge. In his simple,
forthright fashion he dispels the idea of the King having any ulterior
contact with the British Ambassador. In his own words is revealed the
type of man Gardoqui was — modest, direct and sincere.

> "Carmichael has called upon me, to communicate, by order of his Superior,
> that CABARRUS has told him that he will leave tomorrow to go there with a
> certain plan to raise money and, if your Lordship pleases, he will arrange to add
> as much as these people [the Americans] need to succeed. He has paid me the
> honor, which I should be glad to deserve, of suggesting that I lend my weight
> by writing, as I am now, and if you think well of the matter, you will give me the
> details to me. I must advise you that I have informed them that I know nothing
> of any such transaction, but in the course of our chat he seemed rather worried
> because he had heard that CUMBERLAND, [the English Ambassador] has just
> received a certain amount from the King; but I asked him not to believe non-
> sense, that if such were the case, it could only have been given as money for
> prisoners, or something similar. — To Don Bernardo del Campo."

The busy Gardoqui again wrote his friend, del Campo, on October
20th:

> "Sir,
>   I have taken note of the news you kindly sent in your pleasant letter of yester-
> day and am ready to make use of it when convenient. The prize loaded with
> spermaceti I referred to in my last letter, anchored at San Sebastian, where the
> Commander General, or more properly his Secretary, seems to have been lucky
> to have got in touch with [the] approaching Americans, as happened this time.
> But, as I am not sufficiently informed about the state of this matter, I suspend
> judgment, but I believe justice will be done.
>   On the 16th inst. arrived at Bilbao, another American vessel, THE DUKE
> OF LEICESTER, Captain-WARRING, carrying tobacco for my firm. She left
> Virginia on the 15th of September, but since the American, Jay, always sends
> news directly to you I am afraid of troubling you with duplicate news and for
> that reason shorten my information, with the reservation of amplifying at your
> Lordship's pleasure.
>   Your order on this person, who remains praying God to preserve you long
> years. Madrid, October 20th, 1780 — Kissing your hands, Your most obedient
> servant."[2]

The good Don Diego found himself in a position many times to act
as interpreter for the Americans who came within his widespread or-
bit. He was frequently able to smooth out matters without bothering
to take them up with the Court or the Ministry. One instance of this
kind could have caused an international ruckus wherein he proved
himself to be a friend in matters of social significance. Young William

Carmichael, a Baltimorean living in Madrid, had been assigned to Jay as his assistant and secretary. During his stay, he made many friends among the younger diplomatic colony of the city. Lord Cumberland, the British Ambassador, had a large staff and his house was a popular rendezvous for the young blades of the city. The young American was known to be a frequent visitor at the Embassy, both by day and, in the evening, when parties were given there. The close intimacy between the British Ambassador, a shrewd diplomat, and the young secretary to the Minister of the United States began to be the cause of much talk and speculation. Were the Americans perhaps angling for a peace arrangement through Cumberland? After a quiet investigation by Gardoqui through his discreet friends in Madrid, it was discovered that the attraction was a young and very charming lady of Cumberland's household, and that nothing having to do with affairs of State was involved. This case of infatuation seems to have been of no consequence and the courtship soon was broken off, whether by the lady or the young American is not known; but Carmichael soon ceased to be an attendant in her train and continued his duties with integrity and distinction. This incident recalls Lee's injunction to Jay, aforementioned, that "he would do well to hold all affairs of capital importance closely to his breast."

On the 26th of November, 1780, the same Carmichael whose affairs of the heart had given concern to Gardoqui and the Count, addressed a letter to the merchant of Bilbao from which it appears that Jay was already receiving funds under the plan which had been worked out with Floridablanca.

> "Agreeable to the promise given you at San Ildefonso I have made out a list of the bills which Mr. Jay accepted at various times by the direction, and with the permission, of His Excellency, the Count de Floridablanca; some of these become due early next month, and the others, soon after; the amount of the whole is 17,892 dollars, of which the greater part is accepted payable at Bilbao.
>
> I am your obedient servant, Carmichael."[3]

2.

To implement Floridablanca's suggestion during the year 1780, Jay had worked out the arrangement of funds to be supplied by the Court through the Banker Cabarrus with the understanding that for such sums to be advanced he (Jay) would notify the Minister of bills drawn against him in ample time for the Treasury to certify payment to the banker when the demands were made for payment. In February of 1781, a matter of payment arose which was to cause untold embarrassment to the Americans and to arouse a serious question as to their judgment and veracity. A convoy of captured prizes was brought into

Cadiz, loaded with valuable clothing and medicines destined for the British troops in North America. The entire shipment was at once offered for sale in the open market at whatever it might bring. The supplies were of such a nature, and fitted into the immediate needs of the United States so vitally, that the American Agent at Cadiz purchased them at once. His bill was drawn against Jay at Madrid for payment. Funds were not available, necessitating a hurried plea for payment from the banker, without proper notification to the Treasurer of the Court, or, indeed to any one in the Ministry. Jay at once wrote a despatch to the Count de Floridablanca.

"Madrid, 16 Feb. 1781.

Sir,

Mr. Harrison has purchased the Preys clothing at Cadiz, and drawn a bill on me at eight days sight, in favor of the Commissioners of the Convoy for twenty of 128 quarters each, as part of the purchase money. This Bill was presented and accepted this afternoon, as an immediate acceptance or refusal was demanded, I had no opportunity of giving Your Excellency previous notice of it. As it was drawn at an unusual Short Eight, it is necessary to inform your Excellency that the Commissioners would not deliver the Goods until this Payment was made, and as the vessels in which Mr. Harrison expects to ship the greater part of them, will sail very shortly, he was obliged either to agree to so short a day for the payment, or to lose those opportunities for sending the clothing to America, where it is much wanted, and will be extremely welcome.

Mr. Cabarrus' House has offered to advance as much money from time to time in payment of my Bills, as your Excellency is pleased to permit them to pay and to pass the credit of the sum they have contracted to supply to your Excellency. So, Please Sir, favor me with your directions on this matter and permit me to assure you of the regard and respect of —

John Jay"[4]

Jay was in an embarrassing position, since he had considered it of sufficient urgency to accept the bill for partial payment on this prize clothing, not only because of the chance that the Spanish Government would fail to honor the payment of the cost, since they had not been apprised of the matter until after it was an accomplished fact, but, for the reason also, that all prizes brought into Spanish ports were first subject to purchase by the Crown, and in this case, since Spain was herself at war, these supplies might well have been of use to her for her own army. For this reason Jay was all the more grateful to have the Minister agree to cover this unexpected charge and hastened to reassure the Court of his innocence of prior knowledge relative to the purchase, by writing the full details of the matter to Floridablanca. His second despatch was sent on February, 20th.

"Madrid, 20. Feb. 1781

Sir,

I have now the honor of transmitting to your Excellency a copy of Mr. Harrison's contract for the Prize Clothing at Cadiz. He informs me that it is, in his opinion, an advantageous one; and that he would not ship more, by the vessel now at Cadiz, than the amount of his Bill upon me. The Commissioners prescribed the terms of that Bill, and it was not in Mr. Harrison's power to obtain better terms.

I have requested Mr. Harrison to forbear drawing further Bills, without previous advice from me; so in case it should be more convenient to direct the payment of the residue to be made at Cadiz; or in case the clothing purchased should contain articles which Your Excellency may think proper to reserve, there will be sufficient time for these and any similar arrangements.

I cannot quit this subject without again presenting to your Excellency my warmest thanks for your very friendly conduct on this occasion; and assuring you of the respect and regard. . . ."[5]

The following inventory was also sent by Jay and signed by Harrison:

"Feb. 8th, 1781 (copy)
Mr. Richard Harrison, for articles of English Convoy Captured. Debit.

50-Dress Coats with full lining, wool at 135 Reales vellon	3,750
348-Ditto, Sergeant, woolen lining at 117 id. id.	40,716
35-Ditto, linen lining at 107	3,745
371-Dress Coats, soldiers, woolen linings	
396-Ditto, linen lining — (total)-2,767- at 70	193,690
16-Short Dress Coats, Major-at-125	2,000
367-Dress Coats — Soldiers Woolen lining	
100-Ditto, linen lining — (total)-467 at 60	28,020
40-Waist coats, stuff, sleeveless Sergeant at 45	1,800
110-Waist coats, Ditto, Soldiers at 25	2,750
28-Stuff, fore-part waist-coats sergeants at 20	560
559-Ditto, soldiers — at 10	5,590
52-Little waist coats and ticking trousers, sergeants at 40	2,080
225-Ditto, unbleached linen Soldiers at 20	5.100
367-Pairs of linen trousers with lining at 13	4.771
260-Pairs of linen trousers for Majors and Sergeants — 13 & 1 half	8.190
2087-Pairs linen trousers soldiers at 20	41,740
253-Shirts, Sergeants at 18	4,554
3,528-Ditto, soldiers at 12	42,336
3,479-Neck ties, Sergeants & Soldiers at 1 & 1 half	5,218 & 1 half
273-pairs of worsted stockings	

sergeants, 12 pesos a doz. 4.095
3.153-Ditto, soldiers, woolen at 5 19,706
                                           & 1 quarter
287-pairs unbleached thread stockings
   soldiers at 5 1,793
                                          & 3 quarters
2,271-pairs of shoes for soldiers
   at 10 Reales vellon 22,710
112-Flat hats, sergeants at 12 1,344
105-ditto with silverlace
   for ditto at 30 3,150
276-caps with thread lace at 5 & 1 half 1,518
6-Ditto, with silver lace at 15 90
2,280 Hats with thread trimming
   for soldiers at 5 & 1 half 12,540
1,032-Flat ditto, for ditto at 4 .... 4.128
   1-Coat for Major 135
   2-Ditto, sergeant at 117 234
   2-Ditto, soldiers at 70 140
   1-short, for ditto 60
   1-pair stuff trousers for Major or Sergeant 31
                                   & 1 half
   1-pair ditto-for soldier 20
   1-stuff, forepart for soldier, waistcoat or
   Serg. 31
                                   & 1 half
   1-Little waist coat and ticking, thread
   trousers 10
   1-pair ditto, soldier 20
   1-Little waist coat and ticking thread trousers
   for Sergeant 40
   1-unbleached, linen, ditto, soldier 20
   1-pair worsted stockings for sergeant 15
   12-Pair worsted stockings for soldiers 75
   10-pairs unbleached thread ditto for
   sergeant at 9 pesos a doz. 112
                                   & 1 half
   3-pair ditto for soldiers, at 5 18
                                   & 3 quarters
24-Buckles or shoulder-knots embroidered
   in gold at 52 1,260
   1-hat with lace 30
   1-shirt for sergeant 18
   1-ditto for soldier 12
   2-Neck ties - 1 for Sergeant
   1 for soldier at 1 & 1 half 3
   1-waist coat sleevless, stuff for sergeant 45
   1-ditto for soldier 25
302-shoulder knots, or buckles, silk twist, or
   silver and gold, white and in color 1,208
                                      3,512

& 3 quarters
474,198
& 3 quarters

True Copy-Cadiz, 20, February, 1781
by Richard-Harrison"[6]

The listing of clothing above will explain Richard Harrison's feeling of exultation at being able to buy a shipment of clothing so well-fitted for the service of Washington's ragged army even though in so doing he overstepped the regulations by which payment could properly be made. It is also good to find that Floridablanca, recognizing this need, arranged at once with his banker to cover the bill for the purchase. It is self-evident that the articles sent out singly were samples for further orders for the British army in America and that some merchant in England would fruitlessly await future orders, while a few American soldiers made themselves comfortable in his samples.

Having adjusted the matter of the Cadiz prize clothing to the satisfaction of the American Minister and the Spanish Court, it was hoped that no further embarrassing contretemps would arise to ruffle the dispositions of the Court or the American Agents.

The government of Spain had paid the unexpected amount of 12,-000 single pesos to complete the residue of bills due for the Harrison purchase at Cadiz; thus making use of a part of the funds Carmichael had hoped to use in payment of a number of other bills coming due in the ensuing months. At this time the Spanish treasury was short of ready-money for any immediate large advance to Jay, but, before the end of six months, all the remainder of the promised three-millions aforementioned would be completely paid.

Moved by the perilous financial position of the American Minister and his continuous pleas for more money to cover bills maturing each month, Spain advanced additional help during the six-months' period. Thus, we find an additional 14,000 pesos duros being advanced, at the beginning of may, 1781; and again, in July, another advancement of 12,000 pesos fuertes.

3.

September 22, 1781, Jay presented his plan for a treaty between the Court of Spain and the American Congress. Almost before the plan could be considered by the Prime Minister, he found himself faced with the intervention of the French Ambassador, Montmorin, in favor of a further grant of funds to the Americans.

The latter's action was all the more extraordinary to the Minister in view of the fact that, as we have just noted, the arrangement which he had suggested had been put to work by Jay in March and appeared to be serving its purpose very well indeed. Jay, it will be recalled, had been assured that he could incur expenses up to a total of 3,000,000 reales. It seems a fair assumption that the Commissioners in Paris, who had urged the intervention, were unaware of the financial activities of Mr. Jay, in Madrid.

Floridablanca was naturally irked by the failure of the Commissioners and the French Government to follow the courteous and correct procedure of communicating this remarkable request through Aranda, the very able Spanish Ambassador in Paris. The right hand and the left hand were not aware of each other's doings.

This is brought out in Montmorin's assertion that the Spanish Government had made an agreement, dated March 31, 1781, to pay the sum of 89,083 pesos fuertes to the agent of the United States within six months in six equal installments, and, further that only 30,-000 pesos of this amount had been paid to date, leaving (through some strange mathematics) a balance due of 51,083. The Spanish Government was asked to pay over this amount. The amount of 89,083 was to appear later, in March 1782, as the total of bills contracted by Jay and coming due in April.

If the alleged agreement was a fact, surely Jay would have known about it. But that there ever was such an agreement has been challenged by an eminent Spanish historian in these words:

> "The Spanish archives do not reveal such an explicit agreement, therefore we rather think there was an error in the French Ambassador's figures, for the only promise made was relative to the payment, after six months time, of the residue to cancel the 3,000,000 reales promised by Floridablanca to the American Minister, and that had been promised on March 25th 1781"[7]

Jay himself petitioned Floridablanca on November 16th, for loan of 31,809 dollars necessary to pay the bills due in December. The Minister, angered by these two petitions, wrote a note in his own hand on the translation of the treaty as follows:

> "Ask Campo for advice in order to decide on this; contact Muzquiz about the monthly payments on all of which we are indebted, or in arrears, as mentioned in the French Ambassador's note herewith."[8]

Floridablanca's order for the payment of the 51,083 pesos fuertes was issued on November 29th, and Ortiz de la Riva notified him on December 20th, that he had handed the pesos over to Diego de Gardoqui.[9]

On March 2nd, 1782, we learn through a communication from Jay, that he was again embarrassed by the need of money to cover outstanding bills. He was apparently very grateful for 20,000 given by Gardoqui, by which he was enabled to pay the banker Cabarrus for amounts advanced by the latter and we find him asking the Government to guarantee the banker for the amount mentioned on March 2nd.[10] On the 15th, Cabarrus himself is forced to write to the Minister for instructions. We note in his letter which follows, that he is constrained to take this action because the French Ambassador has once again entered into the affairs between the Americans and the Spanish Court.

"Sir,

Mr. Jay sent me a brief letter this afternoon from the French Ambassador in which he advises that, he is in accordance with Your Excellency concerning the payment of some 45,000 pesos in Bills, in Jay's tenure. They were accepted, became due yesterday, they were protested because of non-payment, but they were not returned as was due, and several merchants have kindly postponed their devolution until next Monday.

As we have arranged that I meet this sort of payment only after a plain order from Your Excellency. I have the honor of informing you that I am ready to supply this amount, if thereby I am serving your wishes, provided that orders be given for a Central, or Post Treasury order, to reimburse me for the 900,000 reales, or by any other authority, in four months in four installments of 225,000 each from the 15th of next month.

I shall hope to know your decision in time so that I may cancel the said Bills before Monday.

I remain obedient and respectful to your Excellency's orders and pray God to preserve your life as long as I wish.
Madrid, March, 15th 1782

Exc. your most obedient, sure and grateful servant."[11]

Jay found himself embarrassed not only by the need of money but over the injury to the pride of His Majesty caused by the continued neglect of the Congress to reply to the proposals made by the Government of Spain, especially to questions referring to the vessels asked for in exchange as well as for other points of grave importance to be settled between the two nations. He could only attribute the silence of the Congress to the fact that they were awaiting the arrival of Gardoqui, just assigned to the Congress as the fully authorized representative of the Court.

He was disturbed at the long delay over the matter of the boundaries on the Mississippi. In a despatch of the previous June 28th, Jay had promised that if His Catholic Majesty would oblige himself to answer for certain amounts drawn by Congress, they on their part, would be able to pledge their faith to indemnify for such amounts and to furnish him with certain aid in vessels.

In the same despatch he mentioned that he had been called upon to accept bills to the amount of 10,000 to 11,000 dollars. His letters of

July 11th, 27th and 28th and of August 11th, 16th, 17th, 18th and 25th were devoted likewise to bills presented to him on sight.

In his brief letter to Floridablanca on March 15th, making clear again the urgent need of money, adding a list amounting to 89,083 dollars for bills payable in April, Jay made no mention of the questions Spain had raised concerning timber, ships or navigation of the Mississippi River. Gardoqui was again instructed to inquire as to the status of these matters.

The only answer Jay could give for the continued silence of the Congress was to reiterate that he had no doubt they would give their earliest attention to the all-important questions but he could assure the Court that their reply would be in perfect accord with the wishes of their Good Friend and Ally.[12]

4.

Not long after this last communication another matter arose that disturbed, not only Jay in Madrid, but the Commissioners in Paris. There had developed a recrudescence of privateering. Privateers were preying freely among the Portuguese ships along the coast, and because of the recklessness of their activities, were causing great fear and hardship among the Spanish merchantmen plying the same waters. Many friendly vessels were being captured and their cargoes sold as prize goods. The unbridled actions of these captains at last reached such heights of destruction among Spanish merchantmen that Aranda, in Paris, was constrained to take the matter up with Franklin in person and to ask that Franklin request the Congress to give orders for the protection of Spanish shipping.

Both Franklin and Jay were approached upon the same subject. Franklin's reply indicated that he was not informed about such depredations and he expressed a doubt that American ships were the real cause of such attacks. Jay's answer was much the same.[13]

It was only a short time after this that Jay notified the Minister, Floridablanca, that he had been summoned to Paris at the request of Franklin for consultation and that he therefore would be leaving Madrid.

Floridablanca, having been forced to refuse the final order for 45,-000 pesos, on the terms required by Cabarrus for repayment within six months, for bills drawn by Jay, felt that Jay's summons to Paris was a ruse to leave the country. He is quoted as saying; "It is strange enough that this man should leave on the first occasion that we have refused to hand over money, with the pretext I have mentioned at the beginning of this letter."[14]

It is unfortunate that Jay felt himself to be frustrated in most of his activities while assigned to Madrid. In reality, he had accomplished very practical results favorable to the United States, although his personal humiliation caused by the rigid protocol of the Royal Court forbade the friendly intimacy that existed between himself and the man of business, Diego de Gardoqui. His high standing in the States, together with the prestige he had lent to all the work of the Congress, had led him to expect closer personal relations with the Prime Minister, Floridablanca, and even to believe that an exception should be made in his favor by allowing him to be received by Carlos III, as a fully accredited Ambassador from a friendly nation.

Knowing the rigid customs obtaining at all the Courts of Europe at that time, he might have accepted his own position as a Minister from a new Republic, with the same grace as the representatives from Switzerland or Holland, but for one important factor. Madame Jay was a woman of forceful character; a woman also of bounding social ambition; who had visualized her position at the Court of Spain as one of great splendor and luxury. To feel that she and her spouse, Mr. Jay, were being received almost like beggars, with outstretched hands serving only to plead for more and more aid for their distressed country, was very evidently more than she felt able to bear with good grace.

John Jay held great respect for his wife's opinions and was in the unhappy position of knowing her resentment at not being received at Court, while, at the same time being placed under the necessity of conducting all his business through the Minister or his Secretary, Bernardo del Campo. He was aware that Madame Jay was not a popular figure in the social life of the city and was in no position to ease the situation. It was therefore with, no doubt, a sigh of relief, that he received his orders to join Franklin in Paris. His great admiration and warm friendship for Gardoqui was later to be renewed in New York where Madame Jay herself was to entertain the quiet Spanish Minister with evident pleasure and real affection.

Since many of the attitudes of a people grow out of less important causes than a disgruntled lady's opinion of a society that has not accepted her with the acclaim she expected, it is not surprising to find that in future years the attitude of Madame Jay was reflected in the thinking of many Americans who never glimpsed the Spanish homeland but who remained convinced that Spain was unfriendly to the United States. It is equally plain that Madame Jay was not possessed of the charms of the ladies who so dramatically worked their spells about the Bourbon Court at Versailles. It is also apparent that the lady knew little of the coldly dignified procedure of the most austere Court in all Europe. Be that as it may, the Jays were not happy in Madrid.

FOOTNOTES

[1]Gardoqui to Campo, October 17, 1780, A.H.N.; Legajo 3884.

[2]Gardoqui to Campo, October 20, 1780, *ibid.* Original.

[3]Carmichael to Gardoqui, November 26, 1780, *ibid.*

[4]Jay to Floridablanca, February 16, 1781, *ibid.* Original.

[5]Jay to Floridablanca, February 20, 1781, *ibid.* Original.

[6]Enclosure of Harrison to Jay, *ibid.*

[7]Yela, *op. cit.,* Tomo 1: 448-451.

[8]Note of Floridablanca written on draft of Jay's treaty, *ibid.,* p. 451.

[9]Orders of Floridablanca, A.H.N.; Legajo 3884; also cited in Yela, *op. cit.,* Tomo 1: 451.

[10]Letters of Jay to Floridablanca, A.H.N.; Legajo 3884.

[11]Cabarrus to Floridablanca, March 15, 1782, *ibid.*

[12]Jay to Floridablanca to Aranda, March 15, 1782, *ibid.*

[13]Floridablanca to Aranda, May 5, 1772; Jay to Floridablanca, May 11, 1782; Aranda to Floridablanca, May 18, 1782, in Manuel Conrotte, *La Intervencion de españa en al Indepencia de los Estados Unidos de la America del Norte* (Madrid, 1920), pp. 136-137. See also, Yela, *op. cit.,* Tomo 1: 448-511.

[14]Jay to Floridablanca, April, 1782, Yela, *op. cit.,* Tomo 1: 448-451.

CHAPTER VII

1.

Before going into the mission of Gardoqui to the United States, it seems proper at this point to deal with the brief and unofficial sojourn of the first Spaniard to be assigned to the Congress, and, as an observer, to the headquarters of General Washington from 1777 to 1780, Juan de Miralles.

Early in 1777, Floridablanca recognized the necessity of having more direct information concerning the needs and wishes of the American Congress and therefore of establishing direct contact with that body. Before reaching a decision on a representative, Floridablanca consulted with José de Gálvez, Minister of the Indies and the two men concurred in the opinion that it would be inadvisable to send anyone directly from Spain. Gálvez suggested that an agent coming from Havana would be in a better position to provide the information they would require and transmit news of the progress of the war; such a man could avail himself of the Spanish posts at Havana or those in Louisiana.

A secret letter went out to the Governor-General of Cuba, Don Diego Navarro, authorizing him to choose a man who could proceed to Philadelphia with authority to act as agent for the Government of Spain. The agent he selected should offer all aid possible and facilitate the sending out of information as to the need for supplies and the condition of Washington's army.[1] Navarro accordingly proposed, and Gálvez accepted the name of Don Juan de Miralles, a native-born Spaniard, resident since childhood in Havana, and a wealthy and highly respected landed-gentleman of discretion. Miralles embarked for Philadelphia near the close of the year 1777, and took up his duties under the patronage of the French Ambassador, Monsieur Gérard, the First Minister Plenipotentiary from the Court of Louis XVI, to the Congress. Gérard was an able diplomat with a wide experience. The Spanish Government wanted Miralles to act through Gérard's mediation since it was still maintaining, in 1777, the cloak of secrecy over its operations, a secrecy which it believed vital to the security of its American dominions. News of his arrival in Philadelphia was communicated by Gérard to Aranda in Paris and to the French Ambassador in Madrid and thus circuitously to his own Government.

Miralles' official correspondence was directed to the Minister of the Indies by way of Navarro at Havana. There was little news that he could communicate, other than military, during the first months of his mission since he could not be recognized officially and received as a bona-fide representative of his country. It is certain that he made a most agreeable impression upon those members of the Congress with whom he came in personal contact. His early despatches were all concerned with the urgent needs of the Continental armies. He immediately struck up a warm friendship with General Washington and his staff officers and became firmly attached to the American Cause as soon as he learned at firsthand the incredible hardships under which the new nation was laboring to gain its independence. His partisanship was so strong that he quietly laid his personal fortune on the altar of their necessity at a time when the Continental currency was at its lowest ebb.

Not long after his arrival in the country the Congress issued up to two-hundred million dollars in paper money. Miralles realized that this vast amount of paper was rapidly becoming worthless in purchasing power. By early 1780, one Spanish peso fuerte was valued in Philadelphia at forty American dollars. Miralles generously offered his personal fortune in accepting this paper at a much higher rate of exchange, with characteristic modesty, making no mention of his contribution to the Cause in any of his official correspondence. His action only came to light affter his untimely death, which occurred while he was paying a visit to Washington at the General's headquarters at Valley Forge.[2]

The French Ambassador maintained a scrupulously correct courtesy toward his Spanish colleague, but he was most vitally interested in placing forward on all occasions the contribution of France to the American cause. His practice worked frequently to the marked disadvantage of Miralles and to Spain, whose aid at this time was no less vital. It was not until December, 1778, that Miralles was able to have a conference with the President of the Congress and meet other members of that body on a direct and intimate basis. At this and subsequent meetings, however, the French Ambassador was always present.

There were many matters of deepest concern and mutual interest between Spain and the United States that in no way were related to the fortunes of France, notably; plans for the conquest of the Floridas and the vital matter of the free navigation of the Mississippi. Free navigation of the Great River was at this time being violently contested between the English, who held strategic posts along one bank; and the Spanish, who controlled the opposite bank. Freedom of navigation was of utmost urgency for the United States since war supplies from Spain were being expedited along the waterway. There was under discussion a project to build a canal which would speed the movement of vessels from the Ohio into the Great River. The idea had been suggested by various members of the Congress. Plans were also propounded for the conquest of West Florida, then held tightly in the grip of the English, who were entrenched at Mobile and Pensacola.

These vital matters could be discussed on an intimate basis only with the greatest difficulty. The delicate diplomatic position of Miralles made it all the harder to resolve them with any satisfaction to the two principals. All major recommendations, all plans had to pass through the interested hands of M. Gérard, the French Ambassador. Miralles' position was humiliating. He felt, and not without reason, that the affairs of Spain were being adjusted to the indirect advantage of France rather than to that of his own Court. In a number of instances, Gérard would adroitly interpret a friendly suggestion in such a way that the Spanish Court found its position represented in anything but a friendly light.

Aranda, Spain's very able Ambassador in Paris, was well aware of the situation and much disturbed by the fact that news of Spain's activities and plans for coordination with the Americans was well-known to Vergennes, the French Minister of State and likewise to the French Ambassador in Madrid, before such information was turned over to him. The situation was one of great delicacy. Both José de Gálvez, Minister of the Indies, and Aranda used their influence with Floridablanca to bring about a change in the status of Miralles. But this proved impossible; there was the Family Pact between the two Bourbon thrones and also Spain's need for secrecy. They continued to chafe under the humiliating knowledge that they were receiving reports at second hand. The bulk of Miralles' reports continued to go through Navarro in Havana to the Minister of the Indies and thence to Floridablanca in Madrid and Aranda in Paris. Meanwhile the news was constantly going out from Gérard directly to Paris, a much shorter line of communication.

At the meeting in December, 1778, referred to above, Miralles gave his hearers full assurance that the Americans would be accorded freedom of navigation on the Mississippi and the protection of the flag of Spain, should they need it, for the safety of vital cargoes of supplies for their army. He offered also the fullest assistance in volunteers, supplies and money from the Governor of Louisiana in the contemplated campaign for the American conquest of the Floridas. (In later chapters in this work Spain's important contribution to the final victory will be treated in detail. Don Bernardo de Gálvez, Governor of Louisiana, proved a friend indeed by his personal leadership in the military operations which brought about the fall of British power in the Southeast and Southwest.)

2.

Not all members of the Congress were ready to welcome Spanish assistance in the conquest of the Floridas. The people of Georgia and South Carolina hoped to win the territory unaided and incorporate it within their boundaries. There was also the possibility that Virginia might stand with these two and that her delegates, uniting with theirs, might swing the vote in the Congress against the idea of an American expedition. Miralles, in offering his country's full assistance, was aware that unless some action was taken immediately to weaken the English in this quarter, these southern states were in danger of being overrun by the powerful forces stationed at Pensacola. Acting in concert with the British fleet, British success would mean cutting the confederacy of the United States in two, thereby preparing the way for the eventual defeat of Washington's army in the north.

Washington realized, more acutely than the members of the Congress, the dangerously weak military position of Georgia and South Carolina. He knew he had small chance of sending any detachments from his already dwindling army. Therefore, he stood with Miralles and, approving the latter's recommendations, threw his full support behind the agent of Spain.

The program which Miralles thus presented in December was oriented toward the future conduct of the war. But aid in tangible form had already passed through his hands into those of the Americans, a proof that Spain's promises were real and would be fulfilled. In March, the King had issued orders, in answer to an urgent plea for aid in the South, to send fifty-thousand pesos to the Americans from Havana. He had promised to hand over additional amounts as quickly as possible. Miralles had been authorized to transfer the fifty-thousand pesos at once. Fourteen thousand, four hundred and twenty-four pesos fuertes, two and one-half reales, a sum amounting to approximately $576,960 in Continental currency, was to go directly into the hands of Alexander Gillon, chief of the naval squadron of the state of South Carolina to cover the cost of enlarging his squadron for the protection of the southern states.[3] The almost-vanished credit of the Congress was bolstered further by the aforementioned personal fortune of Juan Miralles, this time to assist the Congress in reinforcing the military position in the south.

No one realized more than Washington the valuable services being rendered by Miralles. His esteem was demonstrated in his personal correspondence following their first meeting. In the most cordial terms he wrote to Don Diego Josef Navarro, Governor of Havana:

> "Headquarters, Middle Brook, March, 4, 1779
>
> Sir:
> A journey to Philadelphia in the winter procured me the honor of Your Excellencys favour of the 11th of March last by Don Juan Miralles, and the pleasure of this gentleman's acquaintance. His estimable qualities justify your recommendation and concur with it to establish him in my esteem. I doubt not he will have informed you of the cordial and respectful sentiments, which he has experienced in this country. On my part I shall always take pleasure in convincing him of the high value I set upon his merit; and of the respect I bear to those who are so happy as to interest your Excellency's friendship. I can only express my gratitude for your polite offer of service by entreating you to afford me opportunities of testifying my readiness to execute any commands, with which you shall be pleased to honor me. With my prayers for your health and happiness, and with the greatest respect I have the honor to be —
>
> George Washington"[4]

The mutual esteem which marked the first meeting between Washington and Miralles soon ripened into a warm friendship. That their relations transcended, from the first, the formalities which are commonly associated with protocol is revealed in a delightful little note which Washington addressed to Miralles in October.

> "West Point, Oct. 16, 1779.
>
> To Juan de Miralles.
> Sir:
> I am honored with your friendly letter of the 2nd of last month (Sept.) Nothing could be more acceptable then your present, but the manner in which it was bestowed. This enhanced its value, because it increased our esteem. I can only send you from this quarter, in return, what you have long had, my very sincere friendship.
> The intelligence you have been pleased to intrust me with, is agreeable, (except that part which relates the loss of your despatches; for this I am concerned). I promise myself the most happy events from the known spirit of your nation. United with the Arms of France we have everything to hope over the Arms of our common enemy, the English. I shall not fail to inform Mrs. Washington of the obligation she is under for your polite attention and remembrance of her. I am sure she will receive your compliments (which I shall make a tender of in my next letter) with gratitude and pleasure as you stand high in her estimation. I shall have the honor, . . .
>
> George Washington."[5]
>
> (Miralles' letter, dated Oct. 2, 1779, is in the Washington Papers. The above-mentioned gift was a sea turtle weighing 100 pounds, and a box of lemons. The good news of which he had informed the General was of the Declaration of War by Spain against England.)

Anyone aware of the scarcity of food during this bleak period of the war can realize the pleasure with which Mrs. Washington received the remarkable gift of a 100-pound sea turtle and the box of lemons, the latter a luxury seldom seen in North America at the time, and the joy, particularly to a woman born and brought up in the Tidewater of Virginia where the preparation of turtle soup had long been a high accomplishment. Washington wrote again to Miralles in early December:

"Morristown, New Jersey, Dec. 7, 1779.
Sir:
    I had the honor of receiving two days since your letter of the 29th of November inclosing a copy of your late representation to Congress. I entreat you to be assured that I esteem myself highly obliged by this mark of your attention and confidence; and that the promotion of the interests of His Catholic Majesty will always be an additional motive to my zeal in the execution of any plan for the achievment of the common cause.
    The subjects you have been pleased to communicate are of the most interesting nature and, have been very seriously considered in concert with the Honorable the Committee of Congress appointed to confer with me on the occasion. Our sentiments were the same; and the result is by this opportunity transmitted to Congress, who, I doubt not will immediately impart it to you with their further resolutions. I therefore beg leave to refer you to them and to repeat the assurances of the respect and great personal esteem with which I have the honor to be."
(A footnote of the Editors — "Congress resolved Dec, 16th, that General Lincoln cooperate with the Governor of Havana in a move against the British in Georgia.")[6]

The important decision to concentrate forces in the Southeast was made only after much serious discussion in the Congress since it required that Washington detach some troops to reinforce General Lincoln in Georgia. There were too few troops for the campaign in the North and there was an urgent need for a foray against the strong British fort at Detroit. Between these two widely-separated points, Washington was hard put to make a choice in sending help, thus weakening his own forces, but his final decision was made after Miralles had presented the strong case for the Spanish plan already undertaken on the Mississippi and along the Gulf Coast. To Major-General Lincoln he wrote expressing his concern, saying:

"From West Point, Sept. 28th, 1779, . . . [The enemy may go South.] The *full* possession of Georgia and the acquisition of South Carolina would be a good counterpoise to their losses in the Islands — They need supplies both on the Continent and in the West Indies, from the superiority in the English Channel, which the juncture of Spain must have produced and the restraint it will impose upon the exportations from England and Ireland."[7]

For this reason he was unable to send assistance to the Northwest although he had expressed himself to the Commander there, Col. Broadhead, in forceful terms when he urged that Fort Pitt be kept strong even though an expedition against Detroit was impossible because of the situation in South Carolina.

Miralles was from that time on in close contact with Washington and the members of Congress. His letters of April 7th, 8th and 10th 1780, treated entirely with the fast-changing scene of operations in Carolina and Georgia, but he did not live to hear the vastly inspiring news of the fall of Pensacola to the forces of Bernardo de Gálvez. He continued to feel depressed because of his lack of official status as an envoy of Spain, knowing that he could be of more service at this time had he been able to present the plans of his country to the Congress in a more direct manner.

He confessed to the Chevalier Luzerne, the new Minister from France who had replaced the veteran French Minister Gérard, that "he had no instructions directly from the Court of Spain; that all his correspondence was with the Governor of Havana; that the Spanish Ministry had signified their general approbation of his conduct down to the end of August, 1779; that he had received a letter from the Minister of the Indies, José de Gálvez, stating that he would be appointed minister to the United States when the King should think proper to send one."[8]

Congress showed every mark of respect to this agent, which was due to his personal character, but carefully avoided treating with him in any public capacity, except through the intervention of the French Minister. Congress would not commit themselves by treating with a person who was not empowered directly by the Spanish Court.

3.

Washington lost no time in sending what troops could be spared to General Lincoln in South Carolina. On the same day we find him writing two letters relative to this strategic decision. The first, to Juan de Miralles follows:

"Headquarters Morristown, Feb. 27, 1780.
Sir,
 . . . The want of any certain intelligence of the fleet, which sailed from New York, I should attribute to their having been disconcerted in their voyage by the tempestuous weather, which prevailed for some time after their departure. A variety of circumstances combining proved that the intention of that embarkation was for the Southern States. All my intelligence agreed in this point. The composition of the detachment; Governor Martin and several refugees from South and North Carolina having embarked in the fleet; the current of the English accounts, by which it appears that General Clinton was expected to be in South Carolina as early as November, in which he was probably prevented by Count d'Estaing's operations in Georgia; these circumstances conspire to satisfy

me, that the Carolinas were the objects. But, notwithstanding this, I think the precautions you are taking to put the Spanish Dominions upon their guard are wise. It can have no ill consequence; and it is advisable to be provided against all contingencies. It would not be surprising if the British General, on hearing of the progress of the Spanish arms in the Floridas, should relinquish his first design and go to the defense of his own territories. I shall with the greatest pleasure comply with your request for giving you information of all the movements of the enemy, that come to my knowledge, which may in any manner interest the plans of your Court, and I have just written to General Lincoln agreeably to your intimation. Every motive will induce him to do whatever may be in his power to effect the diversion desired. If the enemy prosecute the plan, which I suppose to have been originally intended, he will necessarily find his whole attention employed at home on the defensive; but, if they direct their force to another quarter, I am persuaded he will make the best use of his to give them all possible annoyance and distraction. I have the honor to be."[9]

The above letter is further clarified by Washington's letter of the same day to General Lincoln.

"To Major-General Lincoln, in South Carolina, Feb. 27, 1780.
. . . In addition to the advices you were obliging enough to communicate, I have just seen official accounts from the Governor of Havanna [sic], of the success of the Spaniards in Florida. [capture of Baton Rouge and Natchez] if the remaining ports fall, it will be a very important stroke, and in all probability the operations there will have a favorable influence upon our affairs in your quarter: Though perhaps it may not be probable it is not impossible, that the British General, if he has discretionary power, on hearing of the progress of the Spaniards in the Floridas may suspend his original plan and turn his attention that way, and endeavor to defend their own territories rather than attempt conquests, Don Juan de Miralles, the Spanish Agent, in a letter of the 18th communicating the foregoing intelligence, has the following paragraph:
By Royal order, I am very strongly charged to influence Your Excellency to make the greatest diversion with the troops of the United States against those of the enemy in Georgia, to the effect of attracting their attention and disabling them from sending succors to Pensacola and Mobile, which the Governor of Louisiana is to attack, auxiliated with sea and land forces, which were prepared at Havannah [sic] with all things needful, and ready to sail when the station would permit.
. . . You will have since been informed, that your information with respect to the Virginia troops being detached to the Southward was good. Though they could be ill spared from this army, I thought we should have less to fear here than you there, without them; and it appeared upon the whole advisable to throw the weight of Virginia into the defense of our Southern extremity."[10]

It was through Miralles' letter of the 18th that Washington first heard of the rapid campaign of Governor Bernardo de Gálvez against the Mississippi River forts. Miralles quoted the Governor as saying:

". . . The morning of the 7th of September took the Fort of Mantchak by storm. Baton Rouge fort fell Sept. 21 and that of 'Painmure' at Natchez was included in the surrender. Prisoners were 550 Regular troops, 8 vessels and other boats and 50 sailors."

(footnote to letter)[11]

The relief to Washington upon receipt of this encouraging news of the action taken by the Spanish was great. He had written only six months previously to the Congress, from West Point on Sept. 7, 1779 that —

> ". . . If the British lose possessions in the South — they will be amply compensated by the full acquisition of Georgia and South Carolina; both of which are so weak as to be in no small danger."[12]

The situation in the South was indeed perilous and news of Spanish successes in the Mississippi valley were doubly welcome to the harassed General Lincoln. Within three days of the date of Washington's two letters, information was written to the Committee of Foreign Affairs from Charleston by Henry Laurens which bore out the plan of the English fleet mentioned above. In his letter Laurens states:

> "Charleston, February, 14th, 1780
>
> Gentlemen,
>
> My last address went forward, under the 31st. ult. by Mr. Renshaw, one of the Corps of Escorts. The 10th instant, General Lincoln was on the point of ordering the RANGER frigate to conduct me to France. Governor Rutledge had given his consent, and I believe there would have been no opposition in Council, but on the 11th we received authentic intelligence of the arrival of the enemy's troops from New York, at and near Tybee, and the next day of their having landed a large detachment on John's Island, within sixteen miles of this capital. We heard yesterday, that another detachment had landed, and repossessed Beaufort, and we know that two ships of the line, two frigates, and several armed vessels, are cruising near the bar of this harbor. Thus environed an attack upon Charleston, very illy prepared for defense, may be every hour expected.
>
> In these circumstances, were I to study my own private interests and desires, I should remain here, and stand or fall with my country. Whatever her fate may be, exceeding heavy losses to me will be the consequence of my absence at this critical juncture, but the Governor, and other judicious friends urge me to use every endeavor for obtaining a passage through some other channel. Duty dictates the same measure. I shall therefor proceed to North Carolina, where are four vessels belonging to this port and embark immediately on board of one of them, I shall omit no opportunity of acquainting you with my circumstances.
>
> I have the honor to be, . . ."[13]

Henry Laurens had been commissioned by the Congress to go to Europe with the express plan of negotiating a loan from the Low Countries. His journey was to have tragic results; he was captured when his ship was taken by the English and transported to England where he was imprisoned in the Tower of London for over eighteen months. The news was carried to the Committee in the following letter.

> "Vestal-British Frigate,
> St. John's, Newfoundland, September, 14th, 1780
>
> Gentlemen,
>
> I had the honor of writing to the Board of Admiralty, from on board the MERCURY packet, the 23rd ult. (this letter is missing) by Capt. Young, at part-

ing with the SARATOGA. On the 3rd instant, the VESTAL came in view, and after a pursuit of five or six hours, Captain George Keppel took possession of the packet. Mr. Young, Captain Pickles, and myself were conducted on board this ship and yesterday we arrived here.

Certain papers, among which were all those delivered to me by Mr. Lovell, and the Board of Admiralty, fell into Captain Keppel's hands.

These papers had been inclosed in a bag, accompanied by a considerable weight of iron shot, and thrown overboard, but the weight proved insufficient for the purpose intended. Admiral Edwards, Governor of this Island, and commander of the stationed squadron, has ordered me to England in the sloop of war FAIRY, under the command of Captain Keppel. Mr. Young and Captain Pickles will probably go in the same vessel.

I should be wanting in justice, and indeed deficient in common gratitude, were I to omit an acknowledgement of Captain Keppel's kindness to myself, and to everybody captured in the MERCURY. Captain Pickles' conduct, while he had command of that vessel, was perfectly satisfactory to me.

I have the honor, . . ."[14]

As was so frequently the case, all important papers and despatches fell into the hands of the enemy and the plans of the Congress fully disclosed to the British. Seldom, however, did such a catastrophe happen to so important an envoy as Henry Laurens whose loss to the States at this time was most vital. Any plans for assistance or a diversion of American forces in Georgia and South Carolina to direct the attention of the British from Pensacola and Mobile were ended with the arrival of the English before Charleston.

Miralles continued to keep in close touch with the Congressmen and was once again able to further the cause of the Americans by advancing money for financial aid to their agents in Europe. He arranged to purchase their letters of exchange for half their value, without any certainty of repayment, thus absorbing the difference between the depreciated paper money of the Congress and the Spanish peso. Again he made no public statement relative to this valuable contribution to the desperate situation of the Congress.

On April, 17, 1780, he made a visit to Washington's headquarters at Morristown. He left Philadephia with the French Minister, Luzerne, and shortly after his arrival at Washington's quarters was stricken with a fatal malady. On April, 19, he became mortally ill, vomiting blood, and consumed by a raging fever. Doctor Cochran, of Washington's staff, did all that was possible for the dying man; Washington and all his officers offered every aid available at the scantily-supplied post; the Catholic chaplain of the French Ambassador was called upon to administer the last rites; but late in the afternoon of the 28th, Juan de Miralles died. His young secretary, Francisco Rendon, was called from Philadelphia where he was notified of the death of his kindly superior officer by Luzerne.

Washington was much distressed at the tragic end of the sole Spanish representative to the Congress and felt keenly the loss of the friend whom he personally admired for his warmth and generosity of character. He personally arranged for every possible medical attention and physical comfort during Miralles' fatal illness, arranged that all costs should be paid for his burial and delegated twelve captains to carry the coffin of his friend to its final resting place. The highest military honors were rendered as for a fully accredited ambassador; a picked escort presented arms; while a salute of guns was fired every two minutes during the burial service, over which General Washington himself presided, escorted by his highest staff officers. Members of Congress and other high officials of the United States also assisted at the last rites; while a company of Grenadiers rendered the final salutes at the graveside. So ended the career of the sixty-five-year-old gentleman of Havana who, without official status, in a city where no one spoke his language, where his sole interpreter was the representative of a nation not his own, had nevertheless so firmly and ably aided his own country and that of his American friends.[15]

Washington paid his final tribute to his friend in a letter written from his headquarters on April, 30th, 1780, to The Governor of Havana, Don Diego José Navarro, in which he says that the remains were interred — "with all the respect due to his character and his merit." He states that Miralles arrived for a visit to headquarters with the Minister of France and was attacked the same day, was ill nine days during which, "no care or attention in our power was omitted. . . . Ever since his residence with us I have been happy in ranking him among the number of my friends" — "in this country he has been universally esteemed, and will be universally regretted."[16]

FOOTNOTES

[1]Floridablanca to Navarro, A.H.N.; Legajo 3885, exp. 17, num. I; also in Campillo, *op. cit.*, Nota Preliminar y Catálogo.

[2]Jay to Floridablanca, Aranjuez, April 28, 1782, in Conrotte, *op. cit.*, p. 207, footnote 3.

[3]*Ibid.*, pp. 295-296.

[4]*The Writings of George Washington*, John C. Fitzpatrick, ed. (George Washington Bicentennial Ed., 39 vols., Washington, D.C., Government Printing Office, 1931-1944), 14: 192.

[5]*Ibid.*, 16: 470-471.

[6]*Ibid.*, 17: 225.

[7]*Ibid.*, 16: 351.

[8]MS. letter from Luzerne to Vergennes, March 13,1780, in *The Writings of George Washington*, Worthington Chauncey Ford, ed. (14 vols, New York, 1889-93), 8: 208.

[9]*Ibid.*, 8: 207-209.

[10]*Ibid.*, 9: 206.

[11]*Writings of Washington*, Fitzpatrick, ed., *op. cit.*, 18: 55-56.

[12]*Ibid.*, 16: 240.

[13]Laurens to the Committee of Foreign Affairs, in *Diplomatic Correspondence, op. cit.*, 2: 457-458.

[14]Laurens to the Committee of Foreign Affairs, in *ibid.*, 2: 461-462.

[15]Campillo, *op. cit.*, p. XVIII; also in A.H.N.; Legajo 3451.

[16]*Writings of Washington*, Fitzpatrick, ed., *op. cit.*, 8: 209.

CHAPTER VIII

Always in the minds of the negotiators of Spain and the United States and holding first place on their agenda was the haunting subject of Mississippi navigation. While the war went on the Great River, whose banks were held by Spain and England, was considered the main artery through which the lifeblood of supplies could reach the Americans.

Throughout the period of his stay in Madrid, John Jay had endeavored to fulfill the instructions of Congress by obtaining a treaty of commerce and alliance from the Court of Spain. In this he had failed. The one great obstacle, from the point of view of the Spanish Government was "the pretensions of America to the navigation of the Mississippi." Jay's orders on this point were strict and unyielding. He had no room for diplomatic maneuver. "The United States," asserted Floridablanca, "had at one time relinquished all right to the free use of the Mississippi and was now making it an essential point of a treaty." He went on to say that "this is an object that the King had so much at heart that he would never relinquish it."[1]

Some members of the Congress were in favor of abandoning the claim. By the summer of 1780, the delegates of Georgia and South Carolina were in such a state of alarm over English successes in their area that they proposed to yield claim to the exclusive navigation of the river below the thirty-first parallel in return for an immediate treaty of alliance. Virginia backed their proposal and it was passed by the Congress. New instructions in this sense were sent immediately to Jay in Madrid.

It is rather extraordinary that the United States should be so insistent upon the question of free navigation at all when we bear in mind the urgency of their needs in matériel and money. More to the point is the fact that there were at this time no "principles of international law upon which a nation was justified in laying claim to the free navigation of a river whose mouth was held by an alien."[2] The concession which was instigated by Georgia and South Carolina was the result of a state of panic. The people of this region were much more aware of their need of Spanish assistance than the people in the northern states or their delegates in the Congress had begun to realize.

The strategic importance of this southern region was bitterly clear to Washington. He knew only too well the possibilities of catastrophe should the English succeed in conquering it and sever its connection with the North. The next move would be a campaign in which the British would exert irrestible pressure from three sides, the south, the north and northwest and the sea. To forestall this eventuality Washington worked out a plan of operations with the Count de Rochambeau, France's most brilliant commander in America. They would carry the war into the South, at the same time working closely with the Spanish in the Southeast and the Northwest.

It is not our purpose to go into the narrative of the campaigns which followed other than to mention here a forgotten and little-known incident which proved yet again the manifold ways in which vital help was extended by Spain and the Spanish people. The war on American soil was virtually ended by the close of 1781. The battle of Yorktown decided the outcome. In that final and decisive battle Spain's part was indirect, almost casual, but it was also as unique a form of intervention as it was unheralded. It had been agreed by Washington and Rochambeau that the latter should throw the support of his troops into the defense of the southern states. At the time the English were in Charleston and raiding far and wide over the Carolinas. Not neglecting the importance of what would today be called psychological warfare, they were making large and tempting offers of autonomy, trading privileges and protection against hostile neighbors in exchange for a separate peace with the mother country.

Rochambeau, who had counted on the assistance of Count de Grasse and his fleet, found himself unable to secure supplies due to the fact that the fleet was engaged in operations around Santo Domingo. His need for both money and supplies was urgent. In this state of affairs he sent a message to the Admiral commanding the Spanish fleet at Havana, Solano, through de Grasse as intermediary. In answer to the urgent call for help and to facilitate Rochambeau's victory over the English, Solano and the authorities in Havana acted with promptness and impetuosity. They raised, by public subscription, a million and a half libras tornesas (or fifteen million dollars Continental) within twenty-four hours which were put into the hands of Admiral Solano to be put at the immediate disposal of Rochambeau. This extraordinary feat was sufficient to assure his forces the needed wherewithal to engage the English in battle. The brilliant coordination of the armies of Washington and Rochambeau was to bring about the defeat of Cornwallis and the final surrender of the British army at Yorktown on October 17, 1781, thereby ensuring to the Americans the possession of Virginia, the two Carolinas and Georgia. Through this spontaneous action in Havana, Spain took her indirect but important part in the final scene that was to ensure the destiny of the people of the United States.

Rochambeau was neither forgetful nor ungrateful for the timely and remarkably effective intervention of the Spanish people. From his camp at Yorktown he wrote to Aranda in Paris acknowledging his deep gratitude for the million and a half libras tornesas raised at Havana within the space of twenty-four hours and at the most fateful hour in the struggle of the United States.[3]

The war at sea went bitterly on for a year after the great victory at Yorktown. It was imperative to keep the trade routes open among the islands, around Santo Domingo, Guanico and Sta. Eustatia. D'Estaing's return to France with twelve ships of the line for repairs and overhaul created a dangerous situation long foreseen and feared by the American Commissioners in Paris. De Grasse was hard put to it to maneuvre his fleet to a rendezvous with the Spanish troops under the command of Bernardo de Gálvez, the victorious general who had completed the conquest of the Mississippi river posts of the English and the English bastions at Mobile and Pensacola.

The plan for the defense of the West Indies had already been put into operation. Gálvez was in position at Guanico with his troops ready to form a juncture with de Grasse's fleet for the expedition when the tragic news of the debacle of the French fleet reached him. The worst fears of the Commissioners and the Spanish Ambassador in Paris, Aranda, were realized; the fleet was gone. Barnardo de Gálvez had written an almost premonitory letter on the 28th of March, 1782, in which his uneasiness over the projected expedition was expressed. To Don Miguel de Muzquiz, Minister of War, he wrote:

"Excellency, My Lord:
   On the first of last month I left Havana bound for this Colony arriving here on the 27th of last month; here I am, as in all my posts, seeking to serve you and be worthy of your favor. I should be very happy to remain here as short a time as possible, due to the lateness of the season, as well as to what Your Excellency knows we have to undertake as soon as possible; but up to now I have only the troops sent me from Cadiz. The troops from Havana, Brest, and Martinica, although I expect them shortly, have not yet arrived. The days pass, and the heat begins. These worries disturb me greatly, for I have not at hand all the means I need to fulfill, as I must, the King's wishes.
   I trust your Excellency will honor me with your advise, sure that I will be pleased to be of service and follow your wishes.
   Our Lord preserve you many years, GUANICO, March, 28th, 1782.
   Excellency, . . .
                              D. BERNARDO de GALVEZ." (rubric)[4]

His detailed report of the debacle, giving the extent of French losses followed in May:

"Most Excellent Lord.

My Lord,

When we were ready to put into operation the plans of His Majesty, the last battle fought by the French and English Fleets on the 12th of last month, has resulted in the capture of 7 ships of the Line of the former, (including that of the Commandant General, Count de Grasse), of two Frigates; of various artillery, munitions, supplies, and some troops, and the damage suffered by the majority of the French ships: all this has considerably diminished the greater part of the naval strength of our Allies, has augmented the sea power of our enemies, and leaves us only to observe what can result from this latest catastrophe, the details of which I think your Excellency must already have known through the reports which the English, as well as the French sent to Europe immediately, and through the one which I also sent to our Court through the agency of Don Francisco Saavedra. Your Excellency will understand how painful this reverse has been for me, since I desire nothing more than to follow exactly the plans which the Ministry sends me and to do justice in some way to the honors which I have won through the Grace of God.

My just grief has been mitigated in part by the fact that I have just learned of the triumphs of the armies of the King in Roathan, Atila, and Guanaja, taken by my Father, he being the first in reducing them, from the Frigate of His Majesty, the SANTA MATILDE, in company with her Commander, and remaining to continue his expedition.

I beg your Excellency that you count me among the number of your known and devoted, and that you make use of my good will as much as may be your wish.

God keep Your Excellency many years

GUANICO, 17th of May, 1782.

Most Excellent Lord Your hands are kissed by your most attentive servant, D. BERNADO GALVEZ/RUBRIC/. to-Most Excellent Lord, DON MIGUEL DE MUZQUIZ."[5]

(A note on the folder states: "D. Bernardo de Gálvez. The expedition projected having been frustrated as a result of the disastrous battle of the 12th of April, between the Count de Grasse and Admiral Rodney. Answered on August, 11th, 1782.")

During the same month, D. Luis Huet, the naval commander of Spanish units in the area, wrote a short report from Cabo Frances (Cape Francois) to Muzquiz detailing a number of losses to the French fleet:

"Excellency, My Lord,

I take advantage of the first chance I have, to notify you of my arrival at this port, on the eighth of last month, with the army commanded by His Excellency, Don Bernardo de Gálvez, of which force I am Quarter-Master General, should your Excellency find need of my services. In my opinion, our Campaign, for the present, has been frustrated by the unfortunate blow suffered by the French Fleet commanded by the Count de Grasse, on the thirteenth of last month, at the height of Guadalupe, in which battle the French lost five ships of the Line, and at Semana Point, the French lost two ships of the Line and two Frigates: these are: LA VILLE DE PARIS, HECTOR, GLORIOSO, ARDIENTE, CESAR, JASON and CATON and the Frigates, CERES and AMBLE.

If it be no trouble and in accord with the wishes of Your Excellency, that I continue to inform you of whatever occurs worthy of your interest, I shall be gratified to do so, pleased that Your Excellency honor me with your orders.
God preserve you, . . ."6

Both these reports verify the sad news that circulated like wildfire through England, France and Spain. The English were delirious with joy, after the setbacks administered by Washington and the fears rampant in the northwestern territory along the Ohio. The gloom and bitterness in Paris was all directed against the unfortunate Count de Grasse, whose tragedy was certainly not due to his own lack of ability to command, but to the inherent weakness of the French ships. The Count d'Estaing was, for the sake of his prestige as a naval commander, far better off to be in Paris at this time since his fleet would have been almost as helpless against that commanded by the best officer in the English navy, Admiral Rodney, with a fleet of ships in much better condition for battle. At the Court in Madrid the loss of the French ships was a disappointing blow though not as surprising as it was to Louis of France. Carlos III had long known the conditions existing in the three navies and, as mentioned before, had made his views clear in his aforementioned Memorial to Paris. However it was a definite setback to his strategic plans for the use of French ships as convoys for his fighting army under the young commander, Don Bernardo de Gálvez. New methods needed to be worked out at once. The American Commissioners were aware also of the desperate need to proceed with all possible speed in mobilizing ships and supplies from the ports of Spain. Washington must not be suffered to lose ground for lack of reinforcements at this critical hour in the battle for Independence.

FOOTNOTES

[1]*The Correspondence and Public Papers of John Jay*, Henry P. Johnston, ed. (4 vols., New York, 1890-93), I: 316-326, cited in James Alton James, *The Life of George Rogers Clark* (Chicago, 1928), p. 223.

[2]*Ibid.*, I: 435-449, cited in James, *Life of Clark*, p. 223.

[3]Rochambeau to Aranda, Campo de York, October 24, 1781, cited in Conrotte, *op. cit.*, pp. 108-110.

[4]Bernardo de Gálvez to Muzquis, March 28, 1782; A.G.S. Guerra Moderna; Legajo 7303, Folio 300.

[5]Gálvez to Muzquis, May 17, 1782, *ibid.*; Legajo 7303, Folio 305.

[6]D. Luis Huet to Muzquis, May 3, 1782, *ibid.*; Legajo 7303, Folio 282.

CHAPTER IX

1.

All during the cloak-and-dagger period of negotiation between the Spanish Crown and the Colonies in the early days of the war, the quiet merchant of Bilbao acted as the undercover agent for the Court of Spain. After John Jay had been officially assigned to Madrid, the urgent and devious business transactions for supplying aid to the new nation were ably and adroitly carried through by Gardoqui. Thousands of Spanish pounds were transferred to the American Envoy upon Gardoqui's simple receipt. Amidst all the trials of the Americans during those critical and fateful years the figure of Don Diego de Gardoqui is found at the center of all activities, smoothing out the multiple financial, social and personal affairs involved in dealings between the various representatives of the two nations.

Gardoqui remains to this day, in the pages of history, one of the least known, though one of the most effective friends the struggling nation had during the Revolution. Both his family background and his own character had made him the person perfectly qualified for the difficult task he performed so well for so long.

Born Diego Maria de Gardoqui, in Bilbao on November 12, 1735, to Don Jose and Doña Maria de Gardoqui, his ancestors were all Vizcainos of the vicinity of Bilbao. As a member of the great mercantile house of Gardoqui and Sons, he spent the youthful years and the years of his young manhood apprenticed to its business. He was educated in England and thus became master of the language. This knowledge of English, together with his wide acquaintance with both Englishmen and Americans having commercial dealings with his House made him invaluable to the Spanish Court. It is not surprising that he was called upon on numerous occasions to interpret and translate official documents relative to many matters of importance to the state.

Any summation of his character must take into consideration the traits of his province and its people. Vizcainos have long been known for their keenness in commercial dealings, for their knowledge of international affairs, for their quality of cool stability in time of crisis, for their firm, strict adherence to a high code of ethics in matters of conscience and morality. Because of these distinguishing qualities, long recognized both in Europe and North America, this scion of the great House of Gardoqui was unusually well equipped to undertake the difficult assignment as Spain's first Ambassador to the United States.

As the reader will recall, Gardoqui, in a personal letter to his friend Bernardo del Campo, secretary to the Prime Minister, Floridablanca, confessed the reluctance with which he severed all financial connection with the family firm; and uprooted his immediate family from its happy and prosperous domicile in order to assume the responsible mission in America, for which he had been chosen by his sovereign.

His orders to set out for the United States were signed by Carlos III at San Ildefonso on the 27th of September, 1784. His credentials were drawn up in conformity with the formula used for the envoy to Holland, for that nation was considered to be the one most like the United States. Gardoqui was to represent Spain in the capacity of "Encargado de Negocios," with full authority to treat with the Congress on all matters of importance between the two countries.[1]

Orders were sent at the same time to the secretary of the Marine, Don Antonio Valdés, to prepare a ship to transport Gardoqui and his family (whose total maintenance and transportation costs were charged directly to the King) to the nearest post in the United States. William Carmichael, the American representative in Madrid, advised that two pilots of equal experience in American waters be assigned to the vessel in order to expedite Gardoqui's arrival at his post. Spain's first official envoy was to receive a salary of twelve thousand pesos annually, the money to be sent to him from Havana together with all the costs incidental to the performance of his mission. Francisco Rendon, who had acted for Spain since the death of his superior Miralles, was named secretary of the mission at an annual salary of four thousand pesos.

José de Gálvez, Minister of the Indies, instructed Bernardo de Gálvez, then Captain-General at Havana, to place a ship at the disposition of the mission, its sole function to be serving as a despatch boat for transmitting correspondence, personnel and necessities to Gardoqui. It was not to concern itself with carrying commercial products or any other cargo. Gardoqui and his party, including two young men, Don José de Jaudenes of Valencia and Don José de Viar of Bilbao, undersecretaries, sailed from Cadiz October 29, 1784, on the *Gaiman*, Don Domingo Ponte in command.

Gardoqui was destined to endure a long and miserable voyage in spite of the special pains taken to insure a speedy, safe crossing. The *Gaiman* arrived in Puerto Rico after a crossing of twenty-eight days. Here, Gardoqui was forced to a further delay due to the deplorable condition of the ship. The time required for repairs hung heavily upon the impatient envoy who found himself in enforced idleness for the first time. His impatience was ended at last. The voyage was resumed and he reached Havana on December 10. He wrote to the Spanish Prime Minister, Floridablanca, from Havana on January 13, mentioning his disturbed state of mind over the various accidents and the time consumed in repairs during the long voyage. At the same time he brought Floridablanca's attention to the negligence of the ship's captain and other disagreeable details affecting his conduct. This information was sent in confidence to the secretary of Marine, Valdés. Gardoqui's charges were so grave that the captain was relieved of his command and ordered to appear before a Council of War.

Altogether Gardoqui took nearly seven months to reach the United States. Much of the delay was due to the danger of equinoctial storms which are frequent in Caribbean waters in the spring months. The Captain-General of Havana, Count de Gálvez, had ample reason to know the ravages of a hurricane and he refused to risk sending out a ship with Gardoqui on board until he felt sure that all danger was past.

Gardoqui landed with his party at Philadelphia only to find that the Congress had moved its seat to New York. So once more he became a traveller, this time on the last leg of his journey and this time overland. He was welcomed by Rendon who received from him the official orders making him secretary of the mission.[2] The imperturbable Gardoqui, shaken out of his usual calm serenity by the long and hazardous voyage from Cadiz, was greatly relieved to find himself safely arrived at his destination and on *tierra firme*. The conduct of his affairs was once again in his own hands. It seems ironical that this efficient merchant prince, who had for so long supervised the transport of valuable cargoes to the United States, should himself have experienced such a hazardous crossing with his beloved family while affairs of state urgently seeking his attention were held up by circumstances over which he had no control whatever.

In a letter dated the 15th of August, 1785, the Congress wrote to Carlos III:

"Great and beloved Friend,

With great satisfaction we received your Majesty's letter of the 27th September last, which was presented to us by D. Diego de Gardoqui, your 'Encargado de Negocios', on the 2nd of July.

We consider his arrival here in that character as a Proof of your Majesty's friendly Disposition towards us; and we received him in a Manner which was dictated by the same Dispositon in us towards your Majesty.

Permit us to assure you that we entertain the most sincere Wishes for your Majesty's Health and Happiness and that our best Endeavors shall not be wanting to ensure and perpetuate to both Countries the Blessings of Concord, Mutual Friendship and good Neighborhood.

We pray God, great and well beloved Friend, to preserve you in his holy keeping.

By us the United States in Congress Assembled at the City of New York the fifteenth Day of August one thousand seven hundred and eighty five your Majesty's good Friends. Richard Henry Lee, P.-Firmado.-John Jay.-Firmado, Ray un sello de los Estado Unidos."³ (The seal of the United States.)

The President of the Congress, Henry Lee, addressed the following letter to the Count de Floridablanca:

"New York, October 6th, 1785.

. . . The appointment of Mr. Gardoqui gave great satisfaction to the United States, and I flatter myself that the manner in which he was received, and will continue to be treated, will be perfectly agreeable to his Catholic Majesty.

Be assured Sir that it is the sincere wish of this country, not only to be on good terms with, but to cultivate the friendship of the Spanish Monarchy, and I am warranted to add, that the United States will cheerfully join in concerting and concluding such friendly and commercial connections with his Majesty, as by properly settling territorial questions, and regulating the intercourse of the two nations on principles of reciprocity, may produce and perpetuate mutual harmony and good will between them. . . ."⁴

Gardoqui's reception by the Congress and personally by Washington was cordial indeed. His warm friendship with John Jay was rapidly renewed. The admiration for the sure touch which he displayed in his earlier negotiations with Arthur Lee, in the early days of the war, was reflected in the respect tendered him by the President of the Congress. In the social life of New York, the Gardoquis won all hearts by their open hospitality. The luxury to which they were accustomed in Bilbao and Madrid distinguished their style of living in New York. At the balls and receptions that made up the social round of the city they added dignity and grace. John Jay and his lady forgot the frustrations and the grievances over protocol, which were unhappily associated with their sojourn in Madrid and remembered with pleasure, the sympathy and understanding they had experienced in their relations with Gardoqui.

Throughout his life, Gardoqui possessed the rare ability to inspire faith in his personal integrity and admiration for the quietly humorous serenity with which he managed difficult affairs between all types of people regardless of their position, financial, social or official. These qualities made him a formidable adversary where his loyalties were concerned but a warm friend in all matters of the heart.

His openhanded hospitality, the lavish sophistication of his style of living, but above all, his personal charm made him many friends. But Gardoqui had come to the United States to make friends for the Spanish Monarchy and in this major task he was eminently successful. It was a far cry from the former position which Spain occupied in the political and social circles of Philadelphia and New York. Where, heretofore, the agents of Carlos III had been regarded more or less as protégés of the French Ambassador, now Gardoqui was accepted, in his own right as the honored and admired representative of His Catholic Majesty. His whole background provided the solid foundation upon which the popularity of his appointment rested. Because of his special gift for making warm friends, his imperturbility and suavity under the most trying circumstances, Gardoqui earned for himself and his country a place in the American scene attained by few diplomats.

2.

Gardoqui received direct and succinct orders from Floridablanca, as to the matters that must be discussed and agreed upon between the Congress and the Spanish Crown before the final treaty between the two nations could be signed. The Prime Minister's instructions were reduced to four main points and were signed personally by Floridablanca:

"1. To establish the limits within which a solid friendship and open correspondence could be founded and to reduce all possible obstacles to such a clear understanding. On this matter he was to refer to the Count de Gálvez for advice and to work with him in concerted action to establish peaceful agreement, modifying demands if necessary for the love of peace but to cover the entire subject of the boundaries of Spanish establishments in Louisiana and West Florida to the point where West Florida touches the Canal of Bahama.

2. To secure exclusive navigation of the Mississippi, especially from where it enters our limits bank to bank. On this point it is well to inform Gardoqui of the orders for the Indies dictated by me for preventing free navigation for the purpose of engaging in smuggling and to make clear to the Colonists that it is not now permissible to contravene such orders, as they are already aware.

3. Inform the Americans of the United States that it is impossible for us to make special commercial concessions affecting our American dominions or islands because of the existing treaties made with all nations from the treaty of Utrecht, since confirmed and renewed, the latest confirmation having been made in 1783. Convey to Gardoqui a copy of all the articles in those treaties for him to show and make clear to the States that this is not our view or our desire but that it is out of our hands.

4. And finally, that what we can do as a quid pro quo is to give them good treatment in our commerce with Europe and its adjacent islands; to consider the United States as Most Favored Nation provided they will reciprocate and this reciprocation be based upon principles of equity, to which end Gardoqui will bear in mind what we desire with respect to England and the fact that the King of Spain would prefer not to bind himself with pacts but rather with reciprocal regulations, that is to say: that if they should make some regulation favorable to us for our imports and exports, we for our part, will enact another similar one, in so far as it may involve equal damage or profit."[5]

Gardoqui followed his instructions in his own way, quietly but effectively, getting close contact with Gálvez and establishing the routine by which the work of his mission could go forward smoothly. He promptly sent a copy of his instructions to Gálvez together with copies of all the pertinent reports and communications he had found awaiting his arrival in New York and especially the latest despatches received by his secretary, Rendon, during the latter's interim incumbency of the post previously filled by Juan Miralles.

With Gálvez he reached an agreement on the budget for his mission, the cost of running his household, the salaries of Rendon and the two young undersecretaries, Jaudenes and Viar, the cost of travel and courier service, the administrative expense of the legation, and the funds needed for official entertainment. He made every effort to establish at once and to maintain the high tone and importance of the new Spanish embassy.

He presented his credentials to the President and to the Congress and speedily but tactfully made it clear that he would deal separately with any Commissioner of equal standing or any member of the Congress or any committee officially delegated to discuss the diplomatic points at issue as defined in his instructions from Floridablanca.

He guaranteed that Spain would act favorably toward all commercial rights within the Spanish dominions and proposed a defensive alliance with the United States which might later be incorporated into a permanent treaty. For the sake of immediate security he cited eloquently that the situation existing between Spain and the United States was not in any way the same as that existing between France and the United States because of the territorial boundaries, citing the need for speedy agreement over dominion limits to eliminate future questions of defense and commerce. Spain's possessions being adjacent to the United States created far more important problems than those of France, whose sole interest lay in reestablishment of trade and in the northern fisheries.

For the advancement of closer trade relations, he suggested the setting up by Spain of consular offices in American coastal cities and American offices in the port cities of Spain. This suggestion was later incorporated into the permanent treaty signed by Spain and the United States. His expert knowledge of international commerce inspired the confidence of many Congressmen whose backgrounds were not equal to tasks facing the growing number of problems in the far-flung, loosely-knit states.

Gardoqui took infinite pains to clarify the touchy boundary questions as soon as he learned of the havoc being brought about through the early policy of the Dominion of Virginia of paying-off her soldiers, not in money but by land grants in Kentucky. Pennsylvania, Georgia and the two Carolinas immediately inaugurated the same system. In Georgia and South Carolina the situation was particularly grave. There, groups of families and entire neighborhoods were demanding the right to lands as far west as the Mississippi, even into Natchez and the surrounding territory within the Dominions of Spain. These lands had previously been granted to England and Spain in the treaty of 1763, but, since the campaigns of Bernardo de Gálvez they had become Spanish territory by right of conquest.

East Florida rapidly became a country of guerilla warfare and the situation within the border state of Georgia became daily more bellicose. Don Diego managed to expound the position of Spain with sure authority and continued to maintain his poise throughout the many delicate discussions that followed one upon another.

Many men who had served the American Cause with distinction were clamoring for land in the West. A number of these formed groups and drew up formal applications to the King of Spain grants of land across the Mississippi, among them George Rogers Clark, Colonel John Sevier and Colonel Morgan, all of whom had given magnificent service and leadership throughout the Revolution in the West.[6] The men of Kentucky organized to demand the right to become a separate state. Every man's eye was on the western lands.

Throughout this hectic period of settlement and conflicting interests in America, the Spanish Minister remained a calm figure at the very heart of the disputes. His training stood him in good stead in these trying times.

His warm friendship with men of stature and integrity in the Congress enabled him to bring some order out of the chaos of conflicting territorial claims. Although the points listed in his instructions were not to come to full and amicable fruition until after his return to Spain, it was to his clearheaded negotiation and patient understanding that much of the credit for the ultimate solution must be given.

Among all these serious problems one follows with interest and amusement his warmly human approach to matters within his official family. His young secretary, Francisco Rendon, was, during this time, hopelessly in love with one "Señorita Margarita Marshall," daughter of a New York merchant of substantial means. Gardoqui quickly learned upon his arrival that Rendon was of little use to him, since he "mooned about like a new-born calf," haunting the house of his beloved and beseeching Gardoqui to intercede with the King for permission to marry the young lady. Since such permission was required and the delay had extended over four years the good Don Diego consented to use his good offices in behalf of his young secretary.

Since these affairs of the heart were not so freely entered into in the North, where religious differences were more apt to be a factor than in Louisiana where the volatile Creoles and the young Spanish commanders intermarried frequently, Gardoqui took pity on the young lovers. He began a long correspondence with Madrid over the affair, though, albeit with tongue in cheek, since he was not convinced of the necessity for hurry in the matter.

Rendon, at the end of four years, was ordered to return to Spain just when the marriage was about to take place. In his case absence did not make the heart grow fonder and we regretfully learn that the "Pobrecita Senorita Marshall" was left to nurse her sorrow over the perfidy of men while Don Francisco went on to more compelling duties.[7]

Another warm note marks the friendship and admiration that Gardoqui held for the President, George Washington. To Martha Washington, he sent the gift of a beautiful handcarved cradle for a new grandchild. To his Great and Good Friend he sent a pair of jackasses, fine work-animals of the strong strain of the northern Spanish provinces, a gift deeply appreciated by that practical gentleman farmer of Mount Vernon. What a picture of Don Diego, the businessman of Bilbao, the devoted head of an adoring family, and the warmly human diplomat!

FOOTNOTES

[1]Campillo, *op. cit.*, Nota Preliminar y Catálogo, p. XXXVIII.

[2]*Ibid.*, pp. XLI-XLII.

[3]*Ibid.*, p. XL.

[4]*Ibid.*, pp. XL-XLI.

[5]Campillo, *op. cit.*, Nota Preliminar y Catálogo, pp. XXXVI-XXXVII.

[6]Jose Navarro Latorre y Fernando Solano Costa, *Conspiracion Española*, Institucion Fernando el Catolico, Zaragoza, 1949; Vol. I, Appendices 12, 14 and 17.

[7]Campillo *op. cit.*, Nota Preliminar y Catálogo, p. XX.

Part Two

SPAIN AS AN ALLY IN ACTION

IN AMERICA

CHAPTER X

1.

Sometime between 1764 and 1765, three men met in the city of Havana. Their meeting was casual and friendly. They had only two things in common: they were all living far-removed from Ireland their ancestral homeland, and they all spoke Spanish fluently. It was Father Butler, president of the Jesuit College of Cuba, who introduced the other two to each other, Oliver Pollock, late of Coleraine, Ireland and Philadelphia, Pennsylvania and General Alejandro O'Reilly, first officer of the armies of Carlos III and, at this time, Inspector-General of Spanish troops in the New World.

Oliver Pollock was a young and successful trader between the Islands and the ports of the English colonies to the north. He had come to America at the age of twenty-three with his father, two brothers and a nephew from the North of Ireland. At this time he was well- and successfully known all the way from Philadelphia to New Orleans in the trade for flour, molasses, rum, lumber, indigo, spices, sugar and coffee between the ports of the West Indies and those of the Colonies. In the short space of five years he had learned to do business in both French and Spanish and was at home along the Mississippi River posts as well as among the tribes of the Creek Nation. Little is known of his early life but his educational background must have been exceptional. His pleasant and generous personality quickly made him a man of importance whose far-flung contacts were to be of incalculable value to the cause of the Colonies in the coming struggle to win their independence.

Alejandro O'Reilly, regarded as Spain's leading soldier, with the rank of Major-General, and the title of Count bestowed for his long record of service, and for having at one time saved the life of Carlos III, was a man of mature years for the time, approximately forty-five years of age, when he took over his military command in Cuba. He had served in Austria, Portugal, Algeria, France, Italy and Spain and was regarded as a man of the greatest ability and judgment, with a keen eye for administrative detail that was later to be of great value in the organization of the government in Spanish Louisiana and the Mississippi valley.

The casual introduction by Father Butler of his friend, Oliver Pollock, to General O'Reilly was to develop into a friendship extending over the years and instrumental in the forging of close ties between the Spanish Governors of Louisiana and the British colonies along the eastern seaboard. These ties constitute a highly important chapter in the story of Spain's participation in the American Revolution.

In 1768, Oliver Pollock took up residence in New Orleans and that city became the center of all his future ventures in trade and commerce. He married a member of the well-known family of O'Brien, whose ancestry stemmed from the famous Irish family of County Clare and the Kennedys of Ormond.[1] Pollock was to live for sixteen years in New Orleans, during which time he accumulated a great fortune, lived in one of the finest townhouses in the city and maintained two plantations with numerous slaves. He had a happy home life. His wife was later credited by him with having ably assisted in bringing up the large family of four sons and three daughters as well as actively managing the crops and servants on the plantations. She was later to share with him and his children the degradations of debt and poverty, the result of his generous aid to the young nation which he loved so dearly.

A little more than a year after Pollock settled in New Orleans, on August 17, 1769, General O'Reilly made his entry into that city as Governor-General of the Province of Louisiana. Thus the two friends again came together in a vital center that reflected immediately the forceful presence of two vigorous personalities. At this time the province was threatened with famine. There was not sufficient food to feed the newly-arrived Spanish troops, much less a town of two-thousand whites plus as many more of a mixed population of Negroes and Indians. Pollock, by a fortunate coincidence, came into the port at this juncture on board his ship, the *Royal Charlotte*, with a cargo of flour from Baltimore. The flour market was completely under his control, but he offered his entire supply to the Governor-General on the Governor's own terms. The market stood at thirty dollars a barrel, but General O'Reilly purchased the cargo for fifteen dollars per barrel. For this cut of generosity and friendship, Pollock was granted the freedom of trade in Louisiana. "And I did enjoy that privilege," he wrote later, "so long as I staid in the country."[2]

During the years immediately preceding the American Revolution trade along the Mississippi was increasing in volume. Freedom of Navigation on the great waterway was guaranteed by the treaty of 1763, which terminated the war between France and Great Britain. Spain, to whom France ceded Louisiana, and Great Britain enjoyed the same right, as riparian states, to make whatever regulations they might see fit, to regulate trade on their respective river banks. Spain encouraged emigration to such an extent that families were given all necessary tools and domestic animals needed to establish themselves in security. A group of nearly a thousand German families very quickly became a settlement loyal to the government and well-disposed toward the French who had been given posts of honor by the Spanish Governor all up and down the river. A colony from Malaga, the home of O'Reilly's successor, Gov. Unzaga, came in later to settle the country along the Bayou Teche and through their industry made the village of Iberville a rich trading center. By 1776 Francisco Bouligny was writing glowingly of the richness of the Louisiana land and of the products of the forests and rivers.

All young men in the colony were inducted into the Batallion of Louisiana and trained for the defense of the Province under Spanish officers, a policy that was to prove valuable when Spain allied herself with the American Colonies in the approaching years. Schools were founded throughout the territory and the arts of both Spain and France were encouraged in architecture, home-furnishings and dress. Social life followed the pattern of the two mother countries.

Pollock, strategically located at New Orleans, and favored with the freedom of trade granted him by the Spanish Governors, rapidly became the strongest financial power in the Mississippi valley. Up river was St. Louis, founded in 1764, and on the way to becoming the most important fur-trading center of the West. Fur was a magic word. It has been estimated that more than four-hundred traders and merchants were ascending the river during the spring and fall seasons, in fleets of bateaux, each from thirty to forty feet in length and requiring from twenty to thirty men at the sweeps. The journey up the river was long and arduous, sometimes taking nine weeks to reach the upper forts along the river, and to reach the Illinois country. The bateaux were always in danger from marauding bands of Indians who coveted the trade goods and supplies aboard during the up-river journey and the priceless furs brought down river on the return voyage.

Once arrived in the Illinois country, these traders spread out to cover their individual territories, their trade routes carrying them far to the north and west along the upper Mississippi and the Missouri waters. They trafficked along the difficult and dangerous portages of the great lakes. They were well known in the Illinois forts and villages. Kaskaskia, Vincennes and Cahokia brought them into close contact with George Rogers Clark, "The Kentuckian." Out of this indirect and casual link between the government of Louisiana and the colorful frontiersman developed later the direct contact by means of which Spanish aid could be made available to the Americans in the conquest of the Northwest territory. Oliver Pollock was the intermediary through whom that aid was extended. It has been asserted that "lacking the financial support and advice of this trader, planter and diplomat, the cause of the American Revolution west of the Alleghenies would have run a different course."[3] Pollock was able to make his invaluable personal contribution because he enjoyed the confidence of three Governors of Louisiana in succession, O'Reilly, Unzaga and Gálvez.

Between 1770 and 1775, trade at New Orleans expanded enormously. There was a great degree of freedom for the traders of all nationalities who took trade goods into or out of the port. Governor Unzaga became so lenient in the interpretation of the provincial laws that English and Americans were admitted into all the posts along the rivers. Spanish buyers were allowed to traffick with English ships tied up along the Spanish side of the Great River. A captain on the lower Mississippi reported in 1774, that he had seen "seventy sail of vessels" between New Orleans and Manchac (the British fort near Natchez).[4]

Until 1776, the English enjoyed a near monopoly of all this river traffic. It was to get this commerce back for the Spanish and French population of the Province that the government proposed to enforce the trading regulations more stringently against the English and to grant more freedom to merchants operating under the Spanish flag. It was part of the same plan to foster Spanish trade to build strong forts at the mouths of the rivers flowing into the Mississippi, to maintain an army strong enough to defend the Province, to restore the freedom of navigation of the river which was being consistently violated by the English, to protect the trade with Havana and Mexico, should protection be required and, to that end, establish strong posts where the Great River entered the gulf. The provincial government was particularly concerned with the de facto control of commerce in the Gulf exercised by British naval units based at Mobile and Pensacola.

When Oliver Pollock made his personal decision, early in 1776, to support the American colonists in their struggle for independence, he was well on his way to becoming one of the greatest financiers in North America. Free to trade anywhere on the Mississippi, he was also, by contract, sole supplier of flour to the military post of New Orleans. He was personal representative of the powerful company of Willing and Morris of Philadelphia. He was handling commissions for the most important men of Richmond, Natchez and St. Louis. His name was looked upon with respect in Boston and New York. In New Orleans, he stood at the head of all the merchant groups and was a welcome guest at the dinner table of the Governor. Through the great prestige of Conde O'Reilly who, by this time, had returned to Spain, he was in a position to influence the Spanish Court in favor of the cause of the Americans. He counted upon the friendship of O'Reilly's successor, Unzaga, to further that cause and through Unzaga's powerful representation, upon the support of Spanish officials in Mexico and the West Indies. In a matter of months, Pollock was to have occasion to test the strength of his friendships.

2.

On a sultry night early in August, 1776, a small, fast bateau, carrying a party of tired, shabbily-dressed traders from the upper Mississippi slipped into New Orleans and tied up in the shadow of the banks under the city. In less than an hour two of the men presented themselves at Oliver Pollock's mansion. One of them made known his identity immediately, and introduced his companion. From his pouch he produced a letter of urgent importance. Its author was General Charles Lee, who spoke in the name of the Virginia Committee of Safety. The courier, who had just delivered it to Pollock, was George Gibson, captain of a militia company from Fort Pitt, enlisted for the purpose of reinforcing the Virginia line commanded by Lee. Lee was at this time second in command under Washington, his authority being exercised over the Southern District, which comprised Virginia, the Carolinas, Georgia and all country west of the Appalachians.

Captain Gibson, his second in command, Lieutenant William Linn and some fifteen men of his company, known derisively as "Gibson's Lambs," had made a fast journey down the Great River to present Lee's plea for desperately needed powder and supplies. Pollock secured an immediate audience with Governor Unzaga and hurriedly arranged for lodging for the party. He observed strict secrecy in order to prevent knowledge of their mission coming to the ears of the polyglot population of New Orleans. Governor Unzaga also acted to keep the mission secret, receiving Gibson at night. He was courteous but cautious in greeting the American officer since it was necessary for him to maintain an attitude of neutrality as an official of the Spanish Crown.

General Lee's letter, which was addressed to Governor Unzaga, was at once presented to him. It was one of the most forceful appeals for the friendship and support of Carlos III and his Council of the Indies that reached Spain throughout the troubled era of the Revolution. He asked for arms, to be sent by way of the Mississippi and thence overland, because all the ports on the seaboard were being blockaded by the British navy. Addressing himself, through Unzaga to Madrid, he brought out the value of trade between the Colonies and Spain's possessions in the New World and the importance of an alliance between the American Colonies to the East and the Spanish territories in the Southeast and to the West. Allied together these territories would develop such strength that no military force would be brought successfully against them. He made what seems to us, in the light of history, a very modest prediction of both the extent and the character of the new nation's development: ". . . that the colonies, having once established their independence . . . there need be no apprehension that they would molest any other power: for the genius of the people, their situation and circumstances engage them rather in agriculture and a free commerce which are more important to their interests and to their inclination."[5]

He asked for assistance for the American army in the interests of humanity. The courage of the soldiers was not lacking, but they were in dire need of guns, blankets and medicines.

The wind of revolt had been rising at a terrific rate throughout the thirteen Colonies since early in 1775. In January 1776, Lord Dunmore had bombarded Norfolk and landed a party of sailors to fire the town. General Lee reached Norfolk in March, took immediate command of the Virginia troops and forced Dunmore to flee the port. He soon came to realize the perilous position of troops without a source of ammunition. There was at this time an ample supply of powder and guns in Charleston but none could be spared out of the colony of South Carolina for the reason that the British navy was blockading the harbor, ready to swoop upon any ship from the West Indies and the supply would not last out a siege of any length.

Lee's letter to Unzaga carried weight to officials already well-disposed because he was known to have served in England, Portugal and Poland before taking command of Washington's Southern District. Such a military record would carry conviction to General O'Reilly and to the former royal Visitor-General to New Spain, José de Gálvez, now head of the Ministry of Marine and the powerful Council of the Indies.[6]

Captain Gibson and his party of "Lambs" arrived in New Orleans just a month after the Declaration of Independence and he brought the first news of it to reach Louisiana. At that time the situation at Fort Pitt, where Colonel Morgan was in command, and in all the posts along the Ohio, was perilous. The British at Vincennes, with their Indian allies scattered throughout the Illinois country, could descend almost at will to complete the conquest of these posts and close the Mississippi below St. Louis from any aid to the hard-pressed Americans. Britain's Fort Manchac, supplied from Mobile and Pensacola, was in a strong position to support such a conquest. If the British chose to attack New Orleans, with their Indian allies, it would fall an easy prey.

Captain Gibson painted a vivid picture of the plight of the colonial militia as he outlined to Governor Unzaga his plan of operations. Since early in 1775, the armies of the Dominion of Virginia and the scattered companies of militia throughout the southern command had been desperately in need of gunpowder, clothing and medical supplies, particularly vital quinine. England had supplied all military stores until the rising tide of rebellion brought about an order in October 1774, issued by the Earl of Dartmouth to the Governors of America: "It is His Majesty's Command that you do take the most effectual measures for arresting, detaining and securing any Gunpowder or any sort of arms or ammunition which may be attempted to be imported into the Province under your Government, unless the Master of the Ship having such military Stores on Board shall produce a License from His Majesty or the Privy Council for the exportation of the same from some of the Ports of this Kingdom."[7] So it came about that from 1774 on, arms and powder had grown increasingly precious to the men who were in rebellion against the mother country. Meanwhile, England was freely supplying the Indians with all needed war equipment.

Each day the traders, farmers and trappers who composed the militia guarding the frontier became more alarmed at their situation and at their inability to give supplies and medicines to friendly Indian tribes along the rivers. Destitution was rampant. Washington was also facing the problem of feeding and equiping an army.

Governor Unzaga, with a background of forty years of service in the Americas, was able to appreciate the peril in which the western territories stood. His own informants from St. Louis, Fort Chartres, St. Genevieve and the Ohio had already given him clear reports of the rising danger. The official neutrality imposed by the orders of his government placed him in a dilemma: he could not offer aid to either side but his personal sympathies were with the Americans and the need of powder at Fort Pitt was too great to admit of delay. Unzaga made his decision. The powder should go north to the Americans!

But powder was not the only precious war commodity which Spain was in a position to supply if she so willed. Up river there was lead. Since 1770, the lead mines of La Mothe and Herculaneum, near the west bank of the Mississippi, had been the richest in the valley. Fort Chartres, the center of the former French civil government in the Illinois country, was regarded for many years as the strongest fort in North America. It had been the center of the trade in lead until 1753, and the headquarters of the French royal company of the Indies. It had been designed after the plans of the famous engineer of fortifications, Vauban. It had walls two-feet thick plastered over with mortar, making it almost impregnable to any assault that could be

thrown against it. It was a priceless point to hold in the battles for control of the Northwest, about to take place. Could the lead and powder
from that area, added to what Governor Unzaga could supply from
New Orleans, be put at the disposal of the troops of "Gibson's Lambs"
and other troops, such as those of George Rogers Clark, "The Kentuckian," as he liked to be called, these hungry and ill-clothed militiamen might well change the story of British dominion in North
America.

In spite of all efforts to keep secret the news of Captain Gibson's
arrival, it soon spread from the waterfront throughout the city that the
men of the party lately arrived from the upper river were not traders.
Captain Gibson's identity was soon known to the dozens of spies
hovering about the city. Therefore, to quiet gossip, Governor Unzaga
decided upon the ingenious scheme by which he kept up the
appearance of official neutrality. He imprisoned Captain Gibson. The
rest of his party under command of Lieutenant Linn, he arranged to
send back north under Spanish protection.

From this moment on Oliver Pollock became the indispensable intermediary between all those who represented the American cause and
the friendly governors of Louisiana. The ties formed between Pollock
and the Inspector-General of the Spanish armies, Count Alejandro
O'Reilly at the time of the famine in New Orleans, when Pollock had
supplied flour to the starving population, now began to prove their
worth. From now on, first in the form of under cover aid, subsequently
in the shape of open, direct aid from one ally to another, those ties
became increasingly close.

3.

Governor Unzaga and Pollock plotted to send Lieutenant Linn to
Fort Arkansas under military escort, keeping to the Spanish side of the
river route. At Fort Arkansas, Linn's party would be supplied with
food and all needed assistance and speeded on their way to their goal,
Fort Pitt. Pollock outfitted a ship and contracted with Unzaga for the
immediate sale of 10,000 pounds of powder from the Government
warehouse. With 9000 pounds of this purchase Linn set forth in
Pollock's ship on the first stage of his dangerous journey up river, his
men working in shifts day and night to speed their all-important cargo
forward. When they reached the Arkansas Post they were in a state of
complete exhaustion. They were warmly welcomed by the Spanish
commander and spent the winter as his guests. With the coming of
spring they were ready and eager to continue their journey. They were
supplied with food and stores which they paid for with a draft on

Oliver Pollock, acting as agent of the Dominion of Virginia in the amount of $2400. Their supplies were sufficient to take them as far as the Ohio River. From that point Lieutenant Linn was to receive supplies from secret American sources. The party reached Wheeling on May 2, 1777. It was a critical moment in the defense of Fort Pitt. The 9000 pounds of powder saved that fort, a circumstance of vast significance for the course of the Revolution in the West.

Release of 10,000 pounds of powder by Governor Unzaga was the first in a long sequence of interventions which were to have tremendous influence on the fate of the Illinois country and the whole area west of the Alleghenies. It is noteworthy that Unzaga acted in the present transaction without the authority of his government. The powder came from the provincial storehouse at New Orleans. The supplies which kept Linn's party alive during the winter were purchased in a Spanish post. The party had been protected constantly, from one Spanish fort to the next, as they made their way through territory dangerously overrun with the British and their Indian allies.

Captain Gibson, held in prison to quiet the suspicions of the British consul, was released in October, 1776, and permitted to sail to Philadelphia in one of Pollock's ships. A fellow passenger was a Captain Ord whose ship had been captured by the British. Pollock had supplied Captain Ord and his crew with food and clothing at New Orleans until they could be sent home. Both Gibson and Ord were made the bearers of despatches describing the situation at New Orleans, the close cooperation of Governor Unzaga and his personal devotion to the cause of the Americans. Gibson was to report to the Committee of Safety of Virginia, Ord to a committee of the Continental Congress of which Robert Morris was a member. Gibson carried with him 1000 pounds of powder of the 10,000 released from the Spanish stores. Morris and his committee had been at their wit's end to find the ammunition needed for Washington's rapidly dwindling army. This consignment of powder came as if in answer to prayer.

Governor Unzaga had replied to General Lee's letter of May 1776, in warmly sympathetic terms, assuring him that, in so far as possible, all supplies needed by the Americans would be sent along in the most discreet manner possible so that the suspicions of the English consul in New Orleans and the English posts along the east bank of the Mississippi would not be aroused. He, Lee, could depend upon the personal sympathy of the Governor for the cause in which the Americans had engaged their lives and fortunes. A copy of this letter was sent to Spain together with Unzaga's report to the King of what had been done. Carlos III not only approved Unzaga's conduct but issued an order that all possible aid be given from Havana and other

Spanish possessions in supplying arms, ammunition, clothing, blankets and medicines. The order emphasized that all prudence should be exercised in forwarding these goods in order to insure their safe and speedy delivery as well as to maintain the position of official neutrality. To this end, the supplies should be furnished ostensibly in exchange for products of the American Colonies or in the guise of bona-fide sales to known merchants. The King gave unqualified agreement to any plan the Americans might devise for the capture of Pensacola, Mobile and other posts held by the British. Simultaneously with the royal order, the Governor of Cuba was instructed to send Unzaga immediately arms, powder and other war supplies from the factory in Mexico. They were to be turned over secretly to such agent as might be designated.

The order of Carlos III marks the second stage of setting up a Secret Supply Service for the Americans. Governor Unzaga deserved well of the Americans whose cause he had helped by his personal intervention and by the backing he secured afterward from the King. He was soon to be transferred to a post in South America leaving the Louisiana stage for the entry of a much younger, more daring, more romantic representative of Old Spain in New Spain, Don Bernardo de Gálvez.

In 1776, this young Grandee had been ordered to Louisiana as Commandant of the troops of the Province with the understanding that he would eventually assume the governorship when the aging Governor Unzaga should, at his own urgent request, be relieved of the arduous duties of the command. The months following his arrival were spent assiduously in learning the state of defense, preparing himself for the crises arising from the war between Great Britain and her colonies. His introduction to Unzaga was in the usual military form: "Lt. Col. Don Bernardo de Gálvez, Capt. of Grenadiers in the Regiment of Infantry of Seville, has been named by the King Colonel of the permanent Batallion of your city New Orleans." Under the order is a postscript in the handwriting of Count O'Reilly: "The aforesaid bears his instructions and will present them shortly. He is an individual whom I esteem highly, and his Uncle, the minister of the Indies, is my particular friend, wherefore I will thank you for any attentions you can show him."[8]

It is not known at exactly what age Bernardo de Gálvez became Governor of Louisiana. It is possible that he was between 28 and 30. It is certain that he made a most agreeable impression on the people of the city. His youthful face and figure, added to a charm and gayety of manner, lead to the idea that Gálvez was far too young and immature for such a vital post of Empire. After the period of government under Unzaga, whose forty-two years of service in the Americas had aged him in-the-wood of Provincial Command, Bernardo de Gálvez did indeed look like a stripling. His high place in the hierarchy of the great families of Spain laid him open at once to the jealous envy of those who were his seniors in years.

His father, Matias de Gálvez, was the Viceroy of Mexico. His uncle, the head of the powerful Council of the Indies, José de Gálvez, had brought his nephew with him upon his long journey to Mexico, Nueva Vizcaya and Sonora when he was named Royal Visitor-General to New Spain. The family name was, therefore, not strange to North America. At the time of his arrival in New Orleans, the young man had the maturity gained during twelve years of service in the armies of Spain. He was a lieutenant in the war with Portugal in 1762. Later, as captain and second in command, he took part in expeditions against the Apache Indians along the frontier of Nueva Vizcaya. Soon thereafter he was made responsible for the Vizcaya-Sonora frontier. As commander on this frontier he led numerous expeditions against the Apaches in 1769. The following year he demonstrated his great qualities of courage and leadership in a campaign against that warring tribe. Setting out from Chihuahua with 135 soldiers, he pursued them relentlessly for weeks until he reached the Pecos River in Texas. With little food left for starving men and horses, he ordered an attack after a moving address to his men who swore "that they would follow until they died, that they would eat horses, and after that stones, and would never forsake him."[9]

Six months after this incident he was engaged in another campaign during which the prisoners he had captured in the first action accompanied him as guides against their own people. This was the first time that any Apache, the bitter, sworn enemies of all white men, had ever willingly served under a Spanish commander. The Indians recognized and admired his imperviousness to danger and his intrepidity and tenacity in action. He had been wounded three times, by lance and arrow, before he succeeded in bringing peace to the frontier. In 1771, he returned to Spain after having been (temporarily) promoted to lieutenant-colonel. He asked for and received permission for a leave of absence from the Spanish service in order that he might go to France and perfect himself in military science. He enrolled in the regiment of Cantabria and earned promotion to the grade of lieutenant in that regiment. He returned to Spain in 1775, became a captain of infantry under his idol, General O'Reilly, and was slightly wounded as a member of a landing party at Algiers. Later, he was wounded a fifth time, on this occasion, more seriously. After recuperating from his last wound he was promoted to lieutenant-colonel and attached to the famous military school at Avila.

In 1776 came his assignment to New Orleans. After twelve years of service; on the Mexican frontier, in France as a student and outside of

France under the French flag, in Portugal, in Algeria and, as director of training in Spanish military schools, this fresh-faced, charming young man was no tyro at command, though still in his twenties. His acquaintance with France and the French people made him the most popular governor Louisiana had in its entire territorial history. His grasp of administrative detail, his daring and his tactical genius, were to add lustre to his family name and to enshrine him in the hearts of all the people over whom he ruled. He and his lieutenants, by marrying into the established French families, were to align themselves indissolubly with the history of Louisiana. He was audacious, but at the same time gifted with sound judgment. His personal admiration and sympathy for the American Colonists and his future close friendship with Oliver Pollock were to open a new chapter in the history of the American Revolution and turn the tide in favor of George Rogers Clark in the latter's struggle for the Northwest.

FOOTNOTES

[1]James Alton James, *Oliver Pollock: The Life and Times of an Unknown Patriot* (New York, 1937), p. 4. Cited hereafter as James, *Pollock*.

[2]James Wilkinson, *Memoirs of My Own Times* (3 vols., Philadelphia, 1816), II, Appendage 1.

[3]*Ibid.*

[4]Captain Michael Martyn to Rufus Putnam (Ms. letter, Northwestern University). Cited in James, *Pollock*, p. 54.

[5]General Lee to Governor Unzaga, May, 1776 and one from Unzaga to Spain, September 7, 1776, Archivo General de Indias, Seville (cited hereafter as A.G.I.), Estante 87, Cajon I, Legajo 6.

[6]N.Y. Col. Doc's. VIII, 509. See also, James, *Pollock*, p. 62, footnote.

[7]Earl of Dartmouth to the Governors of America, October 19, 1774, N.Y. Col. Doc's, VIII, 509. Cited in James, *Pollock*, p. 61, footnote.

[8]O'Reilly to Unzaga, June 15, 1776; A.G.I., Cuba 18, p. 181.

[9]Cuellar to José de Gálvez, November 23, 1770. Relacion que en (Extracto) Extrado . . . , no. 416, copy Gálvez Papers, Huntington Library. Cited in John Walton Caughey, *Bernardo de Gálvez in Louisiana*, 1776-1783 (Publications of the Univ. of Calif. at Los Angeles in Social Sciences, no. 4, Berkeley, Calif., 1934), p. 63.

CHAPTER XI

1.

January 1, 1777, when Gálvez became Acting-Governor of Louisiana, was an important day in American history. His orders from his uncle, the power behind the throne as Secretary of State and President of the Council of the Indies, were precise. He was to make an immediate survey of the territory from Nachitoches, Opelusas and Attacapas, submit full written reports from all the posts beyond the Arkansas, inform himself fully at once concerning conditions along the English frontier, to map the whole Mississippi and the southern coast from Belize to Bahia del Espiritu Santo. He was to take strong measures against illicit commerce, and curtail the trading activities of foreign vessels. He was to cultivate friendly relations with the Indians. Particularly significant was the injunction to collect all possible information about affairs in the English colonies, through secret agents sent for the purpose.[1]

The coming of Bernardo de Gálvez marked at once a change of policy toward both Americans and English. It meant more vigorous measures to get speedy aid to the former. By July 1777, in answer to the plea of General Lee, the government of Spain had deposited at New Orleans 2000 barrels of powder, a great quantity of lead and large amounts of clothing, subject to the order of Virginia. Spanish aid also meant sanctuary for refugees: Louisiana was rapidly becoming a refuge for hundreds of Americans fleeing the depredations of the English from across the Great River. They flocked into the province with their women, their children and their slaves, and with whatever household possessions it was possible to carry with them. All of them were desperate for food, clothing and ammunition. At all the Spanish posts along the river and in New Orleans they found a haven and the wherewithal to establish themselves in safety.

The English were burning homes up and down the river. They had burned Spanish homes and French homes along with those belonging to Americans. They were firing at ships without regard to their nationality. Their Indian allies were well supplied with British arms and advised by the ablest of all English agents in the South, John

Stewart. By virtue of unlimited supplies and presents he controlled an estimated four or five thousand warriors of the Chickasaw and Choctaw tribes and a possibly equal number of Creeks and Cherokees.

From the Mississippi to the borders of the populated centers of the coast, from the Ohio to the Gulf, along the rivers and trails through the forests, from the outlying settlements of that vast area, the inhabitants were fleeing to the safety of the towns or to sanctuary across the river in Spanish territory. Outlying Spanish settlements were treated with the same insolence as those of the Americans; it made no difference that they were on the soil of Louisiana. England was making use of the tomahawk and scalping knife of her dark-skinned allies through the great woods.

Bernardo de Gálvez was not a man to brook an insult, were it offered to his country, his family or his friends. He reacted against the presumptuous conduct of the British, and their attitude of contempt for Spanish authority, by addressing to his government a peremptory request for two frigates to defend his territory. His sympathy for the Americans was increased a hundredfold by the disregard for Spain shown by the English throughout the area. He early convinced himself that sooner or later the British posts of Mobile and Pensacola would have to be reduced.

The Continental Congress had been considering for some time sending an expedition against Pensacola by way of the Mississippi. For the execution of such a plan an understanding with the Governor of Louisiana would be urgently necessary because the operation would involve the passage of troops over Spanish territory. Furthermore, the open aid of the Governor of Louisiana would be required to provide the expedition with necessary supplies. To assure itself of his aid the Congress would have to depend upon the devotion and influence of Oliver Pollock. So Pollock was asked to broach the subject with Gálvez and report the Governor's views. Gálvez acceded readily to an idea so much in harmony with his own thinking and asked Pollock to assure the Congress that if an expedition were organized, he would assist it with stores, cash, ships and everything needed for the campaign.

Pollock passed this promise on and, at the same time, asked the Congress to send several bland commissions to New Orleans to be issued to American volunteers. He explained that feeling was running so high in the Province against the English that he felt sure of the enlistment of additional men once the expedition reached New Orleans.

The causes of dissension between Spaniards and English continued. Gálvez grew more and more war-conscious. The news coming out of Spain was full of information concerning the aid being given the

Americans by the Spanish Government. Every post in Spain was receiving American ships and supplying them openly with every possible type of war goods and ammunition. The British protested bitterly against the sending of supplies up the river to the Americans in the Illinois country under protection of the Spanish flag.

The extent of Spanish aid afforded ample substance for British protests. By the end of 1777, his first year as governor, Gálvez had loaned Oliver Pollock $74,087. One shipment alone, amounting to 25,000 pistoles worth of blankets, shoes, stockings, shirtings, medicines and great quantities of quinine had been despatched directly from his government warehouse. These shipments, sent up the Misssisippi in heavily-loaded bateaux, sailed under the Spanish flag. They slipped by the English post at Natchez without molestation because they flew the flag of a state neutral in name and still a friendly nation. The voyage up river took from three to four months. The cargoes went to the posts on the upper Ohio which the Americans had recently captured from the British, or, in some cases, to the frontiers of Virginia and Pennsylvania, eventually to reach their destination with Washington's army or with that of General Lee.

Early in 1778, Pollock purchased on his own account merchandise to the value of 10,900 pistoles to be sent up the Mississippi and thence overland to Philadelphia. In his capacity as agent for the Committee of Safety of Congress he gave permission to the commanders of the bateaux to issue desperately needed supplies en route to any officers of American troops descending the river. "In this consignment to the Committee of Congress, besides powder, were gun-locks, musket-balls, and gun-worms, were horn and ivory combs, horn tumblers, scissors, razors, butcher's knives, hinges, nails, brass rings, blue and white handkerchiefs, needles, thread, flannel, cambric, table clothing, napkining, Irish linen, red, yellow and blue calicoes, men's hats, shoes and stockings. Specific needs of the 'gentry' were not omitted, for there was included in the shipment: fine ruffled shirts, metal buttons, red garters, silk breeches, silver breast-plates, wine, brandy and taffia."[2]

Pollock was by now openly accepted as the Official Agent for the American Congress, although actually he did not receive his formal commission for another year. The terrible cost of his transactions was beginning to cause him great distress because he was placing his personal credit behind the purchases he made for the Congress. Governor Gálvez helped him by freely advancing supplies and loans of money.

Due to the effective English blockade of all ports, very few ships got through to New Orleans with fresh supplies. Prices were rising. Men to man the boats plying the Great River were growing fewer in number.

The danger of constant attack from English and Indians caused wages for good river-boatmen to rise astronomically. From 40 pistoles per man they jumped to 70 pistoles. The situation was such that Pollock wrote the Congress begging for an advance of 50,000 pistoles to clear debts already contracted and to reimburse him for cash payments to boatmen. His amount was in addition to the $74,087 which Pollock owed Governor Gálvez and which Pollock told the Congress he hoped it would pay to Gálvez before the end of the year. It appears from a letter of May 7, 1778, addressed to the firm of Willing and Morris of Philadelphia, that he had used much of the balance of their credit amounting originally to $42,000, in remittance to France in payment of purchases for the American Congress. Inasmuch as these remittances represented a diversion of the funds from their intended use for the purchase of supplies in New Orleans, Pollock hastened to assure Robert Morris that the sums thus diverted would be made up in cash by Governor Gálvez although Gálvez had not yet received orders for such an expenditure from his own government.[3]

Secret instructions to officers of the American forces who might have missions taking them down the Mississippi were worked out in careful detail by Governor Gálvez and Pollock. The most dangerous point in the journey was the English post of Manchac from which attacks in force might be expected. The officers were to call at the Spanish posts of Arkansas or Pointe Coupée where they would receive more detailed information concerning the enemy before proceeding further south.

Through timely and regular loans from Gálvez, Pollock was supplied with funds for the purchase of goods to be forwarded to other American agents dealing directly with the Indians of the Northwest. In this way the hard-pressed troops in the Illinois country were able to compete with the British for the friendliness of the Indian tribes. Gifts wisely made to them reduced the risk of scattered attacks on the more isolated posts.

During this period of unofficial Spanish aid, Governor Gálvez had ample opportunity to exercise his ingenuity and finesse. He had to solve the problem of how to carry on his operations in behalf of the Americans in secret when New Orleans was filled with spies and his every move was made under the watchful, suspicious eyes of the British consul. To execute the orders of the King became more and more difficult. One of these required very delicate handling. It read: "The bearer will be a commissioner of a factor of a Spanish merchant who sends various effects to your province for sale there; they are to be deposited in warehouses which must be furnished, and are to be entered free of duty."[4] This order sounds innocent and commonplace enough. The code, which gave it its highly delicate character was in the form of a second, and secret despatch of the same date in which the King explained that the goods belonging to the "Spanish merchant" were in fact the King's own, but since it would be "inconvenient to send them in his royal name to the succor of the English colonies" they were entrusted to a merchant who would be the nominal owner. He would "sell" them to General Lee's Agent, but Gálvez and the other colonial officials were to shun all connection with the transaction "so that England could never argue that Spain had aided her insurgent foes, and that the most she could charge would be that our merchants sold them the necessary goods."[5] The goods in question were invoiced as consisting of 6 cases of quinine, 8 cases of other medicines, 108 bolts of woolen cloth and serge, 100 hundredweights of powder in 100 barrels, and 300 muskets with bayonets in 30 boxes.[6] Since Gálvez, being newly resident in New Orleans, might not know a trustworthy local merchant for such a delicate business, one was to be sent from Havana, one Don Eduardo.[7] Gálvez was told that the King entrusted this important secret mission to him in the hope that he would perform it with sagacity, tact and maturity as well as with vigor and zeal.[8]

Gálvez reported the arrival of Don Miguel Eduardo on May 13, 1777, and pledged his most earnest efforts to carry out the King's orders.[9] But a hitch arose at once. Eduardo had been in the King's service prior to his arrival in New Orleans and this fact soon became known. Consequently the method so carefully worked out for making delivery of valuable goods to the Americans could not serve. The transfer could no longer be disguised as a regular mercantile transaction.

Gálvez was, for the second time now, put to the task of formulating a maneuver that would insure delivery and at the same time not involve his government. His first move was to send Eduardo back to Havana promptly. Next, he let it be known openly that the goods belonged to the King. He gave out word that the powder was sent to replace some that had deteriorated in the warehouse, that the muskets were intended for the Louisiana Batallion, the woolen cloth for the same troops and quinine and medicines for the King's Hospital. He calculated that by giving out this misinformation he would quiet suspicion and that, with the exercise of some ingenuity, all the supplies could be safely conveyed into the hands of the Americans.

His stratagem was clever and yet simple. To transfer the cloth, he announced that it had become moth-eaten and could not be used by the troops of His Majesty. This set the stage for the announcement that it would be sold to a reliable merchant of New Orleans. This merchant, sworn to secrecy, was to forward the cloth clandestinely to its destination. The same merchant was to be the agent for disposing of the powder. He was to inquire for "some barrels of whatever other commodity has about the same weight" as powder; the head of a barrel selected for the purpose would be knocked in, revealing openly that the contents were nonexplosive; then the barrels of powder would be taken away from the warehouse without a voucher from the government superintendent. For transferring the muskets and medicines, the same method was to be employed.[10]

Gálvez was not happy over this operation. In a letter to the Minister of the Indies he urgently advised that all such consignments in future should be either completely smuggled into the province without official bills of lading or received according to the regular system of customs since any digression from routine aroused suspicion and it was impossible to keep such shipments from public knowledge. The King subsequently approved his suggestions and ordered him "to proceed as it might seem most proper and convenient in this so interesting and delicate matter."[11]

2.

The story of the American Revolution along the frontier, in the Illinois and Ohio territory, is not complete or understandable if it is related merely as a struggle between the British forces based in Canada and the frontiersmen whose base was east of the Alleghenies, in Philadelphia and Williamsburg. Within the main struggle were taking place two others; in the one, the English were seeking active military aid, the Americans, military aid or at least the neutrality of the Indian tribes in the area; in the other, the hard-pressed colonials were striving to establish a supply line from Louisiana up the Mississippi which would be more dependable than the long and hazardous overland trail from the eastern seaboard; while the English, who were well aware of this supply problem, were striving to cut the line that ended at New Orleans.

The setting up and the maintaining of this Mississippi supply line was the achievement of three men, Governor Gálvez, Oliver Pollock and George Rogers Clark. By so doing they saved the Northwest Territory for the new American nation. The first member of this triumvirate, Bernardo de Gálvez, assumed the post of acting governor of Louisiana in 1777, and his first acts were no less dramatic than the victories won by General Washington at Trenton and Princeton, victories which did so much to raise the drooping spirits of American patriots. To Oliver Pollock whom Governor Unzaga had commended to him as "a faithful and zealous American in whom he might place implicit confidence" he endeared himself immediately by assuring him that he, Gálvez, would go every possible length for the interests of the Continental Congress. He announced that the port of New Orleans would be open and free to American commerce and to the admission and sale of prizes made by American corsairs or privateers.

This declaration was in conformity with a royal order of October 23, 1776, and it was the first official and public recognition of the United States as a nation and not, as heretofore as only colonies in rebellion against the mother country. Only a month before the King's order, England's Ambassador in Madrid had requested the Spanish Government to close its port to all American vessels on the ground that the Americans were rebel subjects of a power friendly to Spain. Gálvez went beyond the simple promulgation of the royal decree by informing Pollock that he was prepared to suppress all commerce with Great Britain and to engage in trade with the United States.

Within two months he put his promise into action. On April 17, 1777, he seized eleven English vessels engaged in contraband trade and on the following day issued a proclamation ordering all English subjects to leave Louisiana within a fortnight.[12] The effect was electrical all up and down the Great River. The French were assured again of the bulk of commerce long monopolized by the English, the Americans realized that they had at last an ally of real force in the territory. As for the British, they protested angrily that Spain was not at war with England.

Gálvez, coolly appraising the situation, had taken the first legitimate occasion afforded him to further the interests of the United States. He justified his action in these words: "Because an English ship of war had seized three of our boats, which were bringing tar from their land to send from here to Havana, the people began to clamor against this inconsiderate and ungrateful nation, which through the free navigation of the river has obtained the best products of this province. Their resentment showed me that it would be possible to find accusers, though without this occurrence it would have been impossible, and, in fact, taking advantage of the coincidence, I took the most energetic measures to manifest to His Majesty the willingness that I have pledged in fulfillment of his royal orders. Within twenty-four hours after the three mentioned boats of ours had been taken, I confiscated eleven which were employed in the contraband trade in this jurisdiction, and although most of these are entirely useless for navigation and only serve to store goods which have not a quick sale, nevertheless I have dealt them a blow which not only has thrown them into a panic, but which, I believe, is such that for some time they will not think of returning to carry on their clandestine commerce."[13]

Several letters of recrimination were exchanged between Gálvez and the commander of a British Frigate, the *Atlanta*, which had come into the Mississippi from Baton Rouge. In one letter Gálvez protested that her commander, Captain Lloyd, had stopped the French boat *Margarita* and the Spanish boat *Marie* and had ordered them to be detained for search after sending armed parties aboard to wrest control from their crews. Captain Lloyd replied that he had acted on information that the two boats belonged to the Rebels, but that he had allowed them to proceed after learning that they were French and Spanish. He entered a vigorous protest against the confiscation of the eleven British boats, citing the treaty of 1763, which permitted of freedom of navigation on the Mississippi. Gálvez admitted that river navigation was free but that the case in question had to do with contraband trade, not with navigation. He made much of the fact that the vessels he had seized had been tied to the Spanish shore. He called Lloyd's attention to the fact that two of the boats were not British but American. Understandably, he did not add that the two American boats had been quickly and quietly returned to the Americans.[14]

3.

Thus, within the space of three short months the young Governor had shown that he intended to administer his office with vigor and decision. His suave self-assurance and his adroit maneuvering delighted the French and the Americans while confusing and irritating the English. A new feeling of confidence was quietly beginning to permeate the territory. But Gálvez was shrewd enough to know that his position was diplomatically shaky. After all, his own country was not at war with England. He recognized that he would have to maintain at least the semblance of neutrality or defeat the point of his orders.

He adopted an ingenious scheme to help the Americans and at the same time lull British suspicions. He would take over American vessels arriving at the mouth of the Mississippi as Spanish property in order to protect them from the British sloop-of-war patrolling the mouth. Once they were in safe waters he would free them at once to go about their business unmolested. He entrusted the news of this order to Pollock, in secret, in order that it might be forwarded to the Congress in Philadelphia. Pollock chartered a vessel immediately, at a cost of $1,000 and the notification was thus carried to the colonial government, addressed through the recipient, Robert Morris. Pollock wrote in his covering note: "The execution of this will make noise and will, no doubt, create a jealousy between this Government and Great Britain, but as the saying is, 'The more mischief the better sport on the present occasion.' "[15]

Oddly enough, Oliver Pollock, who had already given much in

money and supplies to the cause of the Americans had up to this time no official status as an Agent for the Continental Congress. His commissions had been carried out at the urgent request of his friend, Robert Morris, the financial genius of the new government, or in response to pleas for help from General Lee and Governor Patrick Henry of the Dominion of Virginia. Before Gálvez's time, while Unzaga was still Governor, he had made a valuable contribution to the American cause. Governor Chester, the English commander at Pensacola, had acknowledged as much when he had ordered the captain of a sloop-of-war to seize Pollock and his property. Without official status, Pollock nevertheless had no fear while he operated on Spanish territory and under the protection of Gálvez. "But," he wrote the Congress, with surprising moderation, "in case of an accident which may happen of being taken prisoner I would be happy to have something to show from you either in the character of Civil or Military as you may think proper, so that it would only entitle me to be treated as a Gentleman, for at present I am threatened with Death which in the Service and legally appointed I should not dread."[16]

Pollock had advanced money and goods many times for the Cause and due to the urgency of the need he had kept no formal record. It would seem that his request for some official status might well have been granted long before this. At any rate, his usefulness to the Congress was limited solely by his lack of authority. He asked, therefore, that some form of credit be set up for him in Spain or elsewhere in Europe to cover monies that he himself might advance or for goods and supplies that were being advanced to him through the Spanish Governments in Mexico and the West Indies.

At the same time that Pollock was bringing up the question Gálvez also addressed the Congress making it clear that he would do all in his power to advance the cause of the United States. One would suppose that a communication bearing this assurance would be doubly welcome in Philadelphia at this crucial point in the war. It seems difficult to believe that there was no one in Philadelphia at this time qualified to translate the letter of Governor Gálvez. Yet Robert Morris acknowledged that this was so in the letter he addressed to his agent. Pollock thus became an even more valuable servant of the Continental Congress as the link between it and the Governor of Louisiana, the interpreter of each to the other.

In the first inner struggle on the frontier, mentioned above, the struggle to win over the Indian tribes, the English had the advantage from the beginning. That they did not retain that advantage permanently is due in part to the tenacity of the meagre frontier forces and the daring and intelligence of their leadership: in part also, to the successful establishment and maintenance of a vital supply line between these forces and the Spanish base at New Orleans.

When the struggle began, English power in the Northwest was centered in Detroit. From the English standpoint, the idea of keeping the Indians neutral was really never more than a myth. As early as July 1775, the Earl of Dartmouth issued an order that no time should be lost in inducing the Six Nations and their allies to take up the hatchet against the rebellious subjects of the King. In 1776, Lieutenant-Governor Hamilton, then in command of the Detroit territory, proposed the use of Indian allies against the frontiers of Virginia and Pennsylvania. General Carleton had his formal orders to use every means that "Providence has put into His Majesty's hands for crushing the rebellion and restoring the Constitution."[17]

Commissioners from the Continental Congress and from Virginia strove to offset English propaganda with gifts of wampum and supplies of food and clothing and by speeches urging neutrality. Nor did they fail to appeal to Indian pride. Thus, at a conference called at Pittsburgh, in September 1776, they accorded the usual full military honors to each tribe there represented, a salute of small arms, a flourish of drums and colors flying. Out of that conference came a treaty of friendship to last forever; in this case "forever" proved on definition to mean a little less than two years, but a welcome respite nevertheless.

Hamilton profited from the fact that the Indian tribes were losing their lands to the encroaching Americans and used it successfully as an argument to stir up the Six Nations and Chippewas to such a pitch of hostility that, in 1777, they warned the Virginians and Pennsylvanians against any further advances and ordered them to quit their tribal lands forever, or take the consequences.

When one of the commissioners of the Congress, William Wilson, reached Detroit the same year on his mission of peace and neutrality, he had a taste of Hamilton's methods. Received hospitably enough at the fort, he was very speedily disillusioned, for Hamilton, who was at the moment playing host to the representatives of several tribes, seized the opportunity to humiliate him before the Indians, and through him, the government he represented. Hamilton told the chieftains that the Americans sent to them were enemies and traitors to their mother country, tore Wilson's message to the tribes into bits, cut the wampum belt symbol of peace, which accompanied it, to pieces and incited his hearers to bloody war. Then, as a sequel to his harangue, he ordered Wilson to leave Detroit and carry back to his government the warning of the tribes.

Hamilton did not scruple as to the method of winning over his Indian allies. He and members of his staff, arrayed and painted for war, joined freely in their orgies and savage dances. The odious term "Hair-buyer" was applied to him in 1777. Prices paid for scalps, the careful checking of these bloody tokens, the cruelty permitted the Indians after a successful raid against lonely frontier cabins, caused repercussions in England. Both William Pitt and Edmund Burke rose in Parliament to denounce such unnecessary savagery in war. Said Pitt, who had already spoken forcibly against the use of Germans in the war:

> "But who is the man who has dared to authorize and associate to our arms the tomahawk and the scalping knife of the savage? . . . What! to attribute the sanction of God and nature to the massacres of the Indian Scalping-Knife. . . . They shock every sentiment of honor. They shock me as a lover of honorable war and a detester of murderous barbarity. These abominable principles and this more abominable avowal of them, demand a most decisive indignation."[18]

Hamilton denied the charge that he paid for scalps, but stories of the scalps reported after each attack, of the tortures inflicted on male prisoners in Indian villages, of the enslavement of women are too numerous to brook contradiction. On the other hand, records of the time do not show that Indian women and children were cruelly treated by the Americans.

By mid-year 1777, Hamilton had enrolled over a thousand warriors from all the leading tribes of the Northwest into his army. Indiscriminate raiding by these Indians among the isolated settlements became a regular feature of frontier warfare. The name of Simon Girty, the blue-eyed Indian, became a chilling signal of terror among the terrified women and children along the frontier. Far to the south, at Mobile and Pensacola, the English were also giving license to Indian warfare. The whole frontier, from Pennsylvania through Virgina, the Carolinas and Georgia, was set aflame by warriors in the pay of Hamilton in the North and John Stuart in the South.

The first attack on a fortified post in the North was made against Fort Watauga, in the present state of Tennessee. With only forty men, in a fort crowded with women and children, James Robertson and John Sevier led a desperate defense for three weeks, finally succeeding in beating off the attackers. In this area the Cherokees were the most numerous and powerful nation. Their bloody raids brought about the decision to create a combined force of militia, made up of the men of Virginia, the Carolinas and Georgia, strong enough to take the field and lay waste the territory of the Cherokees. They undertook a campaign of reprisal in the course of which they destroyed the cabins and crops of the tribes, drove their women and children into the shelter of the forests and cut down their warriors on sight. This swift revenge served its purpose: the Cherokees soon submitted to terms for peace.[19]

4.

This was the picture presented along the American frontier when, early in 1777, George Rogers Clark was commissioned by Virginia as a major of militia for Kentucky. He was then already well acquainted with the territory. In 1772, he had started out with a small band of adventurers to explore the country west of Pittsburgh on the upper Ohio and along its tributaries. Kentucky was rapidly being settled and some daring pioneers had even established themselves north of the Ohio. Two years later, so great was the influx into Kentucky that the Indians found themselves being crowded out of their tribal lands. They reacted in the only way they knew and the men on the frontier, led by Governor Dunmore of Virginia, engaged them in a short, but bloody war.

The year 1775 found Clark surveying Kentucky lands for the Ohio Company and staking out lands for himself. While thus occupied, he came into conflict with men who were already settled on lands allotted to his Company and he was obliged to make the journey to Williamsburg in order to press Governor Patrick Henry for a settlement of the disputed claims. While he was in Williamsburg, he also pleaded for precious powder with which to defend the territory against Indian war parties. In the end, Virginia incorporated the area involved in the dispute and assumed responsibility for its protection; she paid compensation to the settlers whose claims were disallowed. Clark returned across the Alleghenies with the powder he so urgently needed.

When he assumed the task of defending Kentucky in 1777, the English were in possession of the posts of Kaskaskia and Vincennes in the Illinois country. Troops stationed at the former place had been removed to Detroit in the spring of the preceding year, affairs being left in the hands of a Frenchman, the Chevalier Philippe François de Rastel. The Chevalier had his eye on the governorship of Louisiana in the event that New Orleans should fall to the British. His orders from Sir Guy Carleton, his superior officer, were "to have an eye on the proceedings of the Spanish and the management of the Indians on that side."[20] Rastel, ever ambitious for promotion, urged Carleton to cut off all Spanish trade along the Ohio, called his attention to the quantity of aid the Americans were getting from the Spanish in New Orleans and declared that their agents were stirring up the tribes along the Illinois River to attack the British posts. During the summer of 1777, he asked: "Shall we make the first move or permit it to be made?"[21]

In March, before Lieutenant Linn had left the Spanish Fort Arkansas with his load of powder and supplies for Fort Pitt and Wheeling, he was informed that he would receive additional supplies and protection to enable him to continue his journey up the Ohio in safety. From whom he received this information is not certain, but without doubt the spies whom Clark had sent into Kaskaskia had made a useful contact with Thomas Bentley whose wife was of a well-known Kaskaskian family and who was suspected of sympathizing with the cause of the Americans. It is clear that Lieutenant Linn had a rendezvous with this man Bentley for Bentley gave him a voucher for the supplies he needed in order to continue on his journey with his precious cargo. His instructions may well have been through William Murray and his brother Daniel, intimate friends of the Bentley family. It is known positively that these two acted as spies for Clark in this area at this time.

Lieutenant Linn charged his purchases, in the amount of sixty dollars, against the account of Oliver Pollock. Then he plunged into the enemy country under a prearranged military escort secretly provided by George Rogers Clark. Clark was aware that Lieutenant Linn was on his way north from New Orleans, but he had no idea where Linn would be encountered. Everyone was keeping an eye out for him. A Colonel Pentecost, for example, instructed one of his own officers: ". . . before you arrive at the mouth of the Ohio I think it necessary that you pass up the Mississippi to the Kaskaskias village, where you will make inquiry and probably meet with Captain Linn with his cargo and if you don't meet him before you get there, when you meet him, you will conduct him with the utmost safety to the said cargo up to the house of James Austurgass on the Monongahela River and immediately advise me thereof. . . ."[22]

While Linn was still at Fort Arkansas he had drawn against Pollock to the amount of $209 for goods bought from Lewis Charlerville of Kaskaskia. Here was a Frenchman doing business with an American, though resident of a town controlled by the British. He represents at once the sympathy of its French inhabitants for the American cause and their understanding that Spain, the donor of Linn's valuable cargo, was backing that cause to the limit.

Fort Arkansas, a Spanish post, certainly furnished Lieutenant Linn with the names of secret friends of the Americans living in Kaskaskia. The importance of the British fort lay in the fact that it commanded the navigation of the Mississippi, in the fact that it furnished quantities of supplies to Hamilton at Detroit, and finally, that it was dangerously placed for the launching of Indian attacks against Kentucky.

Two of Clark's well-chosen spies, Samuel Moore and Benjamin Linn, arrived at Kaskaskia in April, 1777. Disguised as hunters, they remained in the town until they had gathered all possible information, then made their way directly to Vincennes. Two months later, they reported to Clark that Kaskaskia was well supplied with quantities of military supplies, but carelessly guarded; that it was the center for the distribution of presents for the Wabash tribe and was being used fully to bring the Indians into a new plan of attack against Kentucky. They told Clark that throughout their scouting mission they had heard news of Hamilton's determination to launch large-scale war south of the Ohio and, if possible, to destroy the all-important supply route between the Americans and the Spanish at New Orleans.

Providentially, in May 1777, Lieutenant William Linn, with his remnant of "Captain Gibson's Lambs" arrived at a most critical moment at Fort Wheeling with the precious nine thousand pounds of powder, arms, ammunition and medicines supplied by Governor Unzaga of Louisiana. Linn's cargo was to save to the cause of the American colonies a number of Indian allies who were wavering toward Detroit, for it contained the presents to command their friendship. Had they gone over to Hamilton, his control over the whole Northwest would have been complete. It may fairly be stated that the remarkable "Service of Supply" inaugurated by Governor Gálvez and Oliver Pollock at New Orleans dates from the fateful day that Lieutenant Linn set forth with his "Lambs" on the long and perilous journey up the Great River. In the course of 1777, the first year of Gálvez's term as Governor of Louisiana, he sent supplies to the Americans valued at $100,000. In addition there were the shipments made by Pollock. The estimate of the actual value of Gálvez's contribution is conservative on the basis of the records and notes of the recipients.

Clark was fully aware that the frontier he defended was seriously threatened. At this critical hour in the Revolution, loss of the "Middle Ground" might well be fatal. He knew that he was tragically outnumbered by the enemy. If his small army of militiamen should be forced to abandon the Illinois country and Kentucky, and, if the Ohio should be cut off as an avenue of supplies from New Orleans, the colonies would be obliged to depend upon such aid as could reach them through the Atlantic posts. But the British navy watched these ports. Evading them was a difficult business. Clark boldly decided not to wait to be attacked but to be the attacker. He would take Kaskaskia, Vincennes and the smaller British posts. Their fall would make possible his dream of conquering the Northwestern territory. He would attack and take Detroit. He presented his plan for the preliminary campaign against Kaskaskia and Vincennes to Governor Patrick Henry of Virginia. He hoped that the Continental Congress would give him powder and ammunition and that Virginia would contribute armed men. But both the Congress and Virginia were in need of such aid themselves.

Supply! A source of supply! All the success of Clark's bold venture would depend upon supplies! He had great faith in the resourcefulness of Gálvez and Pollock. The three men together could set the plan in motion and bring it to a successful conclusion. Clark had proof enough that Gálvez and Pollock were men of his own kind, in the secrecy and speed with which they arranged for Captain Gibson to reach Washington with his 1000 pounds of powder, and for Lieutenant Linn to get to Fort Pitt and Wheeling with his invaluable cargo. The daring triumvirate, Gálvez, Pollock and Clark, all men of imagination and courage, was now complete. The story of their collaboration would remain forever a glorious affirmation of the friendship between Spain, the forgotten ally, and the struggling new nation of the United States.

FOOTNOTES

[1]José de Gálvez to Bernardo de Gálvez, November 25, 1776, A.G.I., Cuba, 174.

[2]James, *Pollock*, p. 81.

[3]Pollock's letters to Robert Morris and the Congressional Committee, May 7, 1778, *ibid.*, pp. 81-82.

[4]Royal Order to the Governor of Louisiana, February 20, 1777, draft; A.G.I., Santo Domingo, 1598.

[5]Reservada draft, *op. cit.*

[6]Torre, Noticia de los efectos remitidoes a Nueva Orleans, May 9, 1777; A.G.I., Santo Domingo, 1598.

[7]Royal Order to the Governor of Louisiana, February 22, 1777, Draft, *ibid.*

[8]Royal Order to the Governor of Louisiana, February 20, 1777, reservada draft. *Ibid.*

[9]Bernardo de Gálvez to José de Gálvez, May 13, 1777, *ibid.*, carta 52.

[10]Caughey, *Gálvez*, pp. 89-90.

[11]Royal Order to Governor Gálvez, October 13, 1777, A.G.I. Santo Domingo, 1598, copy.

[12]Bernardo de Gálvez to José de Gálvez, May 12, 1777, *ibid.*, Folio 174, no. 40.

[13]Bernardo de Gálvez to José de Gálvez, May 12, 1777, *ibid.*, Folio 174, no. 40. (Continuation of report in footnote 12.)

[14]Bernardo de Gálvez to Lloyd, April, 1777; A.G.I., Santo Domingo, 2596.

[15]Pollock to the President of Congress, September 18, 1772, "Pollock Letters." Cited in James, *Pollock*, p. 75.

[16]James, *Pollock*, p. 76.

[17]N.Y. Col. Doc's, VIII, 596.

[18]William Pitt before the Parliament. Quoted verbatim in Carta del Principe de Masserano to Grimaldi, November 20, 1777 (Reservada), Archivo General de Simancas, (cited hereafter as A.G.S.), Papeles de Inglaterra, Legajo 6912.

[19]James Alton James, *The Life of George Rogers Clark, op. cit.*, pp. 8-9; 46-49.

[20]James, *Pollock*, p. 86.

[21]*Ibid.*

[22]Colonel Dorsey Pentecost to Capt. William Harrod, January 28, 1777, in Reuben G. Thwaites and Louise P. Kellog, Eds., *The Revolution On the Upper Ohio, 1775-77* (Madison, Wis., 1908), pp. 227-228.

CHAPTER XII

1.

Far to the south, at Pensacola, the British stronghold of power commanding the territory of West Florida and the lower Mississippi, Governor Chester was an angry, confused and frustrated man. According to all the known rules of war, this rebellion against the mother country was not going as it should. To his ponderous way of thinking, the treaty of 1763 gave him a freedom of action along the coast and up the Mississippi that should insure control of the territory east of the river. His post at Manchac was strategically placed to stop all aid from getting up the river to the Americans. Carleton, in Canada, held firmly in hand the supply route from Montreal down-river to the Illinois and the Ohio. It stood to reason that the rebels should have been immobilized west of the Alleghenies. Washington, left stewing-in-his-own juice behind his blockaded coast ports, could not be expected to hold his poor and untrained army together for long. The rebellion would surely be put down quickly and its leaders brought before the bar of British justice.

In the year 1777, Spain was not at war with England, yet the Spanish Governor at New Orleans was sending large quantities of supplies to the rebels. The Americans were being received openly in that city as well as in all the Spanish posts along the river. They were permitted to sell their prize ships and to purchase munitions of war with the money made by the open auction of captured goods. They were being given sanctuary against pursuit as well as open assistance in running the blockade England was maintaining at the mouth of the river. Ships were sailing in and out of the port flying the Spanish flag, later to arrive at opportune times where least expected, loaded to the gunwales with supplies for the Americans. American officers and traders were on intimate terms with the Governor, more often guests at his dinner table. Strange conduct for a Governor representing Carlos III, King of Spain and ruler of the largest dominions in America!

Governor Chester was indeed angry, confused and frustrated. All this commerce, while supposedly carried out clandestinely, was an open secret to His Britannic Majesty's Consul in New Orleans. Chester protested indignantly to Bernardo de Gálvez against the sending of arms and ammunition up the river under the protection of the Spanish flag, calling such activities "very extraordinary."[1] Gálvez responded with almost humorous aplomb that he was only offering the usual courtesy and hospitality to the Americans; that if the "Rebels" had been assisted at New Orleans, it was because Governor Unzaga and he "did not know them as such."[2] This display of polite but tongue-in-cheek diplomacy by the impudent young Governor was not calculated to assuage the British Governor's feeling of frustration and the wrath of his officials at Pensacola, Mobile and Manchac. Something would have to be done to put a stop to this flaunting of British authority in West Florida.

All the while Gálvez was in communication with many American officials commanding the destinies of the colonial cause. In the summer he had a letter from Colonel George Morgan, commanding at Fort Pitt. Morgan expressed his deep gratitude for the powder from the warehouse at New Orleans that had enabled the garrison to fight off an Indian attack which took place almost at the moment of its arrival. Lieutenant Linn, he said, had briefed him in detail concerning the generous treatment accorded Captain Gibson and his men as well as given him detailed reports of the generous succor he himself had received at all the Spanish posts along the river.

Bringing up the often-discussed plan of an early expedition against Pensacola and Mobile, he sought assurance from Governor Gálvez that American troops would obtain all the necessary provisions, transports, powder and artillery from New Orleans, clearly acknowledging that such an expedition could not be undertaken without the Governor's full support. This was a truly extraordinary request considering the official mantle of neutrality under which the Governor was compelled to act as the representative of the King of Spain. Nevertheless, the proof of young Bernardo de Gálvez's full sympathy for the American Cause lies in the reply he wrote Morgan: "Although it would please me greatly I cannot enter into it. You may rest assured that I will extend my permission and whatever assistance I can, but it must *appear* that I am ignorant of it all."[3] He guaranteed unequivocally to support freedom of commerce from any point desired and to hold himself responsible for its full protection.

In October, Governor Patrick Henry of Virginia added his plea for aid to those previously made by General Lee, Gibson and Morgan. He set forth, in an eloquent letter, the advantages that would accrue to Spain should she accept; in exchange for substantial assistance she would receive all the trade of the southern part of the United States.

To further such commerce he promised that the government of the United States would build a fort at the mouth of the Ohio for the protection of the valuable cargoes of hemp, flax, furs, beef, pork and tobacco that could be given Spain in exchange for military supplies. He pointed out the value of the vast naval stores then available to the enemy and urged that with Spain's help these stores could be denied to them, thus striking at British sea power. He inquired if American annexation of West Florida would not be of great strategic value to Spain. He pleaded urgently for a *loan* of 150,000 pistoles, offering in return for such a large loan in cash and for other amounts previously advanced by Gálvez: "the gratitude, of this free and Independent Country, the trade in any or all of its valuable products and the friendship of its warlike Inhabitants."[4] He asked Gálvez to consider the possibility of opening a correspondence with the Court of Madrid in the sense of his proposals.

Gálvez already had the confidence of his sovereign when he opened Spanish storerooms and warehouses at New Orleans to every plea for assistance made by the Americans. He had not hesitated to expedite under the security of the Spanish flag the shipment of all goods sent them by Oliver Pollock. But in 1778, he took the further, decisive step of setting up the all-important "Service of Supply" to George Rogers Clark in the Illinois country. The help Clark received from New Orleans was an impressive and vital contribution toward the complete conquest of the Northwest, a contribution especially significant because it was made by Spain when she was still nominally a neutral power. The year 1777 had closed with a notable improvement in the overall military picture from the standpoint of the struggling Colonies. The pincers movement from Canada and New York had come to naught with the defeat of "Gentleman Johnny" Burgoyne and Saratoga was the prelude to the French alliance. But the situation west of the Alleghenies remained fluid and dangerous; there the English appeared to hold all the cards.

2.

As future events were to demonstrate, it was an important event when George Rogers Clark received his commission as colonel in the Virginia militia at the hands of Governor Patrick Henry on January 2, 1778. His first task, to recruit a field force, proved extremely discouraging. It was not until May that he was able to muster a small company of 150 men. At the head of this band he set forth from Fort Pitt, where he received a small supply of arms and powder from the cargo which Lieutenant Linn had brought north from New Orleans.

Descending the Ohio, he was joined by a few Kentucky frontiersmen at the Holston settlement. The party then continued down the river toward the mouth of the Tennessee, eventually leaving their boats and pushing overland toward Kaskaskia. It was a strenuous march of six days. The last two completely without food. On the night of July 4, Kaskaskia was taken by surprise. Clark entered the open gate, captured the commander of the fort, the French Chevalier Rocheblave, whom he found asleep in a comfortable bed and took over the town without firing a single shot. His spies had reported accurately that Kaskaskia was carelessly defended.

The inhabitants were deliriously happy to find that Clark and his "Long Knives" were not the ferocious butchers they had been led to believe. At once they sent hurried messages to nearby Cahokia advising the French at that post that all would be well under "the Kentuckian." So Cahokia opened its gates to Clark. The Indians of the surrounding area flocked into the powwows he called together there with the help of the enthusiastic inhabitants. In a long, fumbling harangue to the assembled savages he made an astounding impression. He was overjoyed and astonished at the success of his effort: "This Speech had a greater effect than I could have imagined, and did more service than a Regiment of Men could have done."[5]

A genius in frontier warfare, Clark immediately let the population know that his next objective was to be Vincennes and with a great show of preparation, he let it be bruited about that an express was to be sent at once to the Falls of the Ohio with orders to a body of troops there to join him so that he would be able to attack Vincennes in force. Little did the people realize that this force consisted of ten men, who had been left behind solely for the duty of guarding the boats of the party.[6]

Many of the inhabitants of Cahokia had friends and relatives living in Vincennes. They were horrified at the prospect facing the latter and at their insistence Father Pierre Gibault, who was well known and loved throughout the Illinois country, persuaded Clark to permit him to make the journey to Vincennes to explain the pacific character of the "Long Knives" and if possible bring about a peaceful surrender of the post. Clark was of course only too happy to be persuaded. Father Gibault hurried to Vincennes and, as a result of his good offices, the post capitulated without the loss of a single life. Captain Helm, with a small company, was sent to take command of Fort Sackville, the bastion of the town.

These bloodless victories brought great prestige to Colonel Clark and made a great impression on the two most important men in Spanish Illinois, Fernando de Leyba, the newly appointed Lieutenant-Governor of St. Louis and Colonel François Vigo, de Leyba's wealthy partner in the Indian trade. De Leyba offered his personal congratulations to Clark immediately following the fall of Kaskaskia, at the same time putting his entire command in St. Louis at Clark's disposal, should Hamilton, the English commander at Detroit, attack the small American forces with his Indians.

De Leyba was a man of seasoned experience in the Mississippi valley, a gentleman of great warmth and courtesy. He and Clark became intimate friends almost at once. All the resources of the St. Louis post were opened to the Kentuckian, soon including the hospitality of the Governor's own home and the warm affection of the ladies of his family. De Leyba had come to New Orleans under the command of Governor Unzaga in 1769. He was serving under the young Gálvez at this time and, at his order, had taken over the dangerous and all-important northern post at St. Louis. Clark was surprised and gratified to find a friend in him and wrote enthusiastically later concerning the warmth and generosity of this Spanish official from whom he had expected only cold austerity, for such was the naive picture of a proud Spanish Don which he had mentally carried concerning all Spaniards.

De Leyba, as soon as he heard of Clark's arrival at Kaskaskia, had written to notify him that he was in possession of a cargo of goods consigned to him by Pollock and subject to Clark's order. There was concrete evidence for Clark that the two other members of the triumvirate, Gálvez and Pollock, were putting the "Service of Supply" into operation. And de Leyba's quick and courteous intelligence added to Clark's confidence in this new friend.

Colonel François Vigo, de Leyba's partner in the fur trade, also gave Clark his warm support. He had served in the Spanish army and had taken to trade in the valley after his discharge in New Orleans. His dealings had already brought him into contact with Pollock and the two had become trusted friends. Vigo was a man of substance and personal integrity and his influence became far-flung within a short time after he took up residence in St. Louis. From his branch trading stores, scattered over a wide area at important points, Clark was able to obtain supplies for which Vigo accepted payment in the form of orders drawn upon Pollock in New Orleans.

Another wealthy merchant, a resident of Kaskaskia, Gabriel Cerre, became an ardent supporter of the American Cause after the fall of that post and, like Vigo, accepted notes against Pollock for supplies furnished to Clark.

All these sources of supplies and credit were especially welcome to Clark at this time because both Virginia and the Continental Congress were in grave financial straits. The paper money issued by the Congress, accepted early in the war, had by this time become valueless in payment for supplies. When Clark set forth on his campaign, he had been promised financial backing by the Congress as well as by Virginia, whose commission he carried. But his hurried preparations had forced him to leave with little clear understanding of how he was to be financed. He had been assured that Oliver Pollock would be able to supply all his needs through Pollock's agreement with Governor Gálvez. He found himself relying heavily upon Pollock.

His first draft was for Father Gibault's peace mission to Vincennes. It was for $285. When Gibault returned to Kaskaskia with the glad news that the American flag was now flying over Vincennes, Clark drew on Pollock a second time, on this occasion for $1260 to cover the cost of the expedition. Having won the territory, he was now much disturbed as to how he could maintain control over it at such a distance from any American base of supplies. During the summer of 1778, he was forced to draw against Pollock many times to cover the cost of goods purchased from the traders and merchants in the territory. Within a few months his drafts on Pollock had mounted to $18,000.

Among his earliest disbursements he listed:

$ 237 for transport of ten men bringing boats from Wheeling to Redstone;
$ 216 for linen boat covers;
$1351 for 12.189 pounds of flour in barrels;
$ 237 for 10 beeves;
$ 30 for a boat anchor;
$ 6 for a treat to Capt. Helm's company - a minute company of not more than five or six men in command at Vincennes;
$ 10 for four pair handcuffs; and
$ 57 for hospital supplies[7]

Salt was in desperately short supply, sometimes being the cause of the loss of an entire winter's hunt. Liquors, rum, whiskey and taffia were a necessary part of the rations. They were valuable items of exchange for provisions and were always short. It became necessary for Clark to cut down the ration to his own men in order to conserve a portion to exchange for provisions. This reduction meant hardship for troops who operated day and night, poorly clad, without sufficient blankets, in all sorts of weather. The men were reduced to the point of supplying most of their clothing needs from the skins of animals. Often they marched over frozen ground without shoes. Cabins and boats had to be constructed and all types of military supplies had to be bought or exchanged at very high cost. The French population supplied only small quantities of goods because their own daily family needs were being supplied at high cost and under difficult transport conditions. Powder was priced at $2 a pound and lead at 50 cents a pound. Bacon and flour were respectively 50 cents and 11 cents a pound and taffia was $6 a gallon. A day's wages for an armourer or carpenter was $1.60.

3.

Clark's accounts with Virginia were well kept and meticulous in detail. He issued vouchers for every item, no matter how small, so that today we have a clear picture of the terrific obstacles he met in conducting such a campaign in the Illinois country in 1778. A few extracts from his accounts will tell their own story:

"Let this man Have 4 lb of pork for the people that are going down the river to Traverse the Horses". "Issue to that Squaw that Funished our men with Provisions one Bushel of Corn and Five pounds of Pork." "Please to issue for the use of the Kaskaskias Indians 40 weight of Flour." "The Commissary of Issues is amediately ordered to prepair one Thousand Rations to have them Ready to Imbark by 12 o'clock;" "Furnish Mr. Edward Murray with five gallons of Whiskey he having agreed to accept that Quantity in full for his Pay as Express form this place;" "As there is a Party of militia going after a Party of Indians as have done mischief you will pleased for to let me have one Pound of Powder and two Pound of Lead we Haveing not a Sufficient quantity for to Persew them."[8]

Clark's commissary, against which these requisitions were made, was supplied with goods paid for by drafts on Pollock. Cerre accepted these drafts for $619, $2000, and $1273; Auguste Chouteau accepted a draft for $2100; one Laffont, a draft for $1000; similarly, a score of other traders for various sums.

Throughout the territory the trade center was New Orleans. There, orders against Pollock were paid in good Spanish dollars or backed up by the treasury of Governor Gálvez. Consequently, the most substantial men in every section of the Illinois supplied the expedition of Clark without hesitancy wherever supplies were available. In addition to the traders already mentioned there were, from the first, the Charleville brothers, three in number. Lieutenant Linn knew them and drew against Pollock for goods purchased from them at some point during his journey up the Ohio River. Clark gave a first draft to Charles Charleville for $200 and a second very soon after for $2000.

Another trader of great influence, Francis Bosseron, was the most influential young man in Vincennes; the House of Bosseron was known from Montreal to New Orleans. At the age of twenty-six, Francis had assumed the headship of his father's great company. He was mayor of Vincennes when Father Gibault made his startling mission to that post. He not only agreed to turn the city over to Clark but also, soon became so valuable to the latter that he was given the first commission issued by Clark in the West. He later became a valuable ally when it became necessary to reconquer Vincennes. His sure knowledge of the northern country all the way to Montreal was priceless intelligence in matters dealing with Hamilton and his Indian allies at Detroit. J. M. P. Legras, another well-known trader of Vincennes, followed young Bosseron's lead. Vincennes could be counted on as a sure source of supplies for Clark's commissary. Ultimately, of course, it was upon Oliver Pollock and Bernardo de Gálvez that Clark depended. Until the final conquest of the Northwest they were inundated with drafts like the following:

"Kaskaskia 2nd Feby. 1779

$1752
Sir

At thirty Days sight of my first of Exchange, second of same tenor and date not paid Pay to Mr. Legras or to his Order the Sum of One Thousand Seven Hundred and fifty two Dollars for sundry furnitures to the State of Virginia and Charge as pr. former advise [sic] from
Sir
Your very obdt. Servt.
G. R. Clark

To Olliver Pollock
Esqr.
New Orleans"[9]

Oliver Pollock was jubilant over Clark's success and happy to have had a part in it. In August 1779, he wrote the Commercial Committee of Virginia: "You'll see he is in possession of the Illinois and that he has drawn bills on me with the expectation of my honoring them for the State of Virginia. There is to the amount of 1,000 Dollars already come to hand which I have accepted payable in January next, and if any more are presented, I shall accept them payable at the same time as I hope before that You'll have it in your power to furnish me with sufficient funds to wipe off the whole. He was already indebted for $42,500 on the same date, because of the accrued debt on behalf of the General Government. His obligations at that time also included $74,087 advanced to him by Governor Gálvez by means of which arms, ammunition and supplies had been furnished the frontier posts of Pennsylvania and Virginia."[10] Approximately $14,445 of this sum had been invested in a cargo of peltries and indigo which he shipped to France, under the French flag, for exchange for goods badly needed by the Commercial Committee. This particular venture had an odd and unfortunate sequel: Pollock discovered that all American agents were not as generous and patriotic as himself; when the cargo reached Cape St. François in the Caribbean it was seized by the agent stationed there, who claimed it in payment of a debt of the American Government. Pollock wrote sadly of the incident: "This was my first reward for serving America." Without resources from Virginia or the Congress to meet Clark's obligations and with his personal funds seriously reduced, he nevertheless wrote Clark: "The cause in which we are embarked urges me to strain every nerve, and luckily having a number of good Friends have hitherto enabled me to serve my Country. In consequence of this I have accepted your bills."[11]

Clark's possession of the Illinois country was by no means secure or unchallenged after the capture of the English strong points. Hamilton, at Detroit, took measures immediately after the fall of Vincennes for its recapture, recruiting forces from Fort St. Joseph and Michilimackinac. In October, he began his descent of Lake Erie, entered the Maumee River, made his way down the Wabash and appeared before Vincennes December 17, with a force of well-armed regulars and their Indian allies, numbering well over five-hundred men. Captain Helm, the young American, with his pitifully small force, had no recourse but to surrender or see the town demolished and the friendly inhabitants at the mercy of Hamilton's Indian warriors.

Among Hamilton's captives was François Vigo, the St. Louis trader. Vigo was permitted to return to St. Louis after he had promised to go home directly and not to stop at Clark's headquarters in Kaskaskia to give news of the fate of Vincennes. Vigo was an astute and observant man of cool judgment. While still Hamilton's prisoner, he had learned that the English commander planned an early spring descent of the Mississippi to coincide with an ascent of the river by Chester, at Pensacola. Their synchronized maneuvers, if successful, would cut Clark off from all supplies from New Orleans. Vigo honorably fulfilled his promise to go directly to St. Louis. Once there, however, he informed his friend and partner, de Leyba, that Hamilton had openly avoured his intention of making war against the Spaniards unless they ceased sending supplies to the Americans, and had warned against giving sanctuary to Americans who would soon be driven out of English territory on the east bank of the Mississippi. Then Vigo went at once to Kaskaskia and revealed Hamilton's plans to Clark.[12]

Clark lost no time in setting out, in February 1779, for the reconquest of Vincennes. His advance was made under incredible hardships: at times his men waded in water up to their waists; they made forced marches, stumbling through flooded woods, and ankle-deep mud over miles of tortuous country. The troops finally appeared before the stockaded walls of Vincennes near the point of complete exhaustion. There was some hot fighting between the attackers and the besieged, during which Clark contrived to send a messenger to the inhabitants without Hamilton's knowledge. The result was that when Clark at last entered the town in the evening, he was joyfully received.

Hamilton became an American prisoner. With the downfall of the "Hair-buyer" the frontier along the Ohio at last became relatively secure.

4.

But the victory in the Ohio country was costly for Oliver Pollock and Governor Gálvez. Clark had depended upon them not only for his essential troop supplies, but also for his Commissary Department, by means of which he supported the inhabitants of the conquered territory and maintained friendly relations with the Indian tribes. It was his Commissary Department which enabled him to hold the Illinois country after the fall of Kaskaskia, Cahokia and Vincennes. Clark was generous in acknowledging the value of Pollock's help. "The invoice Mr. Pollock rendered upon all occasions in paying those bills I considered at the time and now to be one of the happy circumstances that enabled me to keep possession of that Country."[13]

His drafts were a severe drain upon Pollock's resources. Theoretically they were drawn against the state of Virginia, for which Pollock was agent. Actually, they were only negotiable to the extent that Pollock could find means to cover them. That is why he well has been called "the Robert Morris of the West." It must be emphasized, however, that always behind him, and coming to his aid in a financial crisis was Governor Bernardo de Gálvez. By June 1781, Gálvez had advanced him a total of just under $80,000.[14]

It is not the least interesting feature of these transactions that they were all handled between the two principals on the most intimate and personal basis. When the American cause was in urgent need, the young Governor did not hesitate to place his own position in jeopardy by first handing over Spanish funds and later — when the loans were an accomplished fact — reporting what he had done to his own Government. The loans were made chiefly on his own credit; they were delivered to Pollock in the most approved cloak-and-dagger manner, usually at night by Juan Morales, Gálvez's private secretary. Pollock wrote at a later date that these funds were received "as very secret service money." By means of these loans and the monies Pollock was able to raise against his own personal properties and credit, Clark's drafts were covered. When it is remembered that these loans were made in stable Spanish silver dollars at a time when American currency in the Colonies was worth only twelve cents in terms of the Spanish dollar, it becomes apparent that Spanish aid to the Americans in their struggle for independence was far greater, from a purely financial standpoint, than has hitherto been recognized.

But Pollock and Gálvez could not do the impossible and cover every request for help. And Governor Henry's plea for aid, which reached New Orleans in September 1778, met with a polite "non possumus." Henry had asked for an immediate loan of 150,000 pistoles. Gálvez had no recourse but to say frankly: "Were the amount not so large and I had not given to Mr. Pollock the money that I was able to take from the surplus remaining from the sum assigned annually to this Province for its maintenance, I should immediately have resolved to send you a part of it in order to please you and to render that State a service, but this is impossible to me at the present as there is no money."[15] He had in fact scraped the bottom of his treasury for the funds needed by Clark in Illinois and other American parties.

December found Pollock begging the Commercial Committee of Congress for an order to cover drafts amounting to $56,000 which he had honored for the General Government. By that time he had been reduced to selling his slaves and mortgaging almost the last of his remaining properties. Gálvez was at the same time at the end of his treasury resources but he still continued to place the weight of his name and that of Spain behind the loans made by his friend. Later on he was to save Pollock from debtor's prison by personally assuming all the latter's debts.

The Congress was in dire straits at the end of 1778, not only to supply Washington's army but also the men of Count D'Estaing's newly arrived force. To cover these requirements to the best of its ability, it placed an embargo on all supplies. Nothing could be shipped to the relief of Clark's men in the West. Had the partnership between Gálvez and Pollock failed to maintain its "Service of Supply," Vincennes might well have remained in English hands and Hamilton's plan to win control of the entire Mississippi might have cost the Congress the loss of the whole western territory. Had the project of combined operations by Hamilton and Chester come off successfully, the cause of the Colonies in the West and in the Carolinas and Georgia might have been defeated decisively. But Pollock and Gálvez contributed the vital supplies which secured the West for the United States at this most critical hour in the fortunes of the new nation.

FOOTNOTES

[1]Howe to Stiell, April 22, 1778 in Great Britain, Historical Manuscripts Commission. *Report on American Manuscripts in the Royal Institution of Great Britain.* (4 vols., Dublin, 1904-1909). Cited in Caughey, *Gálvez,* p. 92.

[2]Gálvez to Chester, April 4, 1779; A.G.I., Santo Domingo, 2596. Certified copy.

[3]Gálvez to Morgan, August 9, 1777. *Ibid.*

[4]Patrick Henry to Bernardo de Gálvez, January 14, 1778. A.G.I., Cuba, p. 2370.

[5]Clark to Mason, November 19, 1779. Cited in James Alton James, ed., *George Rogers Clark Papers, 1771-1781.* (Springfield, Ill., 1912), collections of the Illinois State Historical Library, Virginia Series, Vol. IV, p. 120.

[6]*Ibid.*, p. 122.

[7]James G. Randall, "George Rogers Clark's Service of Supply," in *Mississippi Valley Historical Review*, VIII (1921), pp. 256-263, cited in James, *Pollock*, pp. 141-142.

[8]James, *Pollock*, p. 143.

[9]"Draper MSS.," 48J33 (Wisconsin Historical Society Library), *George Rogers Clark Letters.* Cited in James, *Pollock*, p. 144.

[10]James, *Pollock*, pp. 144-145.

[11]Pollock to Clark, August 18, 1778, "Draper MSS." 48J33. Cited in James, *Pollock*, p. 145.

[12]Leyba to Gálvez, February 5, 1779; A.G.I., Cuba, 1. See also Caughey, *Gálvez*, pp. 96-97.

[13]Clark to Pollock, August 6, 1778. Randall, "George Rogers Clark's Service of Supply," *op. cit.*, p. xcvii. Cited in Caughey, *Gálvez*, p. 98.

[14]Pollock signed August 26, 1779 an itemized receipt for monies received as follows: $24,023, June 9, 1778; $15,948, October 24, 1778; $22,640, July 3, 1779; $11,478, June 5, 1780. A.G.I., Cuba, p. 569. Approved, José de Gálvez to Bernardo de Gálvez, November 17, 1781, A.G.I., Cuba, p. 175; José de Gálvez to Intendant of Louisiana, March 12, 1782, A.G.I., Cuba, p. 569. See also, James, "Oliver Pollock Financier of the Revolution in the West," in *Mississippi Valley Historical Review*, XVI (1929), pp. 67-80.

[15]James, *Pollock*, p. 153.

CHAPTER XIII

1.

The southern frontier continued to give concern, alike in New Orleans and Philadelphia, after the threat from the north had been exercised. Reinforcement of Manchac by a stronger force sent from Pensacola caused Pollock, in June 1778, to recall all boats going up the river. New Orleans was overflowing with spies, all eagerly watching the activities of Governor Gálvez and Pollock. In spite of their presence he was able, with the help of Gálvez, to fit out his prize ship, the *Morris*, and arm it strongly enough to put it to use as a convoy for cargo vessels sailing to the Atlantic coastal ports. Supplies for these vessels were purchased by means of an advance of $6000 from Gálvez. The Governor reminded his friend that he lacked any authority from his Government and that in case of a rupture with Great Britain, an eventuality for which he earnestly hoped, all his resources would be needed for the defense of Louisiana.[1]

A vivid portrait of Gálvez at this time is painted by Pollock in one of his letters. The young Governor stands out, daring and provocative and self-assured:

> "Tho' I am now despatching the Batteau *Speedwell* under the care of Mons. Connand and goes regularly cleared under Spanish Colours for the Illinois Country, yet so exasperated are they upon the River and at Pensacola that it is a doubt with me whether they will stop her above and perhaps take her tho' Spanish Property as the Governor at Pensacola and the English Sloops from here a few days ago threaten vengeance against the Governor for not delivering up every American here with all the prizes taken and say they will make Reprisals on this Town which in probability will be the means of bringing on further Ceremonies betwixt the Court of Spain and Great Britain. . . . However I cannot conclude this important subject without giving the greatest applause to Governor Gálvez for his noble Spirit and Behavior on this Occasion for tho' he had no batteries erected or even Men to defend the Place against two Sloops of War, the *Hound* and the *Sylph*, and at the Time a small Sloop with 100 men in the Lakes all coming against him with Demands and Threats, yet in this situation he laughed at their Haughtiness and Despised their attempts, and in short they returned as they came. But I have good reason to suppose they are not yet satisfied and only wait for more Force."[2]

Life in New Orleans during this critical period was not exclusively dedicated to such matters as supplies, forays, conspiracies and cloak-and-dagger activities. In the domestic affairs of Louisiana, Gálvez was engaged in the practical demonstration of his gift for governing a province composed of many nationalities. The swift measures taken at the very beginning of his term to wrest the advantage in trade, held by the English, from the expert hands of such men as Stuart, McGillivray and other well-established traders in the territory, and to return it to the French, whose commerce had suffered almost total eclipse since the defeat of France in the Seven Years War and the subsequent Treaty of 1763, brought about an immediate advantage by enlisting the loyalties of the inhabitants. His policy of firm protection of commerce up and down the Mississippi under the Spanish flag added to the security of trade and brought into New Orleans a rapidly growing population and new wealth.

His program of selective immigration resulted in the development of much rich, fallow land in the capable hands of groups of new colonists from Spain, the Canaries, Canada, Germany and the American families seeking safety from Indian attacks east of the Mississippi. Memorials had been sent the Governor from the various groups in which they swore loyalty to the Spanish crown and assured the Governor of their support in all affairs relative to the security and welfare of the province. A town was named "Galvestown" in his honor.

Probably the happiest event to draw the wholehearted support of the inhabitants of New Orleans toward this young man, still in his twenties, was his romantic marriage to the charming Felicie de St. Maxent d'Estrehan, the young and beautiful widow of Jean Baptiste Honore d'Estrehan. This vivacious young lady aroused affectionate enthusiasm not only in the hearts of the volatile Louisianians, but also, at a later date, the acclaim of the populace of Havana and Mexico City where her charm and beauty and winsome manner became one of the chief reasons for her young husband's great popularity as Viceroy. Their marriage, during the ten short years of life that were granted this scion of Spain's nobility, was a romantic idyll that aroused the deepest feelings of pride and affection in the hearts of the Creole population of New Orleans and enshrined them forever in the hearts of the people of Mexico.

Other Spanish officers quickly succumbed to the grace and charm of the New Orleans belles and through marriage tightened the bonds of loyalty to the Spanish Crown. Jacinto Panis, to be heard from many times in the battles of Mobile and Pensacola, fell in love with Margarethe Wiltz, the widow of Joseph Milhet, who had been among those put to death after an abortive insurrection in the time of Governor Ulloa. This marriage of the Adjutant-Major of the Louisiana batallion, endorsed by Governor Unzaga, went far toward erasing the scars left by the rebellion.[3]

A future governor of the colony, the Sergeant Major of the Batallion, Estevan Miro, also fell under the spell of one of the greatest beauties of New Orleans, Marie Celeste Elenore de Macarty. After obtaining a memorial from Gálvez vouching for the lady's nobility and dowry, which was forwarded to the Court, he was granted royal permission for marriage. A history of Louisiana speaks fervently of the love and admiration Miro and his Celeste aroused in the people of the province of their time.[4]

There can be no doubt that Bernardo de Gálvez made a solid contribution to the Government of Louisiana, but probably these three intangibles, the manner in which he carried out his policies, his marriage and his personal charm, went farther toward captivating the Creoles than all his successes as Administrator and Military Commander. According to General Navarro, then Governor of Cuba, "the mildness of the laws and the graciousness and humanity" of the Governor contributed in great part to the happiness of the Louisianians and to their loyalty to Spain.[5]

The daily life in this capital of the West followed closely the manners and customs of Madrid and Paris with the added piquancy of life peculiar to the houses of the American plantation owners and the great traders of the West. At the Governor's table were to be found gentlemen accustomed to the formal courtesy of the courts of Europe seated beside the gauche new officers of the United States; or French chevaliers of Old France seated beside traders whose domain ranged over the wide reaches of the country beyond the Mississippi and the Missouri. At times the courtesy of the house was extended with dignity and grace to the great chiefs of the Creeks, the Chickasaws and the Seminoles.

The ladies who presided over the mansions of New Orleans set their tables with shining silver and rare porcelains from the Old World. Their charms were displayed in the silks, satins and brocaded velvets familiar to the great ladies living at the courts of the Bourbons. Their tables groaned with the venison, fish, fowl and fruits of this fabulously rich country. Formal toasts were washed down eager throats with the finest wines of Spain, Portugal, Madeira and the West Indies. Under the mild soft air of Louisiana, with its great moss-draped trees, its vivid flowers, its potpourri of muted sound from guitar, banjo and fiddle, the mixed voices of Negro slaves in garden and field, the rollicking river songs of dozens of boatmen rambling the streets of this river capital, it is not surprising that a young Spanish Governor and his Creole lady rapidly became the romantic toast of the province.

It was in this highly charged atmosphere that Bernardo de Gálvez played his important part in the American Revolution. His personal generosity to needy refugees swarming the city of New Orleans and all outlying Spanish posts became well known and any plea for help received his prompt and courteous response. While his country continued its policy of neutrality, he facilitated shipping by sea and up and down the Great River. He cooperated with Pollock in sending supplies to Washington's army in the West. As has been noted already, American control west of the Alleghenies is largely attributable to his forceful methods and practical assistance.

American appreciation was not lacking and was expressed often in grateful letters from Virginia and from General Washington and other high officers in the Continental army. But it remained for Oliver Pollock to express the wish to have a portrait of Gálvez made for Congress "in order to perpetuate to your memory in the United States of America, as ranking in your Exalted Nation, as a Soldier and a Gentleman with those that have been of Singular Service in the Glorious Contest of Liberty."[6] Pollock continued to bring the attention of Congress Gálvez's great services to the Nation dating from January 1777, when he first took over control of the Province of Louisiana.

When these two men were making their greatest donations to the cause of freedom there was small hope of their ever being recompensed for their outlays. Pollock laid his personal fortune on the altar of his country completely. Certainly his advances could not have been looked upon at the time as a profitable investment for a trader as astute as he. Later, he learned at what a terrible cost he had sacrificed not only his personal fortune, but also his good name; for he was thrown into a prison in Cuba for failure to pay his creditors in New Orleans for purchases made in good faith for Virginia and the Congressional Committee of Commerce. He was to go through years of poverty and humiliation before he regained enough of the monies he had given the Cause to insure a living for his wife and children.

It was while he was trying desperately to collect from the Congress enough to secure his release from a Cuban debtor's prison that Gálvez providentially arrived in Havana. This was in 1785, and the very hour of Pollock's deepest despair. Gálvez obtained his release and assisted him to return to Philadelphia where he could plead his case in person.[7] Pollock persuaded Gálvez to tell the Congress that he, Gálvez, would hold his friend "personally responsible" for the amount of $74,087. Pollock asked this intervention in the forlorn hope that the

United States Congress might possibly expedite payment of the debt. Gálvez went a step further to help his old friend: he promised that if the Congress failed to repay the sum due to the government of Louisiana, he would personally guarantee payment to the treasury of Louisiana . . . when settlement was finally made, the payment was to Gálvez's Estate.[8] It is possible that Gálvez, realizing to what depths Pollock was reduced, assumed the debt since his own fortunes were advancing rapidly at the time and he was in no need of immediate repayment.

2.

Help for Clark does not mark the only intervention of Gálvez and Pollock in the financing of a colonial enterprise. A second intervention occurred in connection with the Willing Expedition down the Mississippi and had momentous consequences. The expedition itself was of minor importance, a handicap rather than an asset for the Colonial Cause, but it served to bring Spain out into the open as an active, declared ally of the Americans. It started a chain of events ending in the fall of Natchez, Mobile and Pensacola and the secure control of the Mississippi from the most northern post of Fort St. Joseph to the territory of West Florida.[9]

From the time of Colonel Morgan's proposal for an assault upon West Florida until February 1778 when Willing made his descent of the Mississippi, the question of a campaign against the British in this area had been debated by the State of Virginia and by the Continental Congress. One plan for an all-out attack on the Floridas had reached the voting stage in the Congress and it was considered certain that there would be a unanimous vote of funds for troops and supplies for a major campaign. Then Harry Laurens of South Carolina rose to speak in blistering terms of the foolhardiness of the plan. He warned of the danger of defeat for lack of supplies in an area where the waters were patrolled entirely by ships of the English fleet; of the tremendous strength of the English base at Pensacola; of the danger to troops from fever in swamp-fighting. He reminded his audience of the English alliance with the powerful Creek Nation whose warrior bands would be lying in wait athwart the approaches to Pensacola by land; lastly, of the chance of losing the Georgia frontier for lack of troops in that section. All these considerations, he urged, would almost certainly make for a disastrous defeat for such a "hair-brained scheme." Laurens's bitter diatribe convinced a number of wavering Congressmen of the futility of such a campaign and the plan was defeated in the Congress.

It would appear that Willing's expedition down the Mississippi was later agreed upon in lieu of this ambitious program. Although direct orders to Willing from the Congress have not been found, it is considered probable that this small enterprise was ordered by a committee of the Congress and not by the whole body. With or without full Congressional approval, certain it is that James Willing, self-styled "Captain in the service of the United Independent States of America," raided the Loyalist settlements along the lower Mississippi in February 1778.

James Willing had been a resident of Natchez until 1774, where he had been engaged in trade, albeit not very successfully. He was a convincing talker, but a man in whom few in the town of Natchez placed much confidence. His elder brother was a partner in the great firm of Willing and Morris of Philadelphia for which Oliver Pollock was agent and business associate. Through such powerful contacts James Willing had been able to put forward his plan for an expedition, advancing as arguments in his favor his knowledge of the river and his assurance of assistance from Pollock and the Spanish Governor of Louisiana. As a matter of fact, he had had no previous contact with either of the two before he was appointed a captain in the United States navy and assigned command of the expedition. The Congress entrusted him with certain despatches for New Orleans and instructed him to bring back up the river part of the stores which Spain had agreed to deliver there for the use of the United States.

In January 1778, Willing took command of the armed boat *Rattletrap* and with a crew of thirty volunteers set out on a typical swashbuckling adventure. At Kaskaskia he came into contact with the Chevalier de Rocheblave and trader La Chance, a friend of the American Cause whom he relieved of a cargo of brandy. The Bequet brothers of the same place had to surrender their load of peltries. He later unscrupulously intercepted a message from Cruzat, then Spanish Commander at St. Louis, to Colonel George Morgan.[10] Before he reached that Arkansas post he had succeeded in antagonizing the Indian allies of the English so thoroughly that after he quit that place a number of pioneer families fled across the river to the Spanish side to claim the protection of Spain.[11]

By mid-February he reached the plantation of Anthony Hutchins just above Natchez, and promptly seized Hutchins together with all his property and slaves. A few days afterward he took possession of Natchez and declared that the population of the town were prisoners of war. Only after a committee of citizens had taken an oath not to take up arms against the United States of America and not to give assistance to the enemies of that State did he agree to leave them unmolested and in possession of their property. Hutchins was allowed to take the oath at Natchez but, unlike the townsmen, did not have his property restored. Consequently, he became the center of bitter intrigue against the Americans, considering himself and with some justice, unfairly penalized.

Many hair-raising reports followed Willing's progress down the Mississippi. His conduct after leaving Natchez for the lower river seemed to confirm these reports. At Manchac he seized the *Rebecca*, an English armed vessel which had been assigned the duty of securing the river against the Rebels. He confiscated many boats, raided plantations on the Mississippi, on the Amite and Thompson's Creek and burned or despoiled properties generally. He permitted cruelty to the people as well as destruction of their possessions, even going so far as to pursue a few settlers into Spanish territory and despoil them of their belongings on neutral soil.

Dr. Francis Farrell of Natchez reported one of the tragic incidents of this veritable raid. It appeared that the wife of the commander of the fort, "Mary Blommert, having taken a dose of 'Red Precipitate' prescribed by François Dolony, Surgeon to the Rebels commanded by Mr. James Willing, as she was dying cried out with a most lamentable voice 'Oh! Willing! Willing! Willing!' and expired in excruciating pain."[12] The hatred which Blommert later displayed toward the Americans is understandable. There is no reasonable doubt that Willing's wanton depredations at Manchac and along the lower river aroused a ferocious antagonism against him and all Americans. During the course of his journey down river his original party of thirty men had been augmented by a hundred or more adventurers seeking plunder alone and the agreement he made with them to divide the proceeds from the sale of the spoils in New Orleans, half to them and half to his own party, was not calculated to discourage lawless behavior.

Gálvez was deluged with bitter complaints and with petitions for protection. Consternation and fear spread through the West Floridas as rumours of large supplementary forces to follow in the wake of Willing's party were deliberately circulated among the settlers. Willing made impassioned speeches at strategic spots. At the mouth of the Black River, more than a hundred loyalist settlers listened and were swayed by his eloquence as much as by the fear inspired by his name. "Exaggeration of Willing's strength, uncertainty about the loyalism of their neighbors, apprehension of Indian attacks, and the intimidation of Willing's plundering and speaking militated against any organized resistance by the West Floridians."[13]

As the expedition reached the lower Mississippi, volunteers from New Orleans also joined Willing. Oliver Pollock assisted in organizing some of these volunteers. His nephew, Thomas Pollock, joined Willing with a party of fifteen with the idea of participating in the capture of the *Rebecca* but arrived after the event. Another party of twenty-six boatmen under the notorious La Fitte enlisted at New Orleans for the stated purpose of going to Manchac to rescue English property endangered there by Willing's party. Instead, they went down river, and after effecting a junction with a larger party of Americans proceeded to the anchorage of the English brig, *Neptune*. La Fitte tried to persuade the men who were guarding the ship under orders from Gálvez to join with him in taking the vessel. Gálvez's men refused to have any part in the seizure and La Fitte thereupon took possession of the ship.

Because the inhabitants of West Florida had no armed protectors, there began an exodus to the haven of Spanish Louisiana. No exact figures are available as to the number of refugees thus seeking sanctuary across the river, but the stream of desperate people caused Carlos Grand Pre and Juan Delavillebeuvre, the first Spanish officials to encounter them, to offer temporary safety and hurriedly send to the Governor for instructions. Gálvez, as on numerous previous occasions, offered "without distinction to the one or the other the sacred right of hospitality whenever the necessity to claim it should arise."[14]

3.

Pollock had received word of the Willing Expedition from Philadelphia and with his usual promptness had taken up the matter of the reception of the party with the Governor. As early as February he had completed arrangements for their coming with Gálvez. They were offered the freedom of the city. A public building was assigned them as a barrack and Pollock was given permission to auction off their plunder.

For these extraordinary privileges, Gálvez justified himself to his own government in these words:

"In this policy I hope to secure great advantages for the King and for this Province. To the first because all things such as indigo, peltries, etc., which they have salvaged and introduced into our territories are not brought in without my licence and consequently not without paying the regular duties. And to the second because the captured Negroes, as well as those that have been brought for safe-keeping into our Domain whose owners are planning to return to Europe, will be purchased by these Inhabitants at less than half their value."[15]

Pollock's antipathy to Willing because of the latter's arrogance and importunity became so great that before the end of May the two men were no longer on speaking terms. Communication was by letter. On the 30th Willing wrote him:

"In the first place to begin with my Instructions: the following Extracts will serve to specify their tenour. . . . After being ordered to make prize of all British

Property on the Mississippi River I was instructed to apply to the Governor of this Province for Liberty to make Sale of them. That obtained I am Instructed to pay One moiety of the Net proceeds into your hands as Agent for the Congress."[16]

These last words had meaning for Pollock because, when he was still on speaking terms with Willing, he had been informed that the latter brought him official orders making Pollock the recognized Agent of the Congress. Willing had also delivered to him in the period of oral communication authorization to buy and ship $50,000 worth of blankets and other supplies needed by the army. He was directed to send all by fast sailing ships which he was to charter or buy for the purpose. A draft of $30,000 was sent in part-payment for these supplies, the rest to be paid for by shipments of flour. The Congress was dubious concerning the means by which these shipments could be made, the English maintaining a blockade of all the ports.

Pollock communicated the information in Willing's letter to Gálvez and received assurance of the Governor's continued assistance. An additional loan of 4,000 pistoles from Gálvez permitted him to send out a small sloop loaded with taffia, sugar and coffee, three commodities much in demand and by means of which he hoped to make an excellent trade. The proceeds could be added to the fund sent him by the Congress. Unfortunately this trading venture ended disastrously; the ship was captured by the British; the investment was a total loss. The General Government's debt now amounted to some 50,000 pistoles.

Willing and his party proved to be the most unwelcome and troublesome guests Gálvez ever had the misfortune to entertain. The six months following their arrival in New Orleans were the most disastrous for Pollock of all the years he gave to the service of the United States. Both he and Gálvez soon found themselves working as hard to be rid of Willing as they had been working to receive him. Pollock's patience became exhausted. Gálvez found compelling use for all his diplomatic art, regretting ruefully the while his natural inclination to be courteously hospitable to a guest.

But Gálvez and Pollock were not alone in reacting against Willing. The English commander at Pensacola, aroused by the reports of Willing's depredations up and down the Mississippi and throughout the Floridas, and assailed with demands for vengeance sent the armed vessel, the *Sylph*, under the command of Captain John Fergusson, into the river, with orders to seek satisfaction for the victims of Willing's raids. Fergusson demanded that Governor Gálvez make suitable restitution in money for the booty seized by Willing and sold, with the Governor's permission, in New Orleans. He did not fail to remind Gálvez that the Governor had previously restored to the French and

Americans along the river the property taken from them by the English after having refused to permit sale of this property in the open market of New Orleans. He referred particularly to the Governor's action at the time of Captain Lloyd's sojourn in the vicinity.

Gálvez had risked successfully the threat of a reprimand from Madrid over the altercation with Lloyd. Now he found himself in the embarrassing position of having exchanged his former neutrality in favor of a frankly partisan policy. Worse still, the amount of money recovered for the booty actually brought a comparatively small sum in cash but the widespread damage and desolation left throughout the river region amounted to a sum impossible of calculation. The number of petitions from refugees crowding into the lands of Spain mounted day by day and the Governor's problem became increasingly difficult. In order to retain a semblance of neutrality he required Willing to return the possessions of private individuals. Willing complied reluctantly and with bad grace. By May 1, Gálvez was able to make a final settlement of these disturbing accounts. Captain Fergusson, his mission completed, took the *Sylph* down river.

The respite from British threats was but temporary, however. Soon another naval unit, the *Hound,* under Captain Joseph Nunn, appeared before New Orleans to be joined shortly by a second. Meanwhile, Willing was angrily pressing Pollock for a reckoning on the sales of the booty and demanding large sums of money to refit the captured *Rebecca.* His men were becoming a raucous nuisance in the streets. Their brawling, rude conduct very soon disgusted the Spanish and French inhabitants and daily increased the danger of incidents that could bring about a diplomatic crisis. Gálvez strengthened the defenses of the post but knew that they were in no condition to withstand an attack should the English move in force against the city. His men were few and his posts along the river were in a precarious position. Although he maintained an appearance of arrogant assurance toward the English, the young commander was seriously worried over the possible consequences of Willing's Expedition.

From a practical military point of view the raid had only served to arouse the whole country east of the river and in the West Floridas against the Americans. It had verified the shrewd British Indian agent's statements about the barbarity of the "Long Knives." It had aroused an increasing enmity against the Spanish, who received the Americans in New Orleans. It had strengthened English surveillance over the river traffic and thereby weakened the possibility of getting badly needed supplies to Clark in Illinois. Finally, it had served the dangerous purpose of forcing the British to take strong action in reinforcing Pensacola, Mobile and all the posts east of the river.

By May, the Willing group had become so obnoxious that Gálvez felt compelled to write to the Congress of his "critical situation with his neighbors in consequence of the protection and favors shown by him to Captain Willing and his party."[17] When he wrote this he was only too well aware that neither the city of New Orleans nor the province could be defended should the English ships in the river open fire. He knew that if the English closed the lake passage and shut off the badly needed supplies that were being shipped to him by order of the Spanish Court for aid to the Americans he would be powerless to oppose the move. It was with no idea of material gain, therefore, but in the belief that a show of firmness might avert a British attack that he demanded an oath of neutrality from every English subject in New Orleans under penalty of leaving the province immediately in case of refusal. He required the same oath of all Americans in the city. A few English elected to leave. Captain Nunn of the *Hound* protested the order, likewise, at Natchez, McGillivray, the clever half-breed Creek whose word was law among the tribes of the powerful Creek nation of the Southeast. But the captain of the *West Florida*, an English vessel of war cruising the lakes adjoining the post of St. John seized two Spanish boats on Lake Ponchartrain and refused to release them until the Governor rescinded his order. He furthermore warned that no Spanish boat would be permitted to pass anywhere "that the *West Florida* was cruising."

This action of the English officer served to sharpen the fervent hope that Gálvez had secretly held from the beginning of his duty in Louisiana, that Spain would declare open war against Great Britain. Might the open insult to the flag of Spain in Spanish waters bring about the long-desired event? The young Governor was becoming tired of the innuendoes and false courtesies of diplomacy.

4.

As Willing's stay lengthened into months, the cost of the daily maintenance of his party slowly drained away the now slender resources of Oliver Pollock. He and Willing, it will be recalled, had ceased to be on speaking terms. Gálvez was once more called upon for a large loan. The 15,948 pesos were badly needed to build up the defenses of Louisiana, but Gálvez lent them in order to fill out and arm a captured English ship for the journey up the river. The expensive outlay proved to be an utter waste, however, because by the time the vessel was ready to transport the Willing party and valuable war supplies sent from Havana, the British had established an effective patrol over all river traffic.

Willing himself was afraid to make the return journey by river. He knew that Bernardo de Gálvez alone stood between him and reprisals from the enemies he had made. He asked permission to take his party back through Spanish territory where he would be under the protection of the Spanish commanders at the posts along the way. Gálvez, who by this time had no reason to trust Willing's promise to refrain from raids, coldly refused the request. It fell to Pollock to make arrangements for returning Willing to Philadelphia by sea. But this would entail a further loan from Gálvez to prepare the captured English ship for the long voyage. Rechristened the *Morris*, she was loaded with ammunition, powder, muskets, food, blankets and medicines for the Congress from a large supply sent from Spain by way of Mexico. With the unwilling Willing aboard, she set sail for Philadelphia. But she never reached her destination. She became a British prize, and Willing a prisoner of war, later to be exchanged.

Before she sailed, Gálvez, eager to rid himself of the unruly Americans, had acceded to the request of Captain Robert George to lead the men "lately commanded by Willing" north through Spanish territory but he made the Americans swear "to follow the route directly and not to offend or bother during the journey any English subjects, neither their possessions nor their persons, but on the contrary to treat them with the same consideration as if they were Spanish subjects."[18] George and his party took this oath at once. They were furnished a formal safe-conduct to travel north by way of Opelousas, Nachitoches and the Arkansas. Pollock authorized them to draw against him for the cost of supplies they should purchase at the posts along their route. The sums they drew serve to record their progress northward. Thus:

Jan. 8, 1779	$800 at Arkansas
Jan. 21,	$708 and 1 ryal; from the Spanish
	Aux Arcs [Ozarks];
Feb. 4, 1779,	$700 and
	$1000; and on
Feb. 25,	$200 [19]

Willing's stay in New Orleans was disastrous for Pollock, whose fortune was wiped out. His expedition had serious consequences for George Rogers Clark, also, because the British, alerted, had now almost completely closed the river and endangered the vital "Service of Supply." Clark's opinion of Willing was no more flattering than Pollock's. To his friend, de Leyba, the Spanish Governor of St. Louis, he wrote November 6, 1778:

"The intelligence from New Orleans is bad. I don't doubt you have before this been made Acquainted with it. I am now Convinced of what I have long Suspected the bad Conduct of an American Officer in that Quarter. When plunder is the prevailing passion of any Body of Troops whether Great or Small, their Country can Expect but Little service from them. Which I am sorry to find was Too Much the Case with the Party I allud [sic] to. Floriday [sic] on the Mississippi Might have been good Subjects to the States if proper Measures had been taken and probably saved the Expence of a Campain [sic]. I should be happy hereafter to find that I am mistaken on this head."[20]

In 1779, Gálvez would have reason to agree with these sentiments when he faced the strengthened English in open warfare.

FOOTNOTES

[1]Pollock to the Commercial Committee, April 1 and May 7, 1778, cited in James, *Pollock*, pp. 126-127 and 127 footnote. Royal approval was granted August 25.

[2]Pollock to the Congress, May 7, 1778. Extract. A.G.I., Cuba, 2370. Cited in Caughey, *Gálvez*. pp. 123-124.

[3]Jacinto Panis to the King, February 15, 1776 and Unzaga's endorsement; A.G.I., Santo Domingo, 2548.

[4]Bernardo de Gálvez to José de Gálvez, May 20, 1779; A.G.I., Cuba, 2230, no. 284, draft.

[5]James Alexander Robertson, ed., *Louisiana Under the Rule of Spain, France and the United States* (2 vols., Cleveland, 1911) I, 247. Cited in Caughey, *Gálvez*. p. 84.

[6]Pollock to Gálvez, December 18, 1779; A.G.I., Cuba, p. 112. Copy.

[7]Bernardo de Gálvez to José de Gálvez, April 30, 1785; A.G.I., Santo Domingo, 1243.

[8]Pollock to Caron de Let (Carondelet), May 3, 1792; A.G.I., Cuba, p. 184, Copy; also in A.G.S., La Guerra Moderna, Legajo 7235, Folio 401, no. 6.

[9]Caughey, *Gálvez*, p. 102.

[10]United States of America, *Journals of the Continental Congress, 1774-1783* (25 vols., Washington, 1904-1922), X. 275. Cited in Caughey, *Gálvez*, p. 106.

[11]Petition of Fourteen Americans, February 2, 1778; A.G.I., Cuba, p. 191.

[12]Testamentos de las familias Americanas; A.G.S., Guerra Moderna, Legajo 6912.

[13]Caughey, *Gálvez*, p. 110.

[14]Proclamation of Gálvez, March 3, 1778; A.G.S., Guerra Moderna, Legajo 6912; also in A.G.I., Santo Domingo, Legajo 2596.

[15]Bernardo de Gálvez to José de Gálvez, March 11, 1778; A.G.S., Guerra Moderna, Legajo 6912; also in A.G.I., Santo Domingo, Legajo 2596.

[16]Willing to Pollock, May 30, 1778; A.G.I., Cuba, p. 2370.

[17]*Letters of Members of the Continental Congress*, Edmund Cody Burnett, ed. (5 vols., Washington, 1921-1931,) III, 494 n. Cited in Caughey, *Gálvez*, p. 121.

[18]Gálvez to George, August 18, 1778; A.G.S., Guerra Moderna, Legajo 6912; also in A.G.I., Cuba, p. 2370.

[19]Drafts drawn against Oliver Pollock; A.G.I., Cuba, p. 2370. Copies with Pollock's certificate of the reason for their non-acceptance, A.G.I., Cuba, p. 122-1. Also in A.G.S., Guerra Moderna, Legajo 6912 and Legajo 7235, años 1780-1794.

[20]Clark to Leyba, November 6, 1778, A.G.I., Cuba. I.

CHAPTER XIV

1.

Following numerous insults to the flag of Spain along the Great River and in the lakes near New Orleans, Governor Gálvez sent one of the keenest officers of his staff, Major Jacinto Panis, to Pensacola with the dual mission of demanding redress and ascertaining the state of the defenses of that stronghold. In conformity with the diplomatic niceties of the day he furnished his messenger with a personal present of white sugar and a cask of rare wine for Governor Chester. Panis was instructed to press for greater "politeness" on the part of the British and to take up the question of English traders among the Indians in Spanish territory, their presence constituting a growing danger to the tranquility of the region west of the river. He was also to bring to Chester's attention the insulting activities of the British corsair on Lake Pontchartrain. As for the spying aspect of Panis' mission, from the beginning of hostilities between England and her colonies, Spain had issued orders through the Minister of the Indies, José de Gálvez, the Governor's uncle, to use secret agents in an Intelligence Service to gather all possible information relative to British strength and the progress of the war. These secret agents operated out of Havana and New Orleans.

Panis arrived in Pensacola on the 11th of March, 1778, and entered into the business of his secret instructions at once. Outwardly he was a young and attractive officer interested ostensibly in one object, the presentation of his Governor's case for more "politeness" in dealing with the numerous cases annoying both Gálvez and Chester. He dined and wined with various officers of the British staff. But all the while he was making a complete study of all fortifications, enumerating troops and their dispositions for defense and attack, checking supplies available for war as well as for sustaining the post, studying closely the policy of the British toward their Indian allies, marking the movement of ships of war, making maps of the approaches by land and sea. When he took his leave he bore with him a return gift from Chester to Gálvez and a complete plan of Pensacola.

On the return journey to New Orleans he arrived in Mobile in time to hear of the depredations of an American, Captain James Willing, in the course of an expedition down the Mississippi and to find Mobile preparing feverishly to defend itself in the event of attack. Some of the officers at the post were convinced that he knew all about Willing's activities and plans before he left New Orleans.[1] One of them, Major Stevenson, passed on his suspicion to the English commander at Manchac in a letter telling of Panis' visit. Panis could not fail to note this sceptical attitude and it made him uneasy. But the civility and attention of his friends among the officers was scrupulously correct and they accepted his disclaimer of knowledge, in appearance at least.

Panis arrived back in New Orleans in July, to the great relief of Gálvez as well as his young wife. Both the Governor and Señora de Panis had had cause enough for worry, Gálvez because he was badly understaffed at the time when Willing's party was causing annoying incidents almost daily, and Señora de Panis because her love for her husband and her tragic past only emphasized her growing uneasiness over the explosive atmosphere of the city. Major Panis' mission to Pensacola proved of the greatest possible value to Gálvez a year later; Panis' maps then became the invaluable basis of the planned attack against the British stronghold. In his reports to Madrid, Gálvez gave full and generous recognition to this capable officer.

Willing's activities led not only to a hurried request from Governor Chester for reinforcements for Pensacola, Mobile and the posts all along the English side of the Mississippi but also to heightened tension among the settlers over the tightening of the ties between the British and their Indian allies, the Creeks, Chickasaws and Seminoles. Colonel John Stuart, the British Commissioner among the tribes, was sending outrunners and agents with *Platicas* to urge the various clans to fight, plunder and destroy every boat or party of Americans on sight. Runners began crossing the river into Spanish territory, ferreting out and destroying all American refugees living or trading there. The strategic points at the mouth of the Yazoo and the Cliffs of Prudhomme and Margot were most perilous spots for the capture of boats, Spanish or American, coming down the river. The post of Manchac was strengthened and orders were issued for the construction of a chain of forts and batteries along the entire upper reaches of the Mississippi. More British naval units were assigned to guard the lower river against boats running supplies into New Orleans.

Gálvez received intelligence regularly concerning the new British military and naval dispositions. His own assets in terms of trained fighting men were dismayingly inadequate. His militia was fully occupied with the protection of the outlying posts, scattered all the way from St. Louis to Belize. Urgent messages went forth to the Minister of the Indies requesting the immediate despatch of trained veterans for the defense of New Orleans. Meanwhile, hasty entrenchments were thrown up along the waterfront behind which the defenders of the city could gain some slight protection in case of a direct assault. Strategically, what Gálvez needed most was the ability to protect traffic on the great waterway. To that end he ordered three small gunboats to be built, each to mount an eighteen- or twenty-pounder cannon. And here, his tactical sense is demonstrated, for, he pointed out in a letter to his uncle, José de Gálvez, only boats with a very shallow draft and easy maneuverability could be of service along the shallow, winding reaches of the river. Ordinary naval craft would be at a great disadvantage in such waters.

Three specially designed gunboats, manned with well-trained river boatmen could take position at any desired point along the steep river banks and pick off a more clumsy adversary almost at will. They would be capable of navigating the tortuous bayous and small river mouths either under sail or with oars and they would have the added advantage of being able to get supplies and ammunition into or out of any Spanish post very quickly.

Gálvez's spies traversed the routes between Belize, Baton Rouge, Mobile and Natchez by land and by water, marked the well-travelled forest paths of Britain's Indian allies and reported the changing defense plans of the English almost as soon as they occurred. Recruits came in from among the American refugees in Spanish territory. By July 1779, Gálvez had an accession of some 106 men from the Canaries and some 100 from Mexico. Nominally he had some 500 regulars and 10 artillerymen, but half of these, although they were entitled to the pay of regulars, were not combat veterans but raw recruits sent out to him in response to his urgent plea. Among his volunteers were Americans, Frenchmen, Germans, Canary Islanders, Free Negroes and Mulattoes. These men were wholly untrained and came forward only in an emergency. Then he had a far-flung militia, the trained backbone of his forces, under his small, professional corps of Spanish officers. It was a curiously motley army that he began whipping into the loyal fighting force that later he led to a most astounding victory up the length of the Mississippi and then in the Southeast. After his remarkable campaign, the despatches he sent back to Spain cited many of these men for honors for valorous action in combat, among them several mulatto officers, a number of French Acadians and many young American volunteers.

The first, and apparently the only tangible, result of Major Panis' mission at this time was an order from Governor Chester to Colonel John Stuart, the Indian Commissioner, to command his men, then situated at the Wolf River, to confine their spying activities to the

Mississippi Provincial Archives, Spanish Dominion, 1: 299

Americans and refrain in future from molesting any Spaniards engaged in traffic upon the Mississippi. This was surely only a token order because its execution was dependent upon many tribal factors beyond Stuart's power to control. Gálvez was not disposed to rely solely upon Governor Chester in this matter. To minimize the danger of Indian hostility he distributed presents among the Indians on the Spanish side of the river, the Choctaws and a few lesser clans around the Spanish Aux Arcs (Ozarks), those located at Pointe Coupee and at the Arkansas post. Cruzat at St. Louis, with the cooperation of de Leyba and Vigo, acted to hold the Indians in the upper river to Spain by employing them in trade and in the courier service from village to village.

2.

Suffering through the long, hard winter of 1778-9 had been intense in the Illinois country. Clark's force was rapidly disintegrating from wholesale desertions. Many of his men were anxious to get back to Kentucky where they could join their families and take up the task of supplying food and cabins for their own people. Land claims were beginning to deluge the whole Kentucky territory at this time and Clark's men, having claims of their own, wanted to be on the ground to protect their rights. Some of his men were deserting to the Spanish side of the river, lured by the report that quick riches were to be made in New Orleans. Many frontier settlers had lost stock for want of feed; corn commanded a prohibitive price; foodstuffs had reached famine scarcity; due to the intense cold, hunting was difficult and small game, too, had suffered in the bitter winter; ammunition for hunting was also used up. Clark's situation seemed desperate, his task of holding the Illinois country difficult in the extreme. The British now held all traffic on the Mississippi under close surveillance.

At this critical juncture Gálvez and Pollock once again sought to maintain the "Service of Supply." This time their instrument was Colonel David Rogers who had come to New Orleans as the bearer of the letter from Governor Patrick Henry to Gálvez. They managed to assist Rogers to return to St. Louis overland where he was put in possession of goods and ammunition previously consigned there by Pollock for the account of Virginia. From St. Louis, Rogers and his party made their way, unmolested, to the Falls of the Ohio only to be ambushed there by a band of Indians led by Simon Girty, the notorious "Blue-Eyed" half-breed. Out of a party of seventy only thirteen escaped, Colonel Rogers being among those who were massacred. A single boat escaped and returned to Louisville with its cargo of am-

✳ Galvez to Don Diego Josef Navarro N. Orleans 17/8/79

"I hope the nation of Choctaws, who have been aligned with the English by gifts etc. are gained in gt part to my cause. Yet this kind of people, who have offered 1000 times to take up arms in my favor, are accustomed to regard & little their faith & they go with the party that offers them more"

munition, badly needed blankets and clothing. Because the survivors of this disastrous ambush could not complete their mission, the supplies they salvaged were put immediately to use by Clark's ragged men.

Gálvez and Pollock had scraped the bottom of the barrel. Pollock's fortune and credit were at a low ebb and Gálvez was in no position to advance money from his depleted treasury. However, the leaders at St. Louis still had such complete faith in the triumvirate of Gálvez, Pollock and Clark, and in their ability to produce miracles that they continued to advance relief to the troops in Illinois. De Leyba, Vigo and Charles Gratoit honored all drafts against Pollock as they were presented. Montgomery, one of Clark's officers, drew two drafts against Pollock, one for $6,400; another for $12,000. John Todd, another of Clark's officers, purchased provisions for his troops costing $30,000. Knowing how great the need for supplies was at this time and how hard-pressed Pollock found himself, one of his friends rushed into the breech and forwarded Pollock's son a large bateau loaded with merchandise and taffia with instructions that he "should give all assistance and succor to any army or detachment belonging to the United States of America which he might meet with on the Mississippi."[2] In taking this action Pollock's friend was defying the English patrol over the river.

Relations between Spain and England were now rising to the crescendo of tension that was to result inevitably in a declaration of war. Belatedly the news reached St. Louis that the independence of the United States had been proclaimed at New Orleans; that war with England was expected any day; that an expedition, led by Gálvez, was preparing and about to set out against Manchac, Natchez, Mobile and Pensacola. Pollock, though no soldier, was happy over the prospect of being a participant in the coming campaign and recruited some six other Americans to serve under the young Spanish Governor. In a letter to the Continental Congress he wrote confidently: "I make no doubt that he [Gálvez] will soon reduce the British Troops, Tories and Savages, in this part of the World."[3] The news of preparations for war, coupled with a growing admiration for the abilities of the Governor of Louisiana had a tonic effect throughout the valley, especially significant when it is borne in mind that only some two months earlier Washington had put in writing: "If Britain should be able to make a vigorous campaign in America this summer, [1779] in the present depreciation of our money, scantiness of supplies, want of virtue and want of exertion 'tis hard to say what may be the consequence."[4] George Rogers Clark was fired with new determination to go against Detroit, the heart of British strength in the Northwest.

In view of the outright aid and the military support so soon to be thrown into the American Cause in the Floridas and on the Mississippi, it is difficult to understand the curious lack of knowledge among Americans of America's forgotten ally, Spain, in the years of the young nation's greatest crisis. The same holds true for the one figure who, above all others, represents and personifies the role of Spain, Bernardo de Gálvez. During the five years of his contribution, of his friendly liaison between the Spanish Court of Carlos III and the American Government, he at no time received the courtesy of a formal acknowledgement of thanks, not even the courtesy of a response to the letters he addressed to the Congress. We are aware of what we have chosen to call the discourtesy offered our representative, John Jay, in not being openly and formally received at the Court of Madrid, but we strangely have overlooked the discourtesy suffered by Governor Gálvez, the representative of Spain, over a long period of time. But for the friendship of his two American colleagues, Pollock and Clark, his endeavors in behalf of the young, new nation might have been lost in the mists of History. The storm signals of open war between Spain and England were flying in June 1799.

3.

On the 13th of July, a significant group of men made their way through the hot crowded streets of New Orleans to a meeting in the Council Chamber of the Governor of Louisiana. As each man took his seat it must have dawned upon him, glancing about at his companions, that this was no ordinary gathering. Captain Cruzat was there from his post at St. Louis; Captain Juan Delavillebeuvre had come from the southern posts adjoining the routes to Pensacola. Also present were Captain Alexander Coussot from the Arkansas district, and Captains Pedro Josef Favrot, Hilario de Estenoy, Joaquin de Blanca, Manuel de Nava and Martín Mozun, all commanding district posts in the province. The senior officers of Louisiana were already seated in the Chamber; Colonel Manuel Gonzalez and Lieutenant Colonels Estevan Miro and Pedro Piernas, both highly trained and experienced in the difficult business of dealing with the various tribes in the western and northern posts of the province. There too waited Captain Jacinto Panis, Adjutant Major of the Louisiana Regiment, lately returned from a second secret mission to the British stronghold of Pensacola. He was to act as secretary for the meeting.

When all were assembled, Bernardo de Gálvez arose and addressed them in grave tones. This was a "Junta de Guerra," a staff meeting of war. He told them that there had been many indications that Spain would soon cast aside her cloak of neutrality, that messages had lately been intercepted revealing England's intention of making war on the province of Louisiana; that Manchac was now manned by a body of four-hundred trained German veterans, that the full plan for war against Louisiana had been revealed in an intercepted letter from Elias Durnford to William Horn at Natchez. Soon the whole force of the English from Montreal to Pensacola would descend upon the province in a mass attack upon the principal objective, the city of New Orleans. Hordes of savages controlled by Sir William Johnstone, British Agent to the Iroquois, would combine with those of Montreal and join the Indians of John Stuart in the south in a sweeping assault. Regular British troops at Detroit and Pensacola would take part in the campaign. Such was the situation Gálvez outlined to his "Junta de Guerra." With his inimitable manner of impressing his listeners, it is easy to visualize the gravity of the faces of the men in the Chamber when he asked: "Gentlemen what do you advise?"[5] The answer was divided. Some favored the defensive, others the offensive. Gálvez listened and kept his own counsel. He had a plan of his own in mind.

So far as New Orleans knew on that July day, war had not yet been declared. It was not until July 17, that news of the declaration reached Havana. However, the Spanish Government had previously, on the 18th of May, sent out word to all the Colonies that war would be declared on June 21. Word did not actually reach Governor Gálvez until early August. (The reader will be reminded that the events here recounted did not take place in an era of virtually instantaneous communication.) By that time the young commander had his plan of attack well under way. He was ready to begin his campaign. As soon as the news came to him from Navarro, Captain-General of Cuba, he quietly mapped his personal strategy for insuring the loyalty of the inhabitants of the province. Navarro had communicated, in addition to the declaration of war, notice of Gálvez's appointment as Governor of Louisiana, for hitherto he had served in the capacity of Acting-Governor. With his acute sense of dramatic timing, Gálvez withheld the news of the declaration until his forces were ready to move against England's river posts. He also had in mind the proper moment to announce his promotion. This was not the moment, so he made no proclamation.

The hour arrived when all was ready and the inhabitants of the city were called to assemble. Gálvez announced to them that England had declared Spain to be an enemy, that the two nations were at that moment at war "in consequence of the recognition of the Independence of America." He told them he expected an attack upon New Orleans and explained the weak state of the province in view of the strength England was prepared to throw against it. With characteristic

Collell to Galvez 11/8/79 Galveztown
"On 11/8/79 2 large vessels loaded with food & a coy of Waldeckers passed through, allegedly to relieve the old garrison but then went back empty" Miss. Prov Arch 1: 292

simplicity he spoke of his promotion to the governorship of the province. As a youth on the Indian frontier of Nueva Vizcaya, when campaigning against the Apaches of Mesculero, he had early discovered the art of arousing the enthusiasm and loyalty of his followers. Now he made an appeal to the Louisianians which was a masterpiece of humility and dedication.

His hearers responded instantly and wholeheartedly in an outburst of patriotic loyalty and devotion. Juan Antonio Gayarré, head of the Commissary for War, reported his words at a later date as follows:

> "I cannot avail myself of my Commission without previously swearing before the Cabildo that I shall defend the province; but, though I am disposed to shed the last drop of my blood for Louisiana and for my King, I cannot take an oath which I may be exposed to violate, because I do not know whether you will help me in resisting the ambitious designs of the English. What do you say? Shall I take the oath of Governor? Shall I swear to defend Louisiana?"[6]

Thunderous applause greeted Gálvez. The deeply stirred people responded: "Fear not taking your oath of office, for the defense of Louisiana, and for the service of the King we tender you our lives, and we should say our fortunes, if we had any remaining." Once long before, on another American frontier, a similar spontaneous demonstration had gladdened his heart when his exhausted and starving soldiers had sworn to follow him even though "they be compelled to eat stones; they would follow him to their death." This is the stuff of heroes! This soaring, spiritual quality is peculiarly an attribute of the young and fearless. Here is revealed the vivid personality of a born leader. George Rogers Clark, speaking to the Indians assembled at Kaskaskia, had the same quality. It is not surprising that Oliver Pollock was proud to serve in the coming campaign as Aide-de-Camp to the young commander and viewed the outcome with confidence.

Older members of Gálvez's staff all recommended the immediate concentration of defense at New Orleans, fortification of the waterfront, strengthening of the fort at Bayon St. Jean and an urgent call to Havana for the despatch of additional trained troops. Captain Manuel de Nava suggested that the commanders of outlying posts be ordered to surrender on the best terms available should they be overwhelmed by large forces. It was Lieutenant-Colonel Estavan Miro who offered the bolder advice to construct four redoubts below Manchac to command the river above New Orleans. The powerful English fort could then be attacked quickly and possibly taken by surprise; in case of an attack upon New Orleans the same troops could come quickly to its defense, by way of the Iberville. Miro was confident that a small force of some 100 white infantrymen, 100 blacks and 50 white cavalrymen could be raised in the colony.[7]

Gálvez, previously experienced as a frontier commander, understood better than most of his staff the value of the surprise attack. Knowing full well the British plan to overwhelm the province with the large numbers of men at their disposition in the North and South, he realized that, once such forces were assembled and on the move, Louisiana would be impossible to defend. New Orleans would fall and the whole length of the Mississippi, with the commerce of both banks, would be cut off. He resolved to use his slender forces in a swift campaign before the English in the North and South could effect a juncture. In the short space of time between the "Junta de Guerra" and the news of the declaration of war, he appointed Juan Antonio Gayarre as Commissary of War and gave him secret orders for the speedy collection of all possible supplies; he was to commandeer extra boats to add to the Governor's small fleet of gunboats and load them with sufficient food, medicines, ammunition and artillery. Having set the opening of the campaign for August 23, Gálvez issued a proclamation, calling for another assembly of the inhabitants of the city.

Fate intervened at this point. Three days before the date for the assembly, the 18th of August, New Orleans and the immediate vicinity were struck by the most violent hurricane ever to visit the lower Mississippi. In three short hours, all that had been so carefully prepared was lost. Boats were sunk with all supplies on board; all vessels in the river were battered or sunk at their moorings; fields were flooded and foodstuffs ruined; houses in the city were destroyed; householders fled with their women and children to whatever high ground offered safety from the lashing winds and surging waters of the river; the laboriously constructed dirt trenches and walled embankments newly built to defend the city were washed away, leaving the streets a muddy.chaos; merchants surveyed their ruined stocks in warehouses either demolished or submerged by the swirling waters.

Buildings and homes along the river were lost in the whirlpool of wind and waters; cattle and domestic fowls were drowned. Men were carried away or injured by the tumultuous winds in the tragic battle to save their few possessions. For a distance of leagues the countryside was a scene of desolation and destruction. Gálvez described the catastrophe in vivid and colorful language in a letter to his uncle José de Gálvez, Minister of the Indies:

> "For leagues destruction and ruin, all means of livelihood gone, trees flattened, men stunned, their women and children driven into the open country at the mercy of the elements the earth inundated and the river submerging all equally with my resources, my help and my hopes. . . ."[8]

Such was the catastrophe which had befallen the people of New Orleans when they assembled on the appointed day to hear their Governor. When Gálvez, with a defiant courage that was communicated instantly to his audience, disclosed his plans for a speedy campaign against the English forts on the river and called for volunteers to march on Manchac, they rallied to his challenge with shouts that "they would help him defend the province with their lives" and, yet again "we would say our fortunes if we had any remaining."

Unfortunately, the worst effect of the hurricane was limited to the vicinity of New Orleans, so that the heavily defended English forts were spared. This made Gálvez grimly certain that his plan for a quick attack against Manchac must be carried out with even greater despatch than he had calculated before the disaster. Should the English take advantage of the weakened condition of his defenses by a sudden descent upon New Orleans, he would be at their mercy. Preparations for the campaign were accordingly stepped up to a feverish pace. Boats were assembled from points not struck by the hurricane. Four boats that had been sunk were raised from the river bed and loaded with the only ten cannon that remained. By superhuman effort, in less than a week's time, Gálvez was ready. His plan of operations called for a dual approach to his objective, one by a flotilla up the river under the command of Lieutenant Julian Alvarez, the other by a column proceeding overland under his own command. The ten cannon, one a twenty-four pounder, five seventy-eights and four fours, were assigned to Alvarez, the sole artillery officer, whom Gálvez described as a soldier of much zeal and energy notwithstanding the fact that he was at this time very ill. Gálvez did not neglect to make all possible provision for the protection of New Orleans. Lieutenant-Colonel Don Pedro Piernas arrived in the city August 26, after a fast journey from his post and assumed command of town militia. Don Martin Navarro assumed responsibility for the civil government.

On the morning of the 27th, the little army set out, the Governor going ahead to enlist possible volunteers from the German and Acadian settlements. In direct command under Gálvez was Colonel Manuel Gonzalez and second to him, Colonel Estevan Miro. Acting as major of the expedition was Captain Jacinto Panis, adjutant-major of the permanent troops of the Louisiana Regiment. The motley array was composed of 170 veterans, 330 recruits newly arrived from Mexico and the Canary Islands, 200 carabiniers, 60 militiamen, and habitants, 80 free blacks and mulattoes and seven American volunteers. These last included Oliver Pollock serving as aide-de-camp to Gálvez.

The total force of 847 men were "of all sorts nationalities and colors, but without a single engineer and with one artillery officer very sick. They had to march through thick woods and over difficult trails, without tents and other supplies considered indispensible, but they marched on as though to a happy adventure."⁹ Gálvez reported to his uncle, José de Gálvez, that along the way, from the German settlement, Acadia and the Opeluzas, Atacapas and "Punta Cortada" he had been able to add 600 more men of all classes, races and colors, including, in addition, 160 Indians from the vicinity of this last, bringing his strength to a total of some 1427 men. However, the hardships of rapid marches and illness had reduced his number by a third before Manchac was ever reached. It took just eleven days to cover the trek of thirty-five leagues. In order to prevent word of his approach reaching the British garrison, Gálvez took the precaution of arresting one of their Indian agents, Bethune by name, and his companion. Bethune who had gone into Bayon Saint Jean on business, innocent of the state of war between Spain and England, was much astonished and wrote at once to Gálvez and a few days later to Colonel Piernas asking the reason for his detention.¹⁰

It was August 31, before the English commander at Manchac began to be suspicious of Gálvez's intentions, and September 2, before he became certain. Gálvez's own troops were nearly all in complete ignorance of their objective until they came in actual sight of Fort Manchac on the 6th. Then he revealed to them that Spain was at war with England and that he had been ordered to attack their posts along the Mississippi. In spite of their long, exhausting march, they were as enthusiastic over the approaching clash as if they were just taking the road. Only a month earlier, Lieutenant-Colonel Dickson, commanding at Manchac, had ordered his engineer to construct a redoubt on the Watts and Flowers Plantation at Baton Rouge in the belief that the post could not be held against a rumored American attack. So when he learned of the advance of Gálvez he decided to retire behind the defenses at that place.¹¹ Only a small force was left at Manchac to fight off the Spaniards in a delaying action as long as possible.

On the night of the 6th of September, Gálvez stationed his regulars to the north of Fort Manchac to prevent any reinforcements from coming in from Baton Rouge. At first dawn, under cover of the thick mists that hung over the river and through the heavy forest of trees, he gave the order to the militia under Gilbert Antonio de St. Maxent to carry the fort by assault. St. Maxent was the brother of the wife of Gálvez's predecessor, Governor Unzaga, a member of one of the leading French families of New Orleans. Gálvez reported later to his uncle, José de Gálvez, how happy and proud St. Maxent and his militia were to be chosen for the assault. Gilbert Antonio de St. Maxent was the first man to enter the fort. In the obscurity of the misty dawn one officer and five men of the garrison escaped, much to the chagrin of the battle-proud militiamen; one soldier was killed, two officers and eighteen soldiers were made prisoners of war;[12] altogether a small but surprising victory and a valuable one for Gálvez. It gave confidence to his green troops whom their leader had the opportunity to observe for the first time under the test of the battle. The militia had behaved with gallantry. They were later recommended for their discipline and valor.

FOOTNOTES

[1]Stevenson to Patrick Morgan, April 7, 1778; A.G.I., Cuba, 2351.

[2]"Clark MSS," Virginia State Archives, Auditor's Reports, p. 46. Cited in James, *Pollock*, pp. 189-190.

[3]James, *Pollock*, p. 190.

[4]John Jay, Correspondence and Public Papers, H. P. Johnson, ed. (New York, 1890-93) I, 210. Cited in James, *Pollock*, p. 190.

[5]Gálvez to junta de Guerra, New Orleans, July 13, 1779; A.G.S., Guerra Moderna, Legajo 6912, no. 20; also in A.G.I., Cuba, 112 (containing a list of officers present).

[6]Charles Gayarré, *History of Louisiana* (2nd ed., 4 vols., New Orleans, 1879) III, 124; Manuel Serrano y Sanz, ed., *Documentos Historicos de la Florida y la Luisiana, Siglos XVI al XVIII* (Madrid, 1912), pp. 345-346. Cited in Caughey, *Gálvez*, pp. 152-153.

[7]Cuaghey, *Gálvez*, p. 151.

[8]Bernardo de Gálvez to José de Gálvez, October 16, 1779; A.G.S., Guerra Moderna, Legajo 6912. Copy.

[9]Bernardo de Gálvez to José de Gálvez, October 18, 1779; *ibid.*, copy.

[10]Bethune to Bernardo de Gálvez, August 27, 1779; A.G.S., Guerra Moderna, Legajo 6912, copy. Bethune to Piernas, August 29, 1779; A.G.I., Cuba, 192.

[11]Dickson's and Graham's statements, September 22, 1779, *Louisiana Historical Quarterly* XII (1929) pp. 263-264.

[12]Bernardo de Gálvez to José de Gálvez, October 18, 1779; A.G.S., Guerra Moderna, Legajo 6912.

CHAPTER XV

1.

Capture of Baton Rouge presented more difficulties than the taking of Manchac. This fort was much better situated for defense and would take a bloody toll of lives if it were to be won by direct assault. Gálvez knew well the conditions under which his mixed army had been recruited; he realized that news of heavy losses might have the most adverse effect, resulting in wholesale desertions; his men would return to their needy families desperately struggling to survive in the aftermath of the hurricane; he might easily find himself with no troops to complete the conquest of England's Mississippi strong-points. The use of frontier forces, with no tactical training, would be tested for the first time when he attacked Baton Rouge because his training as a tactician had been acquired in French and Spanish schools and Baton Rouge presented very definitely a problem in military tactics. Could the lessons learned be applied successfully with green troops? He dared not risk an assault which would exact a high price in dead and wounded. But he was in the position of having to attack and capture the post quickly before his army melted away.

He described the situation in a letter to Navarro in Cuba and in his later report to José de Gálvez.[1] Dickson was strongly placed at Baton Rouge; the fort was surrounded by a ditch of eighteen-feet wide and nine-feet deep; inside this ditch was an earthen wall enclosed within a formidable wooden palisade; Dickson's armament consisted of eighteen cannon as against Gálvez's ten; he had a garrison of four hundred regulars, reinforced by some hundred and fifty settlers and armed Negroes. In spite of the enthusiasm of his cocky, confident militiamen, who now believed that no English fort could withstand them, Gálvez knew that only a breach in the walls, effected by his artillery and followed by a quick surprise attack could ensure victory without much bloodshed. He considered the strength of attackers and defenders; though the English had eighteen cannon, his own ten were of greater caliber; their veteran troops were over 400 in number, his own only 384 though he had in addition 400 peasants, Indians and Negroes, without discipline or subordination; the English had support from people of this same sort. He had only 14 artillerymen. On the whole, he considered his forces to be definitely inferior to the well-entrenched troops in the fort. He wrote his uncle that he had been able to intercept assistance coming from Pensacola and from Natchez and he called captured Manchac "key to their establishments." He believed that Baton Rouge would fall within two months if he could keep it under siege that long but he would be risking the incidence of sickness among his men and an exhaustion of the supplies, which had been gathered haphazardly because of the hurricane. He would also be gambling against the disintegration of his army.

He rejected the idea of a siege. After scouting the layout of the fort he ordered the digging of a trench that would permit him to bring his artillery into action. The work would have to be done as quietly as possible, to avoid drawing the attention of the English to the spot. In order to accomplish this operation successfully the first move was to divert attention elsewhere. The place chosen for this purpose was a grove of trees reaching out toward the fort far enough to afford the men cover while they worked on a trench from which Gálvez would ostensibly spring to the attack.

On the night of September 20, a detachment of white militiamen, black troops and Indians were sent out to this grove. They were divided into three groups, one to chop down trees, one to throw up earthworks and the third to keep a continuous fire upon the fort as if to cover the two working-parties. The work was to be done openly with the express purpose of attracting the attention of the fort's defenders. The whole operation was a tactical success, the plan of a tactician who had learned his lesson well in Europe. The English fell into the baited trap and fired all night into the grove of trees without wounding a single man. Meanwhile, the trench which permitted Gálvez to bring his artillery into action on the other side of the fort, where the planned assault would take place, was dug without molestation. While the English kept up their bombardment, Gálvez's few artillerymen and veterans worked quietly and feverishly installing their cannon in a garden within musket shots of the walls. When daylight broke the English commander discovered he had been tricked and ordered heavy fire to be directed against the Spanish troops. It was too late. Both guns and gunners were too well sheltered to be reached.

At 5:45 o'clock on the morning of September 21, Gálvez gave the command to open fire. For three hours and a half, Don Julian Alvarez kept up a heavy bombardment of the fort. The destruction was so complete that at three o'clock in the afternoon two officers were sent out to Gálvez to propose a truce. Dickson was required to surrender not only the fort of Baton Rouge but also Fort Pan Mure at Natchez with its garrison of eighty grenadiers. The terms of capitulation granted Dickson twenty-four hours to bury his dead, after which "they [the garrison] sallied forth with all the honors of war for 500 paces with 375 men of the regular troops; surrendered their arms, gave up their flags and became prisoners of war while the habitants and Negroes were freely permitted to return to their homes after giving their promise of neutrality. The regulars were put in the custody of four cadets and the main body of the Spanish army then entered the fort and took possession of their conquest. At the same time Captain Juan Delavillebeuvre, with fifty men, set out to occupy Fort Pan Mure de Natchez.

The fall of this stronghold without a drop of blood being shed was a particularly satisfying victory for Gálvez, because its high-protecting walls would have been difficult to penetrate. Delavillebeuvre carried with him a written order from Dickson, instructing the officer in command to hand over the fort. An officer accompanying the party carried with him a letter from Oliver Pollock addressed to the inhabitants. On October 5 he accepted the surrender of Pan Mure from Captain Forster, the English commander.

Pollock's letter was at once a guarantee that the people of Natchez would fare well under Spanish administration and a testimonial of his admiration for Governor Gálvez.

> "Col. Dickson has capitulated with Governor Gálvez and surrendered his Garrison prisoners of war, he has obliged himself to withdraw the British Forces from your Quarter, and deliver up the Fort to the Spanish Officer who goes for that purpose. The Spirit of Liberty, the protection which every American had received on this River from His Excellency Govr. Gálvez, his generous behavior towards all the Inhabitants, with the advantages which must now spring from an uninterrupted Commerce with New Orleans, where you will meet with a good market for all your Produce, and the necessary supplies for your Families, will I hope be sufficient inducements to you to render all the Services in your Power to his Catholic Majesty's Arms. There is a sufficient Force gone to reduce Pensacola [an anticipation by two years] by which you will be totally secured against the Insults of the Savages. For further particulars I refer you to my good Friend Captn. Barber the bearer hereof. . . ."[2]

Pollock's letter was evidently the first news of the declaration of war to reach Natchez. The settlers surrendered peacefully. A few days later word came to them from the commander at Pensacola, officially advising them that England was at war with Spain and that they should prepare at once for an attack on New Orleans. The leaders of the town had no recourse but to make answer that they were already constrained to take no active part in such an expedition as they had surrendered to Governor Gálvez and given their word not to bear arms against the Spanish Government.

In the meantime Gálvez's commander on another section of the river, moving with great rapidity, had cut all communications between Baton Rouge and Natchez. Carlos Grand Pre, drawing his troops from Pointe Coupee, seized upon the vital British posts located on Thompson's Creek and the Amite. Gálvez rewarded the young officer immediately by putting him in command of the district with small groups of regular troops sufficient to enforce his control.

Gálvez could now return to New Orleans with the satisfaction of a job well done in the face of the most difficult circumstances. Carlos III, in a formal notice, recognized with the "greatest happiness and satisfaction the happy success of the expedition carried out with such great spirit and despatch on the part of the Governor and his men and the great courage and valor shown by his very small company [his few troops], and the Inhabitants of the province, whose fidelity and service to the King presents a picture that is worthy of the highest praise and thanks to the community and to its commander."[3] The struggle for the Mississippi was well launched. Gálvez's leadership and his knowledge of tactical warfare had been proven. His motley army had become a body of men whose loyalty was answering. They had returned to their wives and children with little bloodshed to bring mourning upon the province. With a total loss of one man killed and two wounded, Gálvez could relax and welcome for a few short days the comfort of his own house and the ministrations of the lovely mistress of his heart.

2.

An added satisfaction was the surprising victory of Captain William Pickles, commander of the American corvette *Morris*, which, it will be recalled, was the refitted and armed *Rebecca*, that had cost Gálvez and Pollock so much worry and so heavy an outlay of money. During the hurricane the *Rebecca* had been so badly damaged that she sank at her dock. She had been raised, restored to use and now was in action on Lake Ponchartrain.

Captain Pickles cruised the lake in search of the English vessel the *West Florida* which had dominated the numerous small lakes at the mouth of the Mississippi. He finally caught up with her and closed at once. Out-gunned and out-manned, but undaunted, he called on the English commander to surrender and when the latter refused both ships opened fire. After four men on the *West Florida* had been killed, including her captain, Pickles boarded her and captured her crew. He reported his only loss succinctly:

"Brown Traitor to our Cause swimd [sic] ashore."

The Spanish report of the engagement stated:

"It is unbelievable that he should have captured it because of the disparity in the size of the ships, their armaments, etc."[4]

Captain Pickles' victory may have been "unbelievable." Nevertheless, it cost him the loss of his own vessel which was so badly damaged in the engagement that she sank alongside his capture. Loss of the *Rebecca* or *Morris*, brought about the question from Pollock as to the propriety of making use of the *West Florida* to replace her. Gálvez urged that she be used on the lakes to protect isolated settlers and boats engaged in the valuable commerce of New Orleans against further English depredations.[5] So Captain Pickles continued to cruise the lakes. He later took possession of the northern shore of Lake Ponchartrain, swearing the settlers between Bayon la Combe and the Tauchipaho River, by an oath of allegiance, to become faithful subjects (sic) of the United Independent States of North America with a complete and nonchalant disregard of his Spanish friends and the fact that he was operating in Spanish territory. He later brought some hundred- and twenty-two Indians across the lake to New Orleans and captured a prize with thirteen Negroes aboard later valued at $2,660. With scant education, he would appear to have been a man with a high standard of conduct and motivated by pure patriotism. His personal integrity stands revealed in an atrociously misspelled letter he addressed to Colonel Piernas, commanding at New Orleans:

> "I am informed that theare is a small Vesel afitting out in ye Corrutor of acrusor. I am told she is a privit proporty if so she is only fitting out to go over ye lakes to plunder ye inhabitanes, is so I could Abeen adoing of that, but its my opinion its not right I am sarten we have anumbor of frends theare, & they hav been obliged to stay thear own acct. of theare Familes & what littel proporty they had, & now we to go & take it away from them it undoubtedly will Mak them owner Inemes, in my Opinien its Ower business to make all ye frends we can, in the rume of making Inemes, if I had amind to plundored them i cout adun that sum time ago but my mining is to secure ye lakes, & take care if Enemy dont slip out of ower hands, if ower frends was to be destressed I can soon do that.
>
> I may cum across this vessel in ye night & may do hir som mischeaf dont blame me for it For I trust to none, for what trifel can be got from them is no obgect at this time, & I am shure in my own opinien that so smal a vesel, as I undorstand she is cant be own any other desire only plundering of ye inhabitanes."[6]

Gálvez was no doubt secretly hopeful that Pickles might "cum across" other "vessels in ye night" and do them "sum mischeaf." This American captain was a vast relief after the difficult, blustering Willing.

The Spaniards were also busy in the surrounding waters. At Galvestown, three Galetas and a Bergantin enroute to Pensacola were seized after having taken ammunition to Manchac. In the case of Vizente Rillieux, commander of a small Spanish ship, a victory even more spectacular than that of Captain Pickles had been won. Rillieux had sighted an English transport on its way to Manchac. Landing his small crew at a pass between the lakes, he had set his men to work chopping-down trees to screen from the men aboard the transport. Then as the ship was making its way slowly through the pass, the Spaniards blazed away when it came directly below their concealed guns, all the while keeping up such a blood-curdling racket that the English were sure they were being attacked by hundreds of men. They took fright and hastily ran below deck for cover. At this point Rillieux and his small party of some 14 Creoles jumped aboard and made the entire ship's company prisoners. "What was their surprise to find themselves numbering fifty-six soldiers of the Waldeck Regiment [German mercenaries] and ten or twelve sailors, apprehended by fourteen Creoles, the entire command of Rillieux!"[7]

The proud Waldeck Regiment of professional soldiers seems to have been fated to receive every humiliation possible in the wild western-frontier fighting. These victories on the water brought Gálvez deep satisfaction; they showed that his men could not only act with courage before the walls of English forts, but also, in individual actions, with the imagination and daring with which he was himself so well endowed. He was only too happy to bring these exploits to the attention of the Court. He put them also to good use in indicating his own reckless plan of campaign, adopted against the advice of his senior officers.

The campaign directed personally by Gálvez had exacted a heavy toll from the British in prisoners of war: 54 men, one captain and the lieutenant in command of one company; 28 men of the German Waldeck Regiment, including both officers and troops; one lieutenant-colonel with five captains, ten lieutenants and five sub-lieutenants of the 16th and 60th English regiments; one quarter-master; two commissary officers; one munitions supply officer; three sergeant-majors; 550 regulars and veterans plus unenumerated Negroes and inhabitants who were carrying arms. All were treated as honorable prisoners of war with the pay corresponding to their rank being paid to them according to the articles of war until returned to the point which had been stipulated when they surrendered.

New Orleans, crowded with prisoners of war, became a city boiling with humanity. Food supplies being short, and there being few men to guard the prisoners, Gálvez wrote to his uncle that he hoped the latter would soon be sent to Havana, to be placed under the guard of the second batallion of Spain at the earliest opportunity. Fortunately for the Governor, his friend Navarro, Captain-General of Cuba, had sent him reinforcements from the second batallion to assist in the expedition against the English forts on the river. They arrived too late to be of any help in the river campaign but they now became available and relieved Gálvez and the populace of the town when they were assigned the task of watching over the prisoners and keeping the peace. Should New Orleans be attacked by an army from Pensacola they would give added strength to the defenses.

It was the summer of 1780, before the last of the prisoners left the city for Havana by way of Vera Cruz. Some of the officers were allowed to leave for Pensacola or for England after having given their word not to take up arms against Spain until they were officially exchanged. Colonel Dickson later paid tribute to Gálvez's humane conduct toward the prisoners testifying that they were "treated with the greatest generosity and attention, not only by the officers but even the Spanish soldiers seem to take pleasure in being kind and civil to the prisoners in general."[8]

3.

Gálvez did not underestimate the effect his campaign had had upon British plans in the Mississippi. From Dickson, he received confirmation that an overall attack was to have been made upon New Orleans. His use of the strategy of a swift offense as the best form of defense had been proven correct not only in breaking England's grip on the lower river but also in frustrating the hope of a linking-up of English arms in the north with the forces in the south. His reports to the King were rich in praise for his men; the militia, particularly the Acadians who had long harbored resentment against the English for the harsh treatment received at their hands; the companies of Negroes and mulattoes who had fought with the same courage as the white troops, many individuals cited for valorous conduct under fire and for efficiency as scouts; the Indians who were, under the influence of Santiago Trascon and Joseph Sorelle from Opelousas, respected the Spanish commanders of that district and had refrained from committing the atrocities which were attributed to the Indian allies of Hamilton and Stuart; the Creoles who performed colorful exploits under Rillieux; Oliver Pollock, who served wholeheartedly as the Governor's aide-de-camp; Captain Pickles, who fought with dogged courage; all these were warmly commended in detailed records of their services. All later received citations with appropriate promotions or decorations and the thanks of King Carlos III.

But beyond any question it was to Bernardo de Gálvez that the major credit was due. In less than a month, three forts had been captured, 550 regular soldiers had been taken prisoners, eight boats had been seized. The territory gained was the richest land along the river, the people, the most intelligent and most stable engaged in the river trade. All had come under the banner of Spain. All were loyal to

Gálvez for whom they had great respect and admiration both as Governor and as a brilliant commander in the field.

But Gálvez's military and administrative ability explain his achievement only in part. It was no less due to his spiritual quality, the ability to weld together the heterogeneous groups which made up his army into one enthusiastic whole and to engage behind them the whole civilian population in a concerted effort to support his campaign, a campaign undertaken against the advice of his senior officers and in the aftermath of the most terrible disaster nature could bring against him. The real significance of his campaign was not lost on the English. Their defeat struck consternation in Pensacola and Montreal and forced a complete change of strategy.

The real consequence of this, Gálvez's first campaign, has never been recognized and properly evaluated in the histories which deal with this period. Just as Gálvez, in cooperation with Oliver Pollock, had made a contribution of great significance to the security of the United States by setting up a "Service of Supply" to George Rogers Clark, so now, a second time he had gone into action on the continent of North America in a manner that would have a profound effect upon the struggling new nation. Neither on this nor the previous occasion did the Continental Congress acknowledge its great debt to a defender and friend in the Mississippi Valley.

4.

On February 5, 1779, Leyba, the Spanish Commandant at St. Louis, wrote Gálvez: "Sixteen men, including the drummer, are all the troops I have; of the militia it is true, there are forty able to bear arms, but at this time they are all trading on the Misury."[9] St. Louis, then, was well-nigh defenseless, and so it remained while Gálvez concentrated his attention and the military strength of the province upon the conquest of the English posts on the lower Mississippi. But the Mississippi is a long, long river; while Gálvez was occupied in the south, the English in the north were building up with all haste and a tremendous outlay of money, an army of Indian allies that might swamp the small, isolated garrisons of Spaniards along the upper river and simultaneously sweep all the Illinois country into the British net. Thus Clark, too, though holding grimly to his conquest west of the Alleghenies, would be eliminated.

General Sinclair, commander of the British forces at Michillimackinak, prepared boldly and brilliantly the strategy of a campaign which, had it succeeded, would have crushed the American colonies between British naval power along the Atlantic coast and British military power on the Great River and north of the Ohio. As the army based on Canada proceeded south the army based on Pensacola would cut off the Carolinas and Georgia from sending help westward and take effective control of the English side of the Great River. At some point the two armies would effect their junction and the Americans would find themselves ringed about.

The victories of Gálvez largely destroyed the possibility of carrying out this ambitious scheme. But Sinclair did not abandon his plan to conquer the Illinois country. He was no less determined to capture St. Louis, now that Spain was openly at war with England and already making her entry into the fray with such telling effect upon British strategy. Sinclair's plan involved four distinct operations. First, a detachment of regulars and their Indian allies would make an advance against St. Louis which was expected to fall with little, if any, resistance; this body would then continue down river, reducing the Spanish posts on the west bank, one after the other. Inducements offered to stir-up enthusiasm for these operations were twofold; for the Indians, the chance to overcome their ancient enemies, the Illinois tribes; for the traders, if they assisted in the capture of the Spanish posts, the exclusive right to the rich trade along the Missouri for the following winter.[10] Sinclair's third operation, which he assigned to Captain Harry Bird, was to bring on an engagement with Clark at the Falls of the Ohio.[11] The fourth and last operation was given to a detachment descending from Fort Chicago and centering their attack on the Illinois River.[12]

Money was poured out in lavish presents to the Indian allies to insure their loyalty. The Menominees, Winnebagos and Ottawas were loaded with clothing, trinkets, blankets, guns, scalping knives and quantities of ammunition. The cost to Sinclair was high because the loss of Vincennes and Hamilton's capture had been followed by a conspicious weakening of loyalty toward the English among the tribes of the Northwest. Among Sinclair's Indians was a band of some two-hundred Sioux warriors who were, in his own words, "undebauched, addicted to war and jealously attached to His Majesty's interest." They were led by their war chief "Wabasha," the most feared and respected Indian throughout the Northwest. To the chief of the Ottawas, the vain and cunning "Matchikuis," Sinclair gave the title of General, with the privilege of wearing the Red Coat and Epaulets of his office.

St. Louis was the objective of the troops and war parties under Captain Emanuel Hesse. St. Louis at that time contained a population of about 800 inhabitants, most of them French, but many families allied by marriage with the Spanish, much the same as in New Orleans. It was the leading fur center of the valley, its traders being familiar with the whole Missouri River territory as well as the Illinois and the upper

Mississippi. The people of the town were on friendly terms with many of the tribes, and the Indians entered or left the fortification at will through the open gateway.

To Sinclair, the fall of St. Louis appeared a certainty. "The reduction of Pencour [St. Louis] by surprise, from the ease of admission of Indians at that place, and from assault from those without, having for its defense, as reported, only twenty men and twenty brass cannon, will be less difficult than holding it afterwards."[13] Leyba, likewise, felt that successful defense of the town was hopeless and entertained no illusions. But St. Louis did not fall. How to explain it? Sinclair blamed his failure on the treachery of two men, an interpreter for the Sacs and Foxes, Ducharme by name, who evidently "misinterpreted" and a half-breed, Calvé, Ducharme's trader partner.

Gálvez, according to Sinclair, could have stormed the fort successfully at the head of the Sacs and Outagomies. Instead he had retreated too early in the battle, creating confusion and causing the Winnebagos and Sioux, who were to have stormed the Spanish lines, to become suspicious of being caught between two fires.[14] Whether or not Calvé and Ducharme were traitors to the English, it was not treason alone which explains the salvation of St. Louis. The town was saved by the fact that it received intelligence of the approaching British in time to strengthen the defense. The inhabitants were accustomed to coming and going among the tribes and to visiting the isolated cabins of the few settlers in the area. News travelled fast. So it came about that word of the approaching English-Indian column reached Leyba eleven days before the 300 English and their 900 Indian allies could reach the fort.

Preparations for resistance were undertaken at once. A courier sped to St. Genevieve urging the commander of that post, Cartabona, to march at once for St. Louis. New entrenchments were thrown up and a tower to hold five cannon was erected. Word went out summoning all settlers in the vicinity to report at the fort. Leyba mustered all-told 25 regulars and 289 men from St. Louis and the villages in the area. Three days before the attack Leyba received warning that the enemy was then only twenty leagues from the fort. When the British and Indians came within view of the town they struck swiftly. Within full sight of the palisades, a number of farmers and their slaves, who had ignored the warning to seek safety within the walls, were attacked as they worked in the fields, scalped and butchered.

Leyba's small force fought desperately against the attackers on the 26th of May 1780, and succeeded in beating them off.[15] Sinclair was disgusted with the traders in his war party, whose lukewarm disposition for fighting contrasted with the vigor and zest displayed by the garrison and he threatened to cut them off from all further trading privileges. It was an empty threat because the continued control of trade remained with the victorious Spaniards. Clark arrived in Cahokia too late to take part in the defense of St. Louis but was convinced that his presence in the former had been instrumental in sending the British scurrying back north in defeat. Sinclair never once mentioned Clark in explaining away the failure of his powerful force.[16] But he did list as one of his most important handicaps that he was "unsupported . . . by any other against New Orleans," proceeding to mention "the advances made by the enemy on the Mississippi." This could be taken as an oblique acknowledgement of the importance of Gálvez's campaign against the lower river forts.[17]

Clark, like Leyba, successfully beat off the prong of Sinclair's army thrust out against him. Spanish aid from New Orleans and St. Louis alone permitted him to proceed forthwith on a campaign of retaliation. Clark had consulted with Leyba at an earlier period relative to an expedition against the Indians of the Northwest. Now they could and did translate their plan into action. Leyba agreed to supply Clark with 100 men, completely equipped with boats, arms, artillery and provisions. One of Clark's officers, Colonel Montgomery was placed in command of the joint expedition. At the head of some 300 men he was to strike against the Sac and Fox Indians. As it happened, the enterprise accomplished its purpose without bloodshed. Montgomery proceeded up the Illinois River to Peoria then moved overland to Rock River. When the Indians became aware of his advance they took flight, abandoning their villages and supplies which the invaders put to the torch. Then Montgomery retraced his way. The successful defense of St. Louis and the chastisement inflicted by Montgomery were sufficient to bring the Sac and Fox tribes to a more friendly attitude toward the Spaniards.[18]

Early in 1781 a new commander, Cruzat, succeeded Leyba at St. Louis. Cruzat had absorbed the lesson of Gálvez's campaign on the lower river, that attack is the best form of defense. He decided to protect St. Louis against a possible second attack from the North by making an assault on the point from which supplies for such a raid would come. This point was St. Joseph, an English post on Lake Michigan. He despatched very secretly a small party of Spanish troops and Indians under the command of Captain Eugene Pourre. He wrote Gálvez, by way of explanation:

> "The urging of the Indians, Heturno and Naguiquen [his two chief Indian advisers] to persuade me to make an expedition against the English at Fort St. Joseph . . . forces me to send a detachment of sixty men. . . . It was absolutely necessary to take these measures as I shall explain to you."[19]

First of all, he wrote on, if he had refused to accept the advice of the two chiefs, they might be inclined to go over to the English. The capture of St. Joseph would intimidate the Indians as yet undecided whom to join and whom the English would try to enlist in an expedition against St. Louis in the coming spring. Finally, it would be sound strategy to stir up hostilities against the pro-English Indians of that region.[20]

St. Joseph fell to a surprise attack on the morning of February 12, 1781. The English garrison were made prisoners of war. Everything not divided between the local Indians and those with the party was burned. Captain Pourre took formal possession of the post by proclamation in the name of the King of Spain. The same morning he withdrew with his followers. The proclamation has its importance because it became the basis of the Spanish claim for territory east of the Mississippi in the negotiations for peace between England and Spain. It read:

"I annex and incorporate with the domains of his Very Catholic Majesty, the King of Spain, my master, from now on and forever, this post of St. Joseph and its dependencies, with the river of the same name, and that the Islinois which flows into the Missicipy [sic] River . . ."[21]

FOOTNOTES

[1]Gálvez to Navarro, September 18, 1779; A.G.I., Cuba, 1232, no. 208.

[2]Pollock to the Inhabitants of Natchez District, September 8, 1779; A.G.I., Cuba, 192, copy. Gálvez to José de Gálvez, October 16, 1779, Report (Copy of original certificate, Mexico, November 20, 1779); A.G.S., Guerra Moderna, Legajo 6912.

[3]King Carlos III to Gálvez, January 10, 1780; A.G.S., Guerra Moderna, Legajo 6912.

[4]Piernas to Gálvez, enclosing Pickles' report, September 12, 1779; A.G.S., Guerra Moderna, Legajo 6912. Also in A.G.I., Cuba, 192.

[5]Gálvez to Pollock, October 15, 1779; A.G.I., Cuba, 192.

[6]Pickles to Piernas, September 14, 1779; *ibid.* Quoted in Caughey, *Gálvez*, p. 160.

[7]Bernardo de Gálvez to José de Gálvez, November 18, 1779; A.G.S., Guerra Moderna, Legajo 6912.

[8]Dickson to Campbell, October 20, 1779; A.G.I., 146, 2-7. Bernardo de Gálvez to José de Gálvez, October 16, 1779; A.G.S., Guerra Moderna, Legajo 6912.

[9]Leyba to Gálvez, February 5, 1779; A.G.I., Cuba, I. Also Bernardo de Gálvez to José de Gálvez; A.G.S., Guerra Moderna, Legajo 6912, Folio 6 (Plans for the River and Mobile).

[10]Sinclair Report, *George Rogers Clark Papers, 1771-1781*, James, ed., *op. cit.*, p. CXXVIII, no. 3. Cited in Caughey, *Gálvez*, p. 164.

[11]*Michigan Pioneer and Historical Collections*, (Lansing, Michigan, 1872), X, 395. Cited in James, *Pollock*, pp. 206-207.

[12]"Papers from the Canadian Archives, 1778-1783," *Collections of the Wisconsin State Historical Society*, (Madison, 1855-   ) XI, 151. Cited in James, *Pollock*, p. 207.

[13]Sinclair to Haldiman, February 15, 1780, *Collections of the Wisconsin State Historical Society*, XI, 148. Cited in *ibid.*

[14]Sinclair to Haldiman, July 8, 1780, *Collections of the Wisconsin State Historical Society*, XI, 155-157. Cited in *ibid.*

[15]Leyba to Gálvez, June 8, 1780; A.G.I., Cuba, 193.

[16]Sinclair to Haldiman, July 8, 1780, *Collections of the Wisconsin State Historical Society*, XI, 155-157. Cited in Caughey, *Gálvez*, p. 166.

[17]Sinclair to Haldiman, July 8, 1780. *Ibid.*

[18]Cruzat to Gálvez, November 14, 1780; A.G.S., Guerra Moderna, Legajo 6912, Folio 8. (Gálvez to José de Gálvez asking for aid in the country of the Choctaws). Same letter in Bancroft Library, *Louisiana Collection*. Cited in Caughey, *Gálvez*, p. 166.

[19]Cruzat to Gálvez, January 10, 1781; A.G.S., Guerra Moderna, Legajo 6912, Folio 10. Also in B.L., *Louisiana Collection*. Cited in Caughey, *Gálvez*, p. 167.

[20]Cruzat to Gálvez, January 10, 1781; B.L., *Louisiana Collection*. Cited in *ibid.*

[21]Pourre, Proclamation, February 12, 1781, B.L., *Louisiana Collection*. Cited in Caughey, *Gálvez*, p. 169.

CHAPTER XVI

1.

The expedition against St. Louis and St. Joseph was a Spanish venture, Spanish financed. The campaigns of Clark and his officers were financed through the agency of Oliver Pollock in New Orleans. When Pollock's personal resources were no longer available he drew upon the Continental Congress through a French firm in Nantes only to have his bills returned to him for payment, or discounted to conform to the rate continental currency bore to that of France. The currency issued by the Congress had reached New Orleans by the summer of 1780; it was completely worthless in trade and the holders had no recourse but to offer it to Pollock as the official agent of the Congress. Pollock was forced into the position of borrowing on his home and his plantations, selling his Negroes and petitioning every friend with whom he did business for more time. Gálvez supplied as much in material supplies as could safely be risked on the river at this time. Leyba outfitted Montgomery. Pollock wrote the Congress of the situation of its currency: "In order to support its credit which would have been instantly ruined by a refusal on my part, not only at New Orleans, but everywhere on or near the river, I received and exchanged it for specie." But the supply of specie was not endless and Pollock could not continue to meet the demands of his hungry creditor with promises of future payment. Little specie was available for trade when the population was still struggling to recover from the effects of the hurricane and the specie in the provincial treasury was going into the supplies which were needed for maintaining the war against England. Pollock got neither help out of his predicament from the Congress nor acknowledgement of his letters. But he was nonetheless scrupulous in keeping the Congress informed of the help Gálvez had given him and the American cause. With no expectation of receiving the courtesy of a reply he wrote on one occasion:

"I must then have sunk under the load if I had not prevailed on Don Bernardo de Otter Contador of Louisiana [Governor Gálvez] to lend me 40,000 dollars. My application to him was for money out of the Publick Treasury, but having no orders to warrant it, that could not be done. His friendship however for me, and his regard for the interest of the United States, induced him to make the advance from his own private fortune."[1]

At another time, writing the Congress about the sale of his possessions to cover bills for supplies to the Continental Army and to Clark in Illinois, he ended on this note: "This has laid me under more obligations to this Governor than I would wish and from the *little notice you have hitherto taken* of *his* and *my letters* [author's underlining], has rendered my obligations still more disagreeable."

While Clark was engaged in an expedition against the Shawnees, Fort Jefferson below St. Louis, manned at the time by Americans also, came under siege and strong attack from the Chickasaws and Choctaws. Gálvez had previously written to the Minister of War in Madrid urgently requesting funds and additional troops to build an adequate defense against the powerful Choctaws. Up to this moment he had received no answer. During the remaining months of 1780, Fort Jefferson came repeatedly under attack and the testimony of American officers was that it could not have been saved had it not been for the timely aid given by Pollock. Colonel Montgomery wrote to Governor Thomas Jefferson of Virginia:

> ". . . had it not been for the Assistance of Mr. Oliver Pollock, with whom I am now present, we must undoubtedly evacuate that Post. He well knowing that Govern't having to heart the Setling [sic] a place of so much Consequence and from those good principles he hath always Shewn sent us Relief from time to time both Ammunition and Goods in our Greatest distresses until he has sent his All & is Still Striving to send us further supplies. I am fully Convinced it will not be in his Power to Send further Supplies without Relief. I am in hopes you will take the Speediest Method of Sending him remittances or providing a Fund for our future Relief, as I can see no other Method for the Preservation of the Illinois Country."[2]

Pollock had already pleaded with both Virginia and the Continental Congress for reimbursement for the loan of $74,087 made to him by Governor Gálvez for supplies to aid Clark's earlier campaign in the Illinois country, when Vincennes had been captured. On March 13, 1780, of a harsh and bitter winter, the people of Vincennes were forced to plead with Governor Cruzat at St. Louis to come to their aid with provisions and send them armed protection against the constantly recurring danger of Indian raids.

These Frenchmen had taken the oath of allegiance to the United States when Clark took the post. But the gravity of their plight, in 1780, was offered to Cruzat as their excuse for appealing to him as "good citizens of France" and allies of Spain for Spanish protection and supplies. Cruzat replied with perfect correctness that he considered the people of Vincennes to be subjects of the United States, by right of conquest and that their relief should therefore come from their superiors in Illinois.

Fort Jefferson again sought aid from Pollock in 1781, and received it along with further substantial supplies of medicines and clothing from the Spanish posts along the Mississippi.

Any military summation of this crucial time must take into consideration the significance of the frontier country defended by Clark and his men. Had Sinclair's attempt against Clark in Kentucky and along the Illinois been successful, the famous frontier "Backwater Men," led by Isaac Shelby and John Sevier, would have been forced to fight with their backs to the wall of the Appalachian mountains for the survival of the new settlements in the west, with all the terrible consequences of a war waged against an overwhelming force of British and Indians that would have left the whole frontier a bloody shambles.

It has been asserted, and with some show of reason, that had Sinclair's ambitious program been carried out, the battle of King's Mountain would never have been fought, the turning of the tide of war in the South, by the defeat of Cornwallis, would never have come about, the Carolinas and Georgia would have been lost to the confederation of states. The far-reaching effects of Governor Gálvez's quick and successful campaign along the lower-river posts begins to appear in proper perspective when it is seen with what overwhelming power the English would have entered into the conflict against South Carolina, Georgia and the frontier along the lower river.

2.

From the beginning of Gálvez's expedition against the English forts on the lower river, his mixed troops had come to respect a commander who not only attained his objective but also avoided unnecessary casualties. His impetuosity and his youth alike brought him at times into direct opposition with his seniors in Havana and the officers of the Caribbean Command of the royal navy. But in actual warfare he had already proved the best field tactician of them all. His thoughtful kindness to the families of his officers and men created a warm and indissoluble bond between them and himself. Practically every man who served under him whether in Louisiana or in West Florida or later in Mexico became personally known to him. His recommendations for personal courage or capacity had the solid basis of that close acquaintance.

When Major-General Campbell, who commanded the British troops stationed at Pensacola, first heard of the fall of Manchac and

Baton Rouge, he refused to believe that the news could be true. But a second despatch from the same quarter confirmed the story and he decided to launch a counterattack. He reconsidered when he found that he had insufficient transport for such an enterprise. Instead of taking the offensive he elected to reinforce Pensacola and Mobile, knowing well that they would be the objective of Spain if she were to win control of the Gulf and the Mississippi. Even as far away as St. Augustine there was a feeling of anxiety. The commander there earnestly begged General Clinton for reinforcements as against a possible attack from Havana.

Any intelligent British officer could have guessed correctly the orders which Gálvez received from King Carlos, in a despatch from Navarro in Havana:

> "The King has determined that the principal object of his forces in America during the war against the English shall be to expel them from the Gulf of Mexico and the Banks of the Mississippi where their establishments are so prejudicial to our commerce and also to the security of our more valuable possessions."[3]

The despatch was sent from Cuba in the summer of 1779. Fulfillment had already begun. It remained to expel the British from the Gulf. The King's orders also placed the supreme military responsibility for carrying out the program in the hands of Gálvez, advancing the young Governor of Louisiana over officers who were his seniors at Havana. To lessen the sting, the King went to the trouble of explaining the reasons for his choice; Gálvez had worked out a plan of campaign; he knew the terrain where the fighting must take place; he had been in direct communication with the enemy on several occasions; he had cooperated with the people of Georgia; he had won the approbation of the American Congress; he had gained the friendship of the Choctaws and a number of the Creeks. The King had no need to comment that this was an impressive list of qualifications.

The strategy which Gálvez employed against the Gulf ports was based upon the intelligence reports of Major Jacinto Panis. With the successful river campaign behind him, he was able to proceed with undivided attention on the preparations for his second campaign. During the latter part of 1779, he began to assemble the necessary materiel. With the help of Gayarré, his Commissary for War, he refitted the British boats he had captured as transports. He found it necessary to ask Havana for aid. He could not attack places as strongly fortified as Mobile and Pensacola if his troops had to depend on the slim supplies available in New Orleans.

Unfortunately the two officers in Havana, Navarro and Huet, who commanded respectively the military and naval forces stationed there, were confirmed in their belief that Pensacola could be reduced to rubble by naval bombardment from the sea and without loss of life.

They felt sure that once Pensacola had fallen, Mobile and the other posts would fall automatically in the same manner. They were chagrined when Gálvez informed them that their information was faulty concerning the naval defenses at Pensacola, where there actually were thirty-six and thirty-two pounders both in front of the town and at the harbor entrance, these guns being capable of sinking the Spanish ships before they could move into action. Gálvez maintained that the only way to take the town was to make use of an army. He added his opinion that they should attack Mobile first because it was the source of supplies for Pensacola and the center from which the British exercised their control over the Indians.[4]

The leaders in Havana continued to show great reluctance in supplying the troops and ships which Gálvez required and letters passed back and forth between New Orleans and Havana which did nothing to further the business. Carlos III became "mucho disgusto" with the lack of daring at Havana. Knowledge of his displeasure did not serve to increase cordiality between Gálvez and his correspondents in Cuba. Desperate for help, and losing patience, Gálvez finally sent Colonel Estevan Miro to plead with Captain General Navarro, in person, for "2000 men to be sent to Mobile and Pensacola by the middle of Feb. at the latest."[5]

Miro reached Havana January 24, 1780. There followed a long and discouraging period of frustration and argument. In the end the Captain-General was prevailed upon to release to Gálvez 567 men of the Regiment of Navarro. This small contingent sailed February 10, for Mobile. But they were caught in a gale of hurricane force almost immediately, so that it was well after the middle of February, the deadline set by Gálvez for a juncture with him before Mobile, that the convoy reached the rendezvous.

Meanwhile, at New Orleans Gálvez waited until after Christmas and the "Año nuevo" celebrations before fixing on the 11th of January, for the departure of his army. There was happy feasting and much gayety throughout the Creole city on "Tres Reyes" day, [the Three Kings] the 6th of January, when all the officers and men celebrated with their families and gave and received presents. They visited joyously from house to house, drinking toast after toast to the success of the coming campaign, while their young women looked with proud but misty eyes upon their husbands and lovers.

On the 11th, the population clustered near the wharf to watch as Gálvez reviewed the embarking expedition: 43 men of the Regiment of Principe of the Second Batallion of Spain; 50 of the fixed Regiment of Havana; 144 of the fixed Regiment of Louisiana; 14 artillerymen,

26 carabiniers, 323 white militiamen, 107 free blacks and mulattoes, 24 slaves and 26 Anglo-American auxiliaries — 754 men. The fleet comprised one merchantman frigate, four settees, one packet boat, two brigs, the frigate of war *Volante*, the galliot *Valenzuela*, the brig *Galvez*, armed as a corsair, and the King's brig *Kaulican*.[6]

The fleet descended the river slowly, arriving at its mouth on the 18th. Captain Riaño of the *Kaulican* was sent ahead to make soundings in the southwest pass and returned within two days with the report that there was no more water there than in the east pass. To get through, a few of the vessels had to be lightened. It became necessary to wait until the twenty-eighth for good weather and then all the vessels, with the exception of the *Kaulican*, sailed out upon the Gulf. The latter, due to a failure of the wind, was delayed until the fourth of February.

The entire fleet lay becalmed until the sixth when a strong southwest wind sprang up which carried them along a distance of twenty leagues. Wind, rain, thunder, lightning and hail assailed the convoy during that day and a whirlwind at half-past ten that night. But the ships were not scattered; from the *Galvez* the next morning the commander was able to sight every unit. The following day, however, he could see only four, and one of these was taking water. The next morning the vessels in the van sighted the Perdido River and they turned west toward Mobile. Other ships appeared on the horizon the same evening but fell into a calm before they could rejoin the leaders.

Some time during the night, Riaño, while making a reconnaissance in an armed launch, made out the outlines of an English vessel just inside Mobile Bay. He captured five men of its crew, with the second officer, as they were pulling away from it in a skiff. The prisoners described the ship as a merchant frigate from Pensacola, mounting sixteen guns but with a crew of only twenty men to manage the vessel and handle the guns. Riaño returned immediately to seize it but his galliot ran aground three times. After the third attempt he was forced to give up. On the tenth day, a strong southwest wind, kicking up a heavy sea, determined Gálvez to make for the shelter of the bay. The *Volante* led the way, followed by the *Galvez*. Both vessels went hard aground on the treacherous bar at the entrance. By strenuous efforts the *Galvez* floated free at one o'clock in the morning but she had been badly "maltreated" by the pounding she had taken during the twelve hours she was stuck fast and was taking nine inches of water an hour. The *Volante* and two other ships of the convoy remained firmly grounded on the sandbar.

The eleventh day was too stormy to permit work at freeing these vessels, and on the twelfth, part of the troops could be landed from the sloops that had entered the bay without mishap. Under the direction of St. Maxent, soldiers and sailors were removed from the ships on the bar with the result that the two smaller ships could be worked clear. Hope revived that the *Volante,* too, could be floated free. On the thirteenth day all the laggard ships put in an appearance, expecting the *Kaulican.* Because they had lost their anchors, they were ordered to enter the bay. Two of them crossed the bar safely but the hospital ship was grounded. Taking off men and supplies, and trying to save the stranded vessels, involved more hard work. The English vessel, whose crew had all become prisoners, and the *Volante* were left reluctantly to their fate.

Temporary camp had been set up at Mobile Point. The outlook was discouraging. Weather continued to be the implacable foe of Gálvez. However, his officers and men remained in good spirits and busied themselves with making scaling ladders for use against the high walls of Fort Charlotte. For this purpose they salvaged timber from the abandoned vessels. Gálvez, carefully estimating the losses he had sustained from bad weather, found that his shipwrecks had cost him a great loss in supplies and artillery. He had some 800 men but the dangerous struggle against the sea had put them under great strain. There was no idea, however, of giving up the campaign and retreating. On the contrary, in characteristic manner, Gálvez prepared for attack.

His first move was to place the guns salvaged from *Volante* on the point which commanded the entrance to the bay, his next, to reembark all but the men who manned these guns, and move them up the bay toward the town of Mobile. At this very moment a small ship from Havana sailed into the bay bearing news that reinforcements were on the way. February 20, five ships bearing these reinforcements appeared outside the bay. Two days later, two of the four, having lost their anchors, sailed into the bay, making the treacherous crossing of the bar without trouble in the face of the gaping and astonished troops.

Gálvez moved his men steadily forward toward their objective. By the 25th of February, he was at Dog River, three leagues from Mobile, where he took up headquarters in the house of M. Orbane Demouy, a Frenchman. During the 26th and 27th, more men were landed and a bombardment of the fort was begun from the *Valenzuela's* twenty-four pounder. Gálvez was searching for a good landing-place to bring his artillery off. On the 28th, the troops, advancing across the Dog River, reached a point within two thousand "varas" of the fort. On the 29th, a scouting party of four companies faced enemy fire for the first time when they were greeted with cannon balls and grapeshot, a few of which ripped through the rigging of the *Valenzuela.*

3.

March 1, marked the beginning of one of the most chivalrous ex-changes of correspondence between warring commanders which is recorded to have taken place on the soil of America. It sounds strangely anachronistic in an age when war is waged impersonally and when the distinction between combatants and noncombatants has vir-tually ceased to exist. The exchange began with a polite letter from Gálvez, which his aide-de-camp, Don Francisco Bouligny, delivered to Captain Elias Durnford, the English commander, demanding the sur-render of Fort Charlotte. Durnford's answer was a refusal on the ground that he had the advantage of position and honor forbade a sur-render without resistance. In fact, the garrison believed at this mo-ment that Gálvez had lost seven-hundred men in the shipwrecks. Durnford knew this to be false from an English deserter and a prisoner taken by his men.

Durnford wrote to his senior at Pensacola, General Campbell, that he had derived great pleasure from the visit of Bouligny, an old friend; they had dined together and drunk a "cheerful glass" to the health of their sovereigns and mutual friends. Bouligny, he related, had con-fessed freely that the shipwrecks had caused great damage, but blandly denied any loss of life. He had said quite frankly that the Spanish army numbered some 2500 men. Durnford went on to say that, having been previously informed by trusty Indian scouts that the Spanish forces were largely composed of Negroes and Mulattoes, he had accepted the information volunteered by his friend with equanimity because he considered the statement was only a natural "exaggeration" by a loyal officer. Bouligny had affirmed that the *Valenzuela* had been "just hit." Durnford's conviction was that she had been "well mauled."[7]

The old friends, though national enemies, conversed graciously, dis-cussed mutual acquaintances, inquired concerning family interests, the state of the country and the war until Bouligny took polite and for-mal leave and returned to his own camp to report Durnford's message to Gálvez. As for Durnford: "As soon as Colonel Bouligny left me I drew up my Garrison in the square, read to them Don Gálvez' sum-mons, and then told them that if any man among them was afraid to stand by me, that I should open the gate and he should freely pass. This had the desired effect, and not a man moved. I then read to them my answer to the summons, in which they all joined in three cheers and then went to our necessary work like good men."[8]

A few days later, Durnford sent his foe a handsome present of a dozen bottles of wine, a dozen chickens, a dozen loaves of fresh bread and a mutton. Along with these he sent other provisions which he asked might be turned over to the wife and child of Sergeant Gun and to Charles Stuart, all of whom were prisoners in the Spanish camp. Gálvez responded to Durnford's gesture immediately with the gift of a case of Bordeaux wine, another of good Spanish wine, a box of citrons and oranges, a box of tea biscuits and corncakes and a box of cigars, at the same time assuring the English commander that all prisoners were being well taken care of. But, said Gálvez, he deeply regretted the necessity of introducing into his message "a small reproach." He elaborated:

> "Fortresses are constructed solely to defend towns, but you are commencing to destroy the town in favor of a fortress incapable of defense."

For the sake of the poor citizens of Mobile, he indicated his willingness to promise not to establish any batteries behind private houses if Durnford would forego his plan of burning houses in the town which were strategically located. He would spare the town by attacking the fort from another quarter if no measures were taken to strengthen the fort's defense on that side. Thus, his offer prescribed two conditions.[9]

So the chivalrous correspondence went on with the greatest punctiliousness. Durnford protested that he had meant no discourtesy in sending gifts to the prisoners, that he was sure they were receiving the best possible treatment while they remained in the Spanish camp. He thanked Gálvez for his magnanimous treatment of two townsmen whom Gálvez had released on their simple word of honor. When he came to the subject of the houses surrounding the fort, he acknowledged that the fort had been badly placed, but said that it was beyond his power to remedy this situation and as commander of the fort it was his duty to protect it. The exigencies of his defense compelled him to burn down surrounding houses. His distress over such wanton destruction was no less than Gálvez's. He assured the Governor that few houses had been burned for which his orders were responsible. To the Spanish commander, he conveyed the grateful thanks of the townspeople for his generosity in offering to attack from the other side of town so that the remaining homes might be spared. He then added his opinion, as a military man, that there was sufficient expanse of terrain there from which the Spanish could mount their assault on the fort.[10] This is a truly extraordinary remark to come from a besieged commander to the officer who was about to attack him.

Gálvez had used the phrase "I would promise," not "I do promise" in the offer to Durnford. He was prepared to forego the erection of batteries sheltered by private houses, provided Durnford balanced his generosity by agreeing not to open new embrasures in his fort on its vulnerable side and not to mass men and artillery there. Gálvez came to believe, from Durnford's correspondence, that the offer had been interpreted as an unconditional promise. He wrote Durnford, therefore, to maintain his honor as a soldier that he would like to know whether Durnford considered him bound by his offer. He left the implication that he would act as if his conditioned offer had been a binding promise in the event that Durnford demanded he should live up to it.

Durnford was not to be outdone in observing the code they followed in common. He wrote Gálvez that he was most deeply grateful for his humane and generous interest in the townspeople, but would under no circumstance hold him to his "promise"! He went on to say that he could not promise not to make use of his men and his batteries to the best advantage because honor demanded that he do his duty and defend the fort as long as possible.[11] On this high plane the correspondence ended and both commanders continued the work of setting up their works for attack and defense.

March 7, Gálvez intercepted a letter which carried disturbing news of an expected large reinforcement for the besieged fort from Pensacola. He warned the ship which was stationed outside the harbor to keep a sharp lookout for the approach of such a force by sea. Scouting parties went out along the trails to report any signs of an approach by land.

Durnford's works were designed to hold Fort Charlotte until help came from Pensacola. It was Gálvez's task, then, to capture it before it could be relieved. Both Gálvez and Durnford were handicapped by the dilatory and hesitant manner in which aid was given to them. Gálvez was constantly pleading during the river campaign and now again for sufficient reinforcements for his inadequate, mixed and poverty-stricken army. Durnford looked in vain for the aid he was promised from Pensacola. Yet for the moment the very promise was like an accession of strength. He wrote General Campbell: "Your great good news hath just arrived. I thank you, dear Sir, for the consolation it affords me."[12]

On the night of March 9, after Gálvez had addressed his men in a short speech, 200 armed men and 300 laborers left the camp under cover of darkness. Their mission was to open a trench. Working furiously, by ten o'clock they had dug a shelter and set up a frieze of wooden faggots to hide a battery from the enemy. Before dawn they were relieved, 150 fresh troops taking up the task of guard duty while 150 more erected the battery. At dawn the work was exposed to enemy fire from cannon, grape and shot, from carbines and muskets. Six men were killed within a short time and five wounded. Gálvez recalled the men until nightfall. But the night was stormy and nothing more could be done until the next day.

4.

At this juncture, two scouting parties returned with news that enemy parties had been seen, two English camps, one with twenty tents, the other, showing many fires, with an estimated number of some four- to six-hundred men. Gálvez made every effort at once to avoid a surprise attack from the direction from which the English were approaching the post.

In a vain attempt to draw Durnford's fire away from the newly-dug trench and from the men engaged in placing the all-important battery, he ordered a feinting action by his launches and small craft. They moved back and forth on the front facing the wharf to draw the fire in that direction. The maneuver failed, however. Bombardment continued and the work went on under harassing fire. By ten o'clock in the morning, the Spaniards had finished the desperate undertaking of placing the battery of 18-pounders and one 24-pounder. It opened up immediately and for a number of hours English and Spaniards exchanged shots in a lively duel. Spanish fire was the more effective, every shot doing damage to the parapets and embrasures of the fort. However, the English were able to run a cannon into place as soon as another was knocked out. During the day Gálvez lost four men, one dead and three wounded. At sundown, Captain Durnford, having looked in vain for help, ran up a white flag and sent out an officer to propose a cessation of hostilities.

The final terms agreed upon accorded the defenders of the fort all the honors of war. Certain guarantees were given for the safety of the townspeople. However, unlike the procedure at Baton Rouge, citizens who had borne arms were not released. They were to remain prisoners of war until Gálvez attacked Pensacola, providing the attack came within the ensuing eight months. In the contrary case, they were to be freed upon swearing not to bear arms again during the remainder of the war.[13]

It is easy to imagine the chagrin of Durnford, who was aware that aid was near at hand, and the anxiety of Gálvez, who had the same information. For Gálvez had, as yet, not taken over the fort, though the capitulation had been signed. His Indian allies had reported the presence of General Campbell in the Tensaw district with 1100 men, 2 field-pieces, a howitzer and a large body of Creeks and other Indians. The night following the surrender extra sentinels were placed about the camp and the whole army slept on its arms.

At ten o'clock on the morning of March 14, 1780, Gálvez led his exhausted troops into Fort Charlotte. The town of Mobile witnessed the lowering of the English flag. As the banner of Spain rose to the peak on the walls of the fort it marked the fall of the second strongest English post in the southeast. While the Spanish troops stood to arms, the prisoners of war marched down the breach, 13 officers, 113 soldiers, 56 sailors, 70 hunters and habitants, and 55 Negroes laid down their arms.[14] The Spanish troops continued to stand on formal parade while Gálvez addressed them, thanking them for their zealous and valorous conduct, for the initiative displayed by all, for their fortitude in face of the hardships they had endured to win the victory. He assured them of the gratitude and thanks of the King, in whose name he gave permission for the division of a third of the value of all goods taken in the fort among them.

Within the next few days, four vessels arrived from New Orleans with 30 militiamen who had been left behind for lack of transports, 26 Americans arriving with them. The Americans had started out on the King's barge, the ill-fated *Kaulican*. They had complained bitterly over the long delay at the mouth of the river saying that they had not enlisted in the King's service to be sailors and the captain had returned them to New Orleans. They now arrived by way of the lakes, in the same disgruntled frame of mind, this time because they had arrived too late for even the capitulation ceremony.

The effect of this victory was widespread. News of the fall of Mobile spread through the territory like wildfire. An English trader brought the word to Fort Pan Mure at Natchez, April 25, having travelled through the Choctaw Nation, telling the story as he went. He reported that the Choctaw warriors were already weakening in their support of the British and that the Chickasaws were believed to be wavering. These were glad tidings for Commander Delavillebeuvre at Pan Mure. He hurried off a letter the same day saying:

> "The benevolence of our Governor toward the English militiamen captured at Mobile, which the Englishman who has come from the Choctaws has made known here, seems to have satisfied the people of this vicinity . . . who accord our Governor the praise he deserves."[15]

Within a week after Durnford's capitulation, Gálvez wrote to the Minister of the Indies:

> "I have the satisfaction of relating to you how on the twelfth instant, four days after the opening of the trench, the fort of Mobile with three hundred men of the garrison who have remained prisoners of war, thirty-five cannon and eight mounted mortars, has surrendered to the forces of the King. This capture has cost us some loss and much more time than was expected, because, in addition to its being a fort presenting plenty of resistance, for four months the enemy had done nothing but fortify it, giving its parapets seven feet more thickness than they had in the time of the French. The resistance they made was vigorous, and although this alone would not fail to give sufficient merit to the capture made by troops fatigued, scantily clad, and saved from shipwreck,

there is another circumstance which I believe merits your bringing it to the consideration of His Majesty.

This circumstance is, that after the notice of our shipwreck reached Pensacola, with the exaggeration that we had lost 700 men, General Campbell resolved to leave a small garrison there and to come to attack us by land with the greater part of his forces, with the purpose of deciding here the fate of the Province. He put it into practice and came with 1100 men within nine leagues of our camp. His vanguard was in sight before we had finished opening the trenches; because, having lost most of the launches in the shipwreck, we consequently had to use those that remained to carry supplies for our subsistence and had transported munitions too slowly.

You can understand our situation, on the verge of having our food give out, with very little munitions (for the greater part was lost in the shipwreck), with 1100 men in sight from whose muskets their General had removed the flints in order to attack us with cold steel, with 300 in the fort who with those of General Campbell totalled 1400, a number equal to ours, and with the country on their side, and the protection of the fort.

The whole disagreeable prospect did not take away from our officers and troops the least part of their confidence and hope of victory. On the contrary, believing that new efforts were necessary, they persevered in their labors, opened the trench, established the battery, attacked and conquered the fort in view of the vanguard of the enemy and of General Campbell, who contented himself with observing us. For eight days he was a witness of the valor and courage of our troops, with which, having changed his mind, he broke camp to return to Pensacola with his army, from whose rear guard one of our parties took prisoner a Captain and twenty men.

I cannot give expression to the sentiments with which all the individuals of my small army saw the retreat of General Campbell without coming to grips with us, nor could we reflect without sadness that if the expedition from Havana had arrived to join with us, we could have succeeded over the English the same as at 'Saratoga'. And so that you may know whether this belief is well or ill founded, I would have you know that General Campbell set out with only enough bread for eight days and the meat which was to be found in the houses, counting on arriving at the fort before it was taken; that the road by which they were returning is seven leagues longer than the one we would have taken to cut off the retreat and block the crossing of the Perdido River, indispensable for their return to Pensacola.

I know that you will read with the same feeling with which I write the notice of what has marred an occasion which otherwise would have given us Pensacola, which would have been glorious for the nation, but at the same time I have the pleasure of assuring you that all the officers and troops desire nothing more than to continue proving to His Majesty the resolution which they have of sacrificing themselves in his service, leaving for the next occasion, for lack of time in this, the list of those who must be recommended to his royal compassion."[16]

Gálvez's achievement received prompt and generous recognition from Carlos III. The King ordered his promotion to Field Marshal, and to the supreme command of all Spanish operations in America, with the augmented title of Governor of Louisiana and Mobile. The order conferring these honors was dated June 22, 1780.[17] General Navarro was censured for his hesitancy in coming to the support of

Gálvez. Carlos III publicly eulogized his youthful Field Marshal and the proud but exacting Minister of the Indies wrote in warm terms to his brilliant and daring nephew:

> "Of a truth the capture of an important town, well fortified and defended with vigor, is an act worthy of praise; but how much more praise is due this exploit, accomplished with a meager force, just rescued from two shipwrecks, scantily supplied and oppressed by fatigue, and more so since the attack was conducted under the eyes of a superior force. . . ."[18]

This was not to be the last contribution of Bernardo de Gálvez to the course of the American Revolution. In the campaign about to open at Pensacola he would tie down British forces at a moment when affairs in the southern Colonies were going badly for the American cause.

FOOTNOTES

[1]Pollock to the President of Congress, September 18, 1782. *Pollock Letters.* Cited in James, *Pollock*, p. 214.

[2]Col. Montgomery to Governor of Virginia, January 8, 1781, *George Rogers Clark Papers, 1771-1781*, James, ed. (Coll. Ill. State Hist. Library VIII, Springfield, 1912; Virginia Series III), p. 498.

[3]José de Gálvez to Governor of Havana, August 29, 1779; A.G.I., Cuba, 2358, certified copy; A.G.S., Guerra Moderna, Legajo 6912.

[4]Gálvez to Navarro, October 16, 1779; A.G.I., Cuba, 2351, reservada, no. 228; A.G.S., Guerra Moderna, Legajo 6912, copy.

[5]Gálvez to Miro, December 31, 1779; A.G.I., Cuba 2543; A.G.S., Guerra Moderna, Legajo 6912.

[6]This, and other basic details about the battles of Mobile and Pensacola are found in Bernardo de Gálvez' "Diario . . . de la Expedicion contra Pensacola y Mobile": January 2-March 18, 1780; A.G.I., Cuba, 2351; also, from the same, Gálvez to his uncle, José de Gálvez, Havana, November 27, 1780, with additional personal notes; A.G.S., Guerra Moderna, Legajo 6912.

[7]Durnford to Campbell, March 2, 1780; *Publications of the Louisiana Historical Society*, I, Part III, p. 33.

[8]*Ibid.*, pp. 33-34.

[9]Durnford to Gálvez, March 6, 1780 sic March 5; Gálvez to Durnford, March 5, 1780, "Diario," copies; A.G.I., Cuba, 2351.

[10]Durnford to Gálvez, March 6, 1780, "Diario," copy; *ibid.*

[11]Durnford to Gálvez, March 7, 1780, "Diario," copy; *ibid.*

[12]Durnford to Gálvez, March 2, 1780, *Publications of the Louisiana Historical Society*, I, Part III, pp. 33-34.

[13]Articles of Capitulation; A.G.S., Guerra Moderna, Legajo 6912.

[14]Bernardo de Gálvez, *"Relacion de . . . Prisoneros de Guerra en el Sitio de la Mobile,"* March 20, 1780; A.G.I., Cuba, 2351; Bernardo de Gálvez to Exmo. Sr. Dn. José de Gálvez, Havana, November 27, 1780; A.G.S., Guerra Moderna, Legajo 6912.

[15]Letter of Delavillebeuvre, April 25, 1780, B.L., *Louisiana Collections*. Cited in Caughey, *Gálvez*, p. 185.

[16]Bernardo de Gálvez to José de Gálvez, March 20, 1780; A.G.I., Cuba, 2351, certified copy; also, A.G.S., Guerra Moderna, Legajo 6912.

[17]José de Gálvez to Bernardo de Gálvez, June 22, 1780; A.G.I., Santo Domingo, 2082.

[18]José de Gálvez, June 22, 1780; A.G.I., Cuba, 175.

CHAPTER XVII

1.

The action of Carlos III, in establishing a unified command under Gálvez, was a step forward. But it could not assure the latter of the loyalty of his subordinate officers or the prompt and efficient execution of his orders. It would not guarantee boldness where there was timidity. Captain-General Navarro had embarked a reinforcement of 2,065 men on February 15, 1780, for the campaign against Pensacola; but before they could sail, word had reached him that Pensacola was being strengthened by a great body of ships and troops from Jamaica. On the strength of this report he had ordered the troops to be disembarked.[1] These were the men with whose aid Gálvez believed he could have cornered General Campbell on his retreat to Pensacola and brought about the fall of that stronghold. On March 21, a second expedition sailed, only to return to Havana May 21, "without having accomplished anything because it had not appeared possible to the commander of the squadron for the vessels of war to come near enough to silence the forts which defend the said post."[2]

The reprimand administered to Navarro by the King for his dilatoriness and lack of daring had the effect of prodding him into cooperation with Gálvez. The situation was quite otherwise with the navy. The naval commander, Don Miguel de Coyochea, blandly proposed to the Junta de Guerra, after the abortive expeditions of February and March, that the proper approach to Pensacola would be by way of the Perdido River. Gálvez commented bitterly on this opinion:

> "The project you have indicated to attack Pensacola by a branch of the Perdido is impracticable. Would to God it were as you have been informed and as Don Miguel de Coyochea has explained to me but unfortunately there is a vast difference between the description and the reality."[3]

Gálvez was resolved to attack by sea. The naval officers were aroused by his eloquence to enthusiastic admiration. But they were adamant in refusing to take a squadron under the guns of "Barrancas Coloradas," the fort guarding the entrance to Pensacola Bay. So

Gálvez felt compelled to accept their decision to do nothing until the arrival of two frigates expected as a reinforcement.

While he waited, Gálvez turned his attention to the proper use of Indians by both sides in the conflict and, in correspondence with General Campbell, sought to mitigate the horrors of Indian warfare. He was disposed to limit the employment of Indians, wherever possible to scouting and carrying messages. In his orders to his Indian allies, he stated that they were to refrain from fighting except against their own natural enemies and from engaging in the gory practices against white settlers, so commonly in use by the Indian allies of the British. This stipulation forms a part of each of his treaties with the tribes. In a letter of April 9, 1780, he wrote General Campbell:

> "The Indians who support the side of the English believe that they do them a service by pillaging and destroying all the habitants of the other nation. Those who have embraced the cause of Spain imagine that for the sake of reprisal they can commit the same hostilities against the English habitants. . . . In this war, which we wage by obligation and not by hate, I hope that you will be inclined to join me in a reciprocal convention to shelter us from the horrible censure of humanity."[4]

Campbell, having by far the greater preponderance of Indian allies in the region and having spent large outlays of money to hold them to the British cause, was not disposed to be squeamish over atrocities since his defense depended chiefly upon such allies. Alexander Cameron, Campbell's liaison agent with the tribes of the area stated the case emphatically in July: "I venture to say that the possession of this place [Pensacola] is owing entirely to the great number of Indians who repaired here to assist and who waited near a month for the Spaniards. . . ." It was Cameron who stated that they were well worth the 600-pounds sterling they had cost since March, 1780, and that it was a wise investment to continue to keep them opposed to the Spaniards. There can be no doubt that Indian allies were paid and encouraged to fight for the British in any fashion they chose, without hindrance or restraint, under Campbell, Stuart and Cameron in the south as under Sir William Johnston, Hamilton and Sinclair in the north.

For a whole year following the fall of Mobile, Gálvez was balked at every turn in his plans for an attack on Pensacola. Meanwhile, since April, 1780, a large fleet carrying a formidable array of troops had been in the throes of preparation in Spain for support of his expedition. Every national facility for making war was put to the task of supplying the troops destined for America. Letters passed almost daily between the Count de O'Reilly, Inspector-General of the King's forces and José de Gálvez, then Minister of Marine and the Indies.

Numerous orders from the latter went out to Lieutenant-Colonel John Vaughn, assigned as aide-de-camp to Cagigal, commander of the crack Regiment of Hibernia, going to America. An immense amount of supplies was listed in the official correspondence of this period — weapons, clothing, medicines, rations and blankets, all allocated to the expedition to be conducted by Bernardo de Gálvez. In the archives are preserved, on page after page, the records of supplies for the fleet that was being assembled at Cadiz from every post in the nation, records of the officers and men assigned to the regiments chosen to go to the scene of conflict.

As the most promising young officers, from every great family of Spain, urgently petitioned the King for permission to join these regiments, a wave of excitement swept over Spain. Gálvez had become the symbol of all that was romantic, daring and glorious. Veteran service commanders, as well as junior officers, begged for transfer from home assignments. Costs mounted astronomically as supplies poured into Cadiz. Supplies for one regiment alone ran to $3,330 or 8,325 pesos.

One day before sailing, the evening of April 23, 1781, the squadrons from Barcelona and Malaga arrived at Cadiz in time to join the fleet. Even so, there were not enough ships to transport all the troops, horses and artillery assembled. Every ship in the fleet was dangerously overcrowded. Some regiments had to be left behind for later sailing. The hospital ship itself was crammed to suffocation with eager young troops aglow with the adventure of service in America. During the final days of the embarkation, English squadrons had been sighted cruising dangerously near the port. The ships based on Gibraltar had been alerted to intercept the two groups which came down the coast from Barcelona and Malaga. A flotilla of enemy vessels to the number of 22 ships of the line and 15 frigates was reported converging on the fleet from the southern coast of Portugal.

A foe more subtle than British men-of-war had threatened the expedition; it was an epidemic in the north which delayed the famed veteran regiments of Guadalajara and Aragon in filling their complement of men and officers. An exhausting, long overland march to the port of Cadiz further delayed their arrival so that line troops already embarked had to be redistributed in order to keep vital commands intact.

The armada, under way at last, in spite of these hazards and obstacles, met with appalling conditions during its long and violent voyage. Sickness among the overcrowded troops took a fearful toll. The terrific heat, together with turbulent seas, made a stinking hell of many vessels and forced a stop in the Canaries where hundreds of men were left. Every island port of call made drains upon the scant medicinal and food supplies. One event alone gave ground for rejoicing during the Atlantic crossing: the capture of a prize whose cargo proved to be powder and ammunition for the British forces in the south.[5]

2.

As Gálvez waited month after month for signs of activity by the Junta de Guerra in Havana, his patience became exhausted. He decided, as a last resort, to force aggressive action by going in person to Havana. On August 11, the Junta succumbed finally to his eloquence and decided to send 3800 men against Pensacola with provisions for six months. To this number were to be added 2000 more from Mexico and Campeche, with as many additional men as could be spared from Puerto Rico and Santo Domingo. Officers sitting in this important Junta were Major-General Don Diego Josef Navarro of Cuba, General Victorio de Navia, lately arrived in advance of the fleet from Cadiz along with two other officers from Spain, and Bernardo de Gálvez.[6]

Spirits in Havana soared high as the work of fitting-out the convoy progressed rapidly. On October 16, the troops sailed from Havana. Navarro had given wholehearted support to the preparations for the coming campaign. All Havana had fallen to with a will to help the popular and appealing young marshal. The name of Gálvez was on every lip and the expedition was the main topic of all the talk in the streets and in the homes of the inhabitants. Prayers were said in all the churches and every bell in the city rang out in benediction over the placid blue waters of the harbor, as the convoy sailed away to the conquest of the great English bastion of Pensacola.

The youthful leader of the expedition, pacing the deck of his ship, must have gazed out over the calm waters of the southern seas with hope and exaltation as his convoy stretched out far to the horizon. It was the glorious month of October, when seasonal disasters were considered to be well over for the year. Twice before his expeditions had been threatened by the dangers that whistled in the heart of Caribbean hurricanes, the curse of these waters in August and September. All that Gálvez needed now was smooth sailing to his goal. Then would follow a quick attack against the forts guarding the entrance of Pensacola. Two days later, on the 18th, when the fleet was well out in the Gulf of Mexico, nemesis struck for the third time, a hurricane of terrible power which raged from the 18th through the 23rd of October. Many vessels were hopelessly crippled, one was sunk without a trace. The entire convoy was scattered in all directions. Warships that attempted to stand in for Cape Françoise were dismasted, transports seeking cover were driven to Mobile, some as far as New Orleans. A great number ended up at Campeche.[7]

Gálvez worked desperately to reunite what remained of his fleet, but he faced a hopeless task. At the end of a month he returned to Havana, stunned, saddened and exhausted, but undaunted to face again the problem of gathering new supplies and troops. The aim of subduing the English at Pensacola now seemed almost unattainable. For the ardent young Field Marshal, this third and crowning disaster from the heavens must have brought his darkest hour. This was indeed an "Iron Star"! But Gálvez was a soldier of iron. He would follow his star even though heaven and hell appeared to be against him! He would never rest until the flag of Spain flew over the stronghold of Pensacola!

The disaster to the expedition gave the British commander at Pensacola a welcome reprieve. Writing in January 1781, General Campbell said he was encouraged to believe that the destruction of the Spanish fleet would now make possible the relief of some of his troops, together with the large body of Indians he had been holding all winter in the hope of recapturing Mobile. He added that he was hopeful that the Spanish forces at Mobile had not been reinforced since the disaster to the convoy.

Gálvez, after the catastrophe, was not unaware of the dangerously weak condition of Mobile but he was unable to send even the smallest aid to Ezpeleta, his commander there, although he attempted immediately to do so, until it was too late to be of help in resisting the attack of the British.

The troops General Campbell sent to recapture Mobile were among his best: Colonel von Hanxleden with 60 men of the long-suffering and bitterly complaining veteran Waldeck Regiment whose troops had been humiliated in every action against Gálvez's untrained militiamen and bore an undying grudge as a result; 100 men of the Sixtieth Regiment; 11 militia cavalrymen; approximately 250 men of the Pennsylvania and Maryland loyalists, and about 300 Indian allies.[8]

The assault on the garrison of Mobile occurred at daybreak, January 7, 1781, a Sunday. Ezpeleta's small force was taken momentarily by surprise and there were some losses before the post could rally to fight off the attackers. Action was centered on the small village of Mobile which lay across the bay from the main defenses. "Under the command of the officer in charge of guarding the approach to the town, young Ramón de Castro, Lieutenant of the Principe Regiment, the small Spanish force repelled gloriously a corps of three-hundred English veterans and three-hundred Indians who attacked them during a tempestuous night, having left their dead in the very fort into which they had begun to penetrate, the Waldeck Colonel who led the attack and who was the best officer of Pensacola, a sergeant major, an adjutant, a captain of grenadiers and sixteen men were killed in the forefront."[9]

This gallant defense of Mobile by so small a force galvanized the commanders at Havana into life and a sanguine outlook toward a new expedition against Pensacola. A small detachment of spirited, courageous men had defeated the finest troops Campbell could send against them and forced the survivors to scurry back to Pensacola, under the command of a militia officer. Ezpeleta had lost fourteen killed and twenty-three wounded, a high price for the small garrison to have paid for victory. If Campbell were to make a second attempt with the overwhelming forces at his command, the few men left to Ezpeleta would be crushed. Gálvez realized that the fall of Mobile would entail the loss of all his earlier conquests. His River Campaign would then have lost all significance. His strongest argument now for renewed efforts to organize a campaign for the capture of Pensacola was the strategic importance of Mobile, the meaning of the valiant defense which had kept it in Spanish hands.

In the despatches which he sent to the court of Spain, filled with detailed descriptions of personal heroism and extraordinary courage, is revealed the pattern of a very real democracy; the actions which are so vividly recounted were ascribed to their authors without regard to race, creed, or color and with no favoritism on account of nationality or social condition. A few individual cases illustrate the point in accordance with the prevailing Spanish military custom. Gálvez recommended for a commission in the veteran regiment of Cantabria a "Ysidro Roig," for having distinguished himself gloriously in resisting an attack in the Aldea vicinity against 200 English troops and 500 Indian allies, and being so cruelly injured that he died of his wounds while still fighting against overwhelming numbers. The commission was requested for Roig's son, then only a boy, the pay to be sent to his young widow for her use throughout her life. Dying gloriously beside Roig was Lieutenant Don Marcelino de Cordova, whose young brother, a sub-lieutenant of the cadet class, Gálvez recommended for promotion to the higher grade of his fallen brother for valorous conduct in the same action. For, Gálvez explained in his citation, the younger brother had fought madly while standing over the body of the slain elder, resisting its mutilation by the bloodthirsty savages who swarmed all about the tiny detachment of 150 men. Gálvez made an eloquent plea that the pay of the slain officer be continued and that it go to his mother whose younger sons would also, in their time, serve the King in the magnificent way of the ancient House of Cordova.

He spoke with tender solicitude for the mother, Doña Gertrudis Bruillos, widow of an earlier Captain Cordova, "dead for Spain" these many years, whose slain son's body would remain forever beside the. dark, wooded trail, in the gloom-shrouded forests of Louisiana. He begged this heroic mother and the equally courageous mother of Ysidro Roig, to be consoled by the thought of the high service their sons had rendered the nation and the exalted example given by these two men to all those who lived and fought beside them; they would never be forgotten; their names would ring always, high, clear and proud in the ears of the grateful people of Louisiana.

He asked for the grant of permanent pensions to two soldiers of the "Milicianos de la Louisiana," Juan Hebert and Maturino Landry, the first of the company of the "Costa de Iberville," the second, of the "Compañia de la Fourche de Chatimachas," both fine volunteers. They had fought for three days, had been mutilated for life and left for dead by the attacking savages who "crowded through the deep forests as numerously and as silently as the countless leaves on the trees." Their citation read: Throughout these three dreadful days and nights these two men moved about the swampy terrain as quietly as animals leaving no trace of their passing, and through their intimate knowledge of the bayous and the tortuous winding paths under the great moss-hung water oaks. Their sure-footed knowledge of wood-craft among the snake-infested deep-kneed swamp cypresses, their intimacy with the sounds of the black forests by day and night, were able to save their small unit of Milicianos who would otherwise have fallen victims to the deadly silent knives of the savages. In hand-to-hand fighting they were both badly wounded and maimed for life. Gálvez stated flatly that without their knowledge and their fearlessness in exposing themselves to every danger in that country, the battle could not have been won. He therefore recommended their promotion to the permanent grade of sergeant, with full retirement pay in that grade for life.

He asked for a pension of 380 pesos a year for Madame Borell in memory of the glorious death of Lieutenant Don Pedro Borell, also of the "Militia of Louisiana." He recommended to the attention of His Majesty, the King, Don Inriquez Desporez, a captain of the Militia Regiment of New Orleans, and asked that he be promoted to "Teniente de Infanteria" Lieutenant of Infantry, a permanent grade in the career army with the hope of a transfer to the regulars in Mexico where he could be given advanced military training. This officer deserved recognition for his courage and zeal in the battle for Mobile. Gálvez asked that pensions be given to the scouts of the Negro company. He accorded them the highest praise for their fearless action in making contacts directly with Indian allies of the English and returning with highly important information which led to the capture of valuable prisoners of war.

3.

To Chester, a prisoner of war at Mobile, he wrote proposing they agree that all free Negroes who had worked on fortifications be given papers permitting them free return to their home on either side of the river. Gálvez wanted to limit the use of the term "prisoners of war" to military personnel in the strict sense, that is, to persons who had borne arms. In a moving passage found in one of his lists of recommendations for awards, he stated, that while he carried on his own body the scars of three wounds garnered in the service of the King, he had never before witnessed such valor and tenacity, such stoic courage under unimaginable hardships, such steadiness in the face of overwhelming odds, as he had been privileged to witness with his own eyes on this frontier. He confessed that he felt humbled before men whose physical endurance, coupled with almost unquenchable gayety, often found an outlet in rollicking Creole songs, at times filling the dark forest and the winding reaches of the bayous with a singular beauty. This young Spanish Grandee had a thorough respect for the men who made up his mixed army. He had also a sense of the heights to which men of humble origin could rise in their stern, grim world of almost unearthly beauty.[10]

In his last and successful personal appeal for action before the cautious "Junta de Guerra" at Havana, Gálvez brushed all excuses for further delay aside. He answered those who posed the problem of a lack of supplies for a new expedition and those who timidly suggested that the troops who would be requisitioned were needed for the defense of the island, by quietly but firmly reminding them: that his orders were to lead an expedition against Pensacola; that troops and supplies had been sent from Spain for the furtherance of such an expedition; that the Junta either had them or they did not. On the subject of food supplies he remarked pointedly: "Either we have them or not. If we have them, it is the same to eat them here or elsewhere."[11]

His argument that the hurricane had not singled out the Spanish fleet for destruction but had hit the British forces on the seas with equal ferocity was unanswerable. It was presented with fiery eloquence and characteristic tenacity in pursuit of an objective:

> "The English, departing for Charlestown, encountered weather which scattered their squadron and drove some of the convoy as far as the very coasts of England. This is more or less what happened to us. But the English were not dismayed; they found themselves, reunited and attacked with happy results as you know. Are we not capable of so much? Has the military virtue that was

characteristic of our nation deserted us and passed to the enemy? Have we so little constancy and tenacity in the continuation of the enterprise that a single tropical storm suffices to halt us? Such will be the idea formed of us, and that a single blow has vanquished us, unless it was not thought an object of greater consequence. If this is so, I retract whatever I have said, for, occupied with the advantages of the nation, I have sacrificed my personal affairs as is my obligation. I am the first who would desist from my importunity and would see with satisfaction and without envy the glories of another, but I fear that advising a lesser program from economy and parsimony will also be useless.

Let us reflect a long time on what is to be decided. The King decreed that the theatre of war should be in America, and perhaps our compatriots in Europe with less hope of obtaining, have succeeded in conquering while we tranquilly waste time that might be employed more gloriously. At any moment peace can surprise us, and if this should happen, all the other branches of the service will rejoice in the happy hour. But we military men, whom the King, after maintaining during peace, found useless during war — with what grace can we continue to wear a sword covered with rust, which was not drawn when the occasion demanded! Protesting again that if all or any part of my application is contrary to the purpose of later orders to desist further (as I have already said), I ask that I be blamed only for an earnest desire to fulfill the first orders while I did not know the later.''[12]

All Gálvez's thinking was centered on Pensacola. His successes up to this point had been only so many advances toward that ultimate goal. But the Junta, though profoundly moved by his appeal, challenging them as patriots and as career officers to strike a blow for their King and country, remained fundamentally as timid and cautious as ever. They voted unanimously for another expedition, but they were not thinking of an expedition which would sail against Pensacola. In their minds, the expedition they authorized was to be limited in its purpose to the securing of the ground already won by reinforcing Mobile, New Orleans and the river posts.

The decision was taken in November 1780. It was not until February 13, 1781, however, that the task of preparing the expedition had been completed and Gálvez boarded his flagship, the *San Ramon*, and simultaneously assumed supreme control over all forces, naval as well as military, which had been assigned to him. The fleet was not large enough for an assault on Pensacola. But Gálvez never intended it should be used for any other purpose and he wanted his authority to be clearly understood from the start, so that any refusal to obey his orders would be a clear case of insubordination. No specific objective was mentioned in the action taken by the Junta, so that Gálvez was technically within his rights in interpreting the intentions of the Junta. Furthermore, there were the orders of the King; certainly the fall of Pensacola would be in fulfillment of the wishes of Carlos III.

The troops sailed, proud and happy to be under a leader in whom they had an abiding faith. No one but the leader knew that their destination was Pensacola. None knew that the strain under which the leader had been living was already taking its toll, that the years of life left to him were numbered. He came aboard the *San Ramon* still not fully recovered from a dangerous hemorrhage. But Gálvez was living in the exciting present, in the exhilarating atmosphere of action, as he stood on the deck of the *San Ramon* and surveyed his flotilla as it sailed out of Havana in formation: the *Santa Cecilia* leading, the *Santa Clara* bringing up the rear, the flagship *San Ramon* to windward, the *Chambequin* and the *San Pio* shepherding the transports. Within three hours, the fleet was out of sight of land.

Across the sea, the blue waters of the Gulf loomed ahead — Gálvez's last and greatest adventure. His most strategic operational gift to the cause of freedom from British control over North America was under way. England's future on the southern frontier was bound up in this venture which would yield up the final answer to the question who should control the territory from the east bank of the Mississippi to the Appalachian Mountains. This time victory sailed with Gálvez, victory after so many heartbreaks. His recompense would be a royal-worded crest as poignant as ever graced the escutcheon of a Grandee of Spain, "Yo Solo!" (I alone!) Down the centuries it would be a clarion call to the chivalry and youth of Spain, a fitting accolade for this scion of a proud house of a proud race, whose roots lay buried deep in the soil of Andalucia, whose bones were to rest forever in the soil of New Spain.

FOOTNOTES

[1]Navarro to José de Gálvez, February 26, 1780; A.G.S., Guerra Moderna, Legajo 1753, Folio 6, reservada; *Historia de la Mobila* "Internas y Gracias conceder por Ellas," Legajo 6912.

[2]Saavedra to José de Gálvez, February 16, 1781; A.G.I., 1578, no. 3; also, A.G.S., Guerra Moderna, Legajo 7303, cartas (Originals) nos. 156, 182-192.

[3]Bonet to Gálvez, March 15, 1780; A.G.I., Santo Domingo, 2543, no. 14; Gálvez to Bonet, March 22, 1780, *ibid.*, no. 16.

[4]Gálvez to Campbell, April 9, 1780; A.G.I., Santo Domingo, *ibid.*, no. 27, copy.

[5]Log of the *San Luis* and daily letters and reports from Don Josef de Solano; A.G.S., Guerra Moderna, Legajo 7303, Folios 93-169. March and April 1780; see especially Cartas 156, 159, April 23, 1780 and April 28, 1780 (Report of Strength); Cartas 176-181, Havana, August 28, 1780 (Affairs of the Fleet); Cartas 182-192 (Report of Voyage to Pensacola, listing men aboard, then reduced to 627, listing the dead 1249 from the regiments of Aragon and Guadalajara alone, listing 1013 prisoners of war); Carta, reservada, 183 (Navia to Conde de Ricla concerning troops destined for Pensacola to the order of "Mariscal del Campo Don Bernardo de Gálvez"). All Cartas originals.

[6]Junta de Guerra, Havana, August 27, 1780; A.G.I., Santo Domingo 2082.

[7]Saavedra to José de Gálvez, February 16, 1781; A.G.I., 1578, no. 3; A.G.S., Guerra Moderna, Legajo 7303, reservada, no. 192; Navia A.G.S., Guerra Moderna, Cartas 192, 193.

[8]Campbell to Henxleden, January 4, 1781; A.G.I., Cuba, 2359; also cited in Caughey, *Gálvez*, pp. 194-195.

[9]Saavedra to José de Gálvez, February 16, 1781; A.G.I., 1578, no. 3.

[10]Bernardo de Gálvez to José de Gálvez, Item "Campo de Pensacola I de Cuyo (sic) de 1781"; A.G.S., Guerra Moderna, Legajo 6912 (Años 1779-1789).

[11]Gálvez before the Junta de Guerra, Havana, June 17 and October 14, 1780; A.G.I., Santo Domingo 2083. Cited in Caughey, *Gálvez*, p. 196.

[12]Gálvez before the Junta de Guerra, Havana, November 30, 1780; *ibid*. Cited in Caughey, *Gálvez*, p. 197.

CHAPTER XVIII

1.

The blue waters of the Gulf of Mexico were at last kind to the Spanish fleet. On March 8, Gálvez sighted his first objective, the island of Santa Rosa, and immediately prepared to silence the battery on the western tip of the island. Under cover of darkness on the night of the 9th, he landed without opposition at the head of a party of grenadiers and light infantry and proceeded on foot to Siguenza Point. He found the fort there, containing three dismounted cannon, deserted. Early the next morning, he took his first prisoners, a party of nine men who had come over from the English frigate, *Port Royal*, to look after the cattle on the island. When these men failed to return to the ship, the English became alarmed and learning of the presence of the Spaniards, opened fire both from the *Port Royal* and from the fort at Barrancas Coloradas.

The first action in the siege of Pensacola was now joined. Gálvez ordered two 24-pounders and some smaller artillery to be landed with 150 campaign tents, erected a battery to bring the *Port Royal* and a second British vessel within range and forced them to withdraw from their exposed position.[1]

On the 11th, the Spanish fleet weighed anchor, preparatory to entering the bay. The captain of the *San Ramon*, which was to lead the fleet in, insisted that Gálvez, who had come aboard, return to the island. Much against his own wishes, Gálvez complied, for he wanted to make the entrance at the head of his men. He was obliged to watch the operation from shore. The *San Ramon* went aground on the first sandbar, then slowly worked herself free and returned to her former anchorage outside the bay.[2]

Gálvez was deeply concerned. He was stranded with his small force on Siguenza Point. Should rough weather overtake the fleet in its exposed situation it would be forced to sail away or risk being dashed against the shore. The commander and his men would be left without war supplies or provisions and at the mercy of the British. Two tasks were of the utmost urgency; first, the landing of sufficient supplies to give security to the troops on Santa Rosa Island; second, bringing the fleet within the shelter of the bay at the earliest possible moment. Calbo, the commander of the fleet, worked strenuously to lighten the flagship, but in spite of the removal of some two-thousand hundredweight of ballast and much valuable firewood, she could not be eased over the bar.

On the 12th, Gálvez went aboard to urge Calbo to send his frigates and transports into the bay ahead of the flagship. By so doing he would avoid the danger of blocking the entrance if the *San Ramon* again went aground. Calbo was not only adverse to the suggestion but reluctant to attempt an entrance again under the guns of Barrancas Coloradas. Feelings between the two men became tense as they argued over this vital question. Gálvez had been named supreme commander of all forces involved in the expedition. Now the senior naval officer balked at risking his ships without the certainty of being able to bring them into the bay.

Gálvez could not allow the disagreement to end with inaction. To do so would mean an end to his hopes for the capture of Pensacola. He chose to ignore Calbo and the vessels under his command and to act audaciously with only the few Louisiana ships which formed part of the expedition. These units had never taken orders from the naval command at Havana. The units thus at Gálvez's disposition were the sloop *Valenzuela,* under Captain Riaño of Mobile fame, and the brig *Galveztown.* Gálvez's desperate plan was to force an entrance into the bay with these two vessels, in the hope that his daring move would stimulate the units of Calbo's fleet to follow him. He, Gálvez, would personally take the two ships under the guns of Barrancas Coloradas.

Now, as ever the master of the dramatic gesture, he sent an officer to the flagship bearing the message to the crew:

> ". . . that a thirty-two pound shell, received in the camp, which he brought and presented, was one of those fired by the fort at the entrance, but whoever had honor and valor would follow him [Gálvez], for he was going in advance with the GALVEZTOWN to remove fear."[3]

The message did nothing to soothe the ruffled feelings of Calbo, who was standing on the deck of the flagship while it was delivered. On the contrary, his anger was aroused to such a pitch that he declared before his entire crew that Gálvez was "an audacious and unmannerly upstart, a traitor to his King and Country." He promised them to make a full report to the King of the insult offered to himself and the entire navy and concluded his tirade by expressing the choleric hope that he would have the satisfaction of personally hanging Gálvez to the yardarm.[4]

Gálvez was in too much haste to get under way to be concerned by Calbo's hostility. He hoisted the flag of a rear admiral over the *Galveztown,* ordered a salute of fifteen guns, an act of sheer bravado addressed to the army, the fleet and the enemy that there should be no doubt as to who was in charge of the operation, and ordered his tiny squadron to stand in toward the bar, with all sails set.

They came rapidly into the channel and were presently under the fire of the guns of Barrancas Coloradas, the *Galveztown*, which flew the admiral's pennant from her masthead, bearing the brunt. Through the barrage of fire, the *Galveztown* sailed calmly into the bay. Although some twenty-seven or more heavy caliber shots fell around her, she sustained no serious hit and proceeded to an anchorage under the shelter of the Spanish battery on Siguenza Point. As Gálvez was sailing in past Barrancas Coloradas to the "extraordinary applause of the army, who with continuous cheers demonstrated to the general its delight and loyalty to him," he ordered a salute of fifteen guns, loaded only with powder, to the English fort, a gallant and flamboyantly youthful gesture which added immeasurably to the delight of the troops and fanned afresh the smoldering anger of Calbo, who stood discomfited on the bridge of the *San Ramon*. It increased enormously the awesome respect of the British, sheltered behind the heavy guns of their powerful fort for they were now brought face-to-face with the defiant young commander whose name had already brought fear to Pensacola for many months.[5]

The pride of Calbo's captains was touched to the quick by Gálvez's challenging and spectacular gesture. Where this small Louisiana squadron could go, under such a heavy barrage, and under the lead of a man who knew little of naval tactics, they could go. They demanded that Calbo should order the whole fleet to weigh anchor and follow Gálvez into the bay. Calbo became even more adamant in his refusal and forbade any ship to move without his express order. That night he received a message from Gálvez, giving full details of the channel and finally yielded to the repeated pleas of his captains by agreeing to order the fleet to sail in the morning.

It was afternoon of the following day when the fleet, with the exception of the flagship, *San Ramon*, began to enter the channel. For one hour, as the ships passed under the guns of Fort Barrancas Coloradas, they were subjected to a heavy bombardment of over 140 cannon shots, but again none was damaged. While the admiral watched the action from his flagship, the irrepressible young field marshal took up a position, in his gig, in the center of the danger, to encourage and assist the fleet units. For the entire long hour, the fearless commander led a charmed life in the heart of the bombardment.[6]

This display of personal disregard for danger was the last straw for the pride of Admiral Calbo. He announced forthwith that his participation in the expedition was over, now that he had safely delivered the fleet inside the bay, and that he was returning in the *San Ramon* to

Havana. He no doubt hoped thus to be in a position to report the insulting actions of Gálvez before the doughty officer had time to make his own report of the same. Unfortunately for Calbo, his return to Havana was regarded with disfavor, his explanation that he was unable to take the *San Ramon* into Pensacola Bay only adding to his ignominy "Pobrecito! Pobrecito Calbo!" In the "Diary of the events of the Squadron"[7] (Logbook), the squabbles between the navy and the young field marshal were to fade before the greater glory of the expedition.

2.

During the days immediately following the successful entry of the fleet into the bay, Gálvez spent his time in the usual formal correspondence with the British commander of Pensacola while awaiting the additional forces which he had ordered into action from New Orleans and Mobile. On February 1, before leaving Havana, he had sent orders to Piernas at New Orleans to mobilize all available forces there, including the men who had taken part in the earlier, disastrous attempt ruined by the hurricane and the party of nearly five-hundred men, under the command of Rada, who had arrived too late to assist in the defense of Mobile. March 1, he sent orders to Ezpeleta to march at once from Mobile by way of the Perdido with all the men he could muster.[8]

General Campbell indicated his willingness to cooperate with Gálvez in saving the the town of Pensacola and proposed that both sides spare the buildings and pledge themselves to safeguard all noncombatants. The bearer of this message was Colonel Dickson, paroled since his surrender at Baton Rouge. Gálvez received him graciously and agreed at once to Campbell's terms. During the time that Dickson remained with Gálvez, an overnight delay in the writing of a formal acknowledgement and agreement, forced by a return of the illness from which Gálvez had been suffering when he sailed from Havana, Campbell burned the houses near his fort. This precipitate action, taken while his messenger was still in the Spanish camp, infuriated Gálvez who regarded it as a gross breach of faith. He told Campbell in no uncertain terms what he thought of his conduct:

> "Most Excellent Sir, My Dear Sir: At the time we are reciprocally making one another the same propositions, for both of us aimed at the conservation of goods and property of the individuals of Pensacola, at the same time, I say, the insult of burning the houses facing my camp on the other side of the bay is committed before my very eyes. This fact tells of the bad faith with which you work and write, as also the conduct observed with the people of Mobile, a great many of whom have been the victims of the horrible cruelties protected by your Ex-

cellency; all proves that your expressions are not sincere, that humanity is a phrase that although you repeat it on paper, your heart does not know, that your intentions are to gain time with which to complete the destruction of West Florida; and I, who am indignant at my own credulity and the noble manner in which it is pretended to halucinate me, must not [hear], nor do I wish to hear, other propositions than those of surrender, assuring your Excellency, that as it will not be my fault, I shall see Pensacola burn with the same indifference, as I shall see its cruel incendiaries perish upon its ashes. God keep your Excellency many years."[9]

Soon after the beginning of formal negotiations, seven men who had been made prisoners of war in the previous campaigns and released on parole, thereby enjoining themselves against taking any action on the side of the English, came out to surrender to Gálvez in accordance with their pledged word. Colonel Dickson was one of these seven. They brought with them their families, their slaves and, in the case of Dickson and one of the other officers, three servants.[10]

During the tense week while Gálvez awaited the coming of his troops from Louisiana, another incident occurred which further angered the already-aroused young field marshal. Three Spanish sailors escaped from prison in Pensacola and reported being badly mistreated by their English captors. Gálvez had always been scrupulous in his treatment of all prisoners who fell into his hands and his humaneness had been well vouched for by them after they had been freed to return to their own forces. Gálvez was now so outraged that he dismissed Campbell's representative, then in his camp, and flatly refused to listen to any further proposals.

Ezpeleta and his men arrived on the 22nd, by way of the Perdido. Gálvez took a party of 500 men across the harbor to act as guards while the weary troops rested from their arduous overland march from Mobile. On the afternoon of the 23rd, the squadron from New Orleans sailed into the bay with not a single loss from the concentrated fire of the fort. With these additions to his strength, Gálvez now commanded an army of some 3553 men.[11] But they remained scattered units until the 24th, when Gálvez united the entire force by bringing the troops from the island of Santa Rosa to the mainland. The main attack for the subjection of Pensacola was about to begin.

During March and April, the Spanish forces came into direct contact with the enemies they dreaded most, the Indian allies of the English. They paid in blood through slow attrition for advancing the main plan of occupying Pensacola and capturing its fort. Almost every tribe in the Southeast had contributed to the forces of Campbell and these warriors were ably led by either white officers or half-breed chieftains well-trained in the arts of war, and unrestrained in the practice of it according to their own savage rules.

Warriors from the Choctaws, Creeks, Seminoles and Chickasaws were all called into action for the defense of Pensacola. The British spent thousands of pounds to hold them to the cause and placed over them the shrewdest leaders ever assembled at any one point: Alexander McGillivray, Benjamin James and Alexander Fraser. (After the Revolution, these men associated themselves with the Spaniards and became valued friends in maintaining control over the tribes of the old Southwest.) Others, like James Colbert, his half-breed son and Alexander Cameron, remained through the years sworn-enemies of the Spaniards. These men were responsible for much of the British strategy in the battle for Pensacola. Had it not been for the powerful Indian allies of the British, the task of capturing Pensacola would have been much simplified, the loss of life much smaller. They initiated, successfully, scores of attacks and bloody skirmishes.

A trader in Pensacola, Farmar by name, who kept a journal, was an eyewitness of the activities of these Indians during the period of the campaign:

> "The Indians report that they killed and wounded a number of the enemy but could not get their hair . . .
> The Indians brought in with them a scalp . . .
> The Indians came about 2 o'clock and brought a great number of scalps, firelocks and bayonets . . .
> The Indians brought in a prisoner which they took close to the enemy work. It was with difficulty they gave him up . . .
> They returned in short time with ten scalps. . . ."[12]

3.

April 19, was a day of great rejoicing in the Spanish camp: a fleet of more than twenty sails was sighted off-shore which proved, upon closer view, to be the long-awaited squadron of reinforcements from the mother country under the command of Josef Solano. On board his transports were 1600 trained troops under the very capable Field Marshal Juan Manuel de Cagigal. The backbone of the finest soldiers of Spain had arrived at last, after a long and violent voyage from Cadiz to Havana and thence to the rendezvous with Gálvez. Four French frigates, carrying 725 more Spanish soldiers, formed part of the flotilla. At last Gálvez had an army capable of fighting the battle which would decide the fate of England along the southeastern frontier.

Solano was a man of very different caliber than Calbo. He had brought Spain's finest troops across the seas and he placed them immediately at the disposal of Gálvez. Cagigal, also a man of energy and courage, assumed command of his own two groups of soldiers and also the crews of Solano's ships to the number of 1350, along with the best naval gunners and equipment of the fleet. For the moment, heavy seas kept the fleet from the bay. Nevertheless, within three days almost 3675 men had been transported by launches to the camp before Pensacola, and Gálvez's forces were augmented to more than 7000.

The young Field Marshal had been slightly wounded in an Indian foray several days before the arrival of the fleet. His joy knew no bounds, now that he found himself at the head of such a formidable body of trained soldiers.[13]

He reached a decision as to the best method of reducing the powerful British stronghold after he had devoted more than an month to a minute study of the terrain and the position of the English artillery in Fort George. He refused to consider an open assault which would leave many hundreds of dead before the walls. Using his old tactics of camouflaging his artillery in covered-camouflaging trenches, he detailed hundreds of men to the task of digging a trench, almost a tunnel, from his lines to a small hill from which his artillery, once emplaced, could command the English forward redoubt. His men worked for three nights to complete the tunnel and on the night of May 1, placed a battery of six twenty-four pounders at a point where their fire would protect his engineers. Then the latter continued their digging until they reached the vulnerable Pine Hill and began at once to erect a powerful battery there.

The first battery to be set up had already taken heavy toll of the English and they reacted desperately when they discovered that another battery was being placed on Pine Hill. They laid down a terrific artillery barrage while their infantry charged under its protection to save their forward redoubt into which Spanish troops had infiltrated. The attack was successful and the Spanish troops were forced back in hot hand-to-hand fighting, bayonet to bayonet.

The gallant captain and lieutenant of the Hibernian Regiment, as well as the officers of the Regiment of Mallorca, fought like tigers in defense of the vital trench. They were captured at last, badly wounded, unable to withdraw to the first trench while guarding the guns not yet in position; but intended for holding the redoubt. The English, in turn, retired after spiking four field-pieces, taking with them the wounded Spanish officers, before Gálvez was able to get reinforcements to his badly mauled party. In this short action, 18 men were killed and 16 wounded.[14]

When Gálvez had reoccupied the hotly contested point, the battery was repaired and the Spanish laid down a continuous bombardment against the crescent-shaped wall of the fort. Colonel Ezpeleta was ordered to make the first assault against it in the early dawn hours of the 7th. As his party approached, it was forced to change direction, delaying the timetable, and dawn found them exposed to a barrage that would have again meant the loss of many men. The assault could be effective only by the element of surprise. Meanwhile the heavy bombardment continued, shell after shell cannonading into the fort as the Spanish artillerymen sought for a vital weak spot in the walls. The cannon of the British forces kept up a continuous din as Indian scouting parties scoured the outposts and trails about the camp.

Early on the morning of the 8th, a Spanish shot found its mark. The powder magazine of the crescent blew up with a mighty explosion. The mighty crescent, heart of the defense of Pensacola, was a mass of splintered and smoking ruins in a matter of seconds. Between eighty and a hundred men were blown to instant death. Cagigal hurriedly sent an urgent message to Captain Alderete, commander of a frigate, to bring the guns of his ship into action against the walls of Fort George in a powerful bombardment. Again the navy was to move reluctantly. The bombardment did not materialize.

Ezpeleta and his Lieutenant-Colonel, Giron, rushed light troops into the smoking wreck of the crescent. Howitzers and cannon from the redoubts were hurriedly brought forward and directed a heavy barrage against the center redoubt, wounding the English Lieutenant Ward, commanding that point and wounding thirty of his men so badly that many of them died before the end of the fateful day.

Gálvez now ordered a mass assault against the fort. The whole fort was now exposed to a withering fire and the fall of the bastion became only a matter of hours. Once the assault got under way the hand-to-hand fighting became a ghastly picture of smoke, confusion and death. General Campbell recognized the hopelessness of his position and at three o'clock on the afternoon of the 8th, ordered the running up of the white flag of surrender.

"In Order to prevent a further Effusion of blood, I propose to your Excellency a Cessation of Hostilities until tomorrow at noon, in which time Articles of Capitulation shall be considered of & prepared, provided your Excellency is disposed to accede to Terms honourable to the Troops under my Command, and such as may afford Safety, Security and Protection to the Inhabitants."[15]

The conference over the terms of the capitulation continued on until one o'clock in the morning of the 10th. In the end, Campbell surrendered to the young Spanish Field Marshal the entire province of West Florida, including the long-feared and powerfully placed fort at Barrancas Coloradas (the Red Cliffs). All English troops were promised the full honors of war; noncombatants were to be protected, along with all unarmed laborers; slaves were to be restored; prisoners were to be sent to any desired port, except Jamaica or St. Augustine.

In the final words of the capitulation agreement, Gálvez again demonstrated his generosity of spirit and his conception of high conduct. "The full and entire Execution of the present Capitulation shall be observed bona Fide, and where doubts shall arise not provided for in the preceding Articles it shall be understood to be the Intention of the contracting Parties that they be determined in the manner most Conformable to Humanity and Liberality of Sentiments."[16]

The formal surrender of the fort took place on the afternoon of May 10, 1781. After taking over the great fortification at Barrancas Coloradas the following day, the great and happy task of evacuating the Spanish troops to Havana began. The number of prisoners of war and the number of returning troops have been listed in the reports of Ezpeleta, Cagigal, Gálvez and the Naval Command. Gálvez's own report to his uncle, José de Gálvez, written on May 26, 1781, and later printed triumphantly in the *Gazeta de Madrid* on August 7, 1781, brought about one of the greatest waves of national pride and exultation ever to sweep the nation. At Havana the victory celebration began with the wild ringing of every church bell in the city and lasted for a full week of fiestas, in which the entire population forgot everything but the acclamation of the returning heroes. It is heart warming to imagine the bursting joy and pride of the Governor's Lady, in her house high above the Mississippi in the Creole city of New Orleans.

4.

The fall of Pensacola was a stunning blow to English prestige in North America. The Continental Congress had considered plan after plan for an attack against this powerful and strategic center which held the southern state in a grip of terror. The news of its fall to the young commander from New Orleans was the cause of joy and profound relief to the harassed armies under Washington. Since his rapid and daring attacks on the river posts and Mobile, his priceless defense of the Illinois country through his System of Supply, his defense of the upper river from St. Louis, this young Spaniard had given the most vital aid contributed by any one man to the struggling American colonies. In winning this triumphant victory over the last great British outpost, he had not only served his King to the limit of his strength, but had made to the United States the most important gift an ally could offer: the security of their southeastern and western frontiers.

Enormous supplies fell into Spanish hands with the capture of Pensacola, supplies that could not now be used against the Americans in South Carolina and Georgia. Nor could they continue to be used in arming the vast hordes of Indians, long in the pay and service of the British. They could no longer be used to supply the forts of the west and along the Mississippi. It is certain that the fort at Pensacola did not fall for lack of supplies. It also is certain, that with the conquest of the almost impregnable Fort George, the British found themselves for the first time without Indian allies to carry on further depredations against the settlers in the country.

By June 1, all the prisoners had set sail for Havana or New York in Spanish ships. Gálvez left the post soon afterward, but not until he had set up a government guaranteeing the inhabitants the same privileges they had previously enjoyed. He appointed Arturo O'Neill as the new commander of the post of Pensacola, with strict military orders concerning its defense. Having been waited upon by a delegation of the merchants of the town, who were deeply concerned as to their legal status, he at once ordered O'Neill to promulgate the Code O'Reilly which had been the basic law of Louisiana since 1769.

Gálvez had observed, with obvious satisfaction, that the defenses of Fort Barrancas Coloradas had been wholly ineffective against the entry of hostile fleets into the bay. Before he left, therefore, he ordered an engineer's survey to be made of the place and a relocation of the cannon so that entry in the bay would be closed more effectively. He urged that the improvements be made with speed, in order to avoid any chance that the fort would prove equally ineffectual in the event that the English should try to recapture the stronghold.

He gave orders that the defenses at Point Siguenza and on the beach in front of the fort were to be set up as soon as practicable. Approaching the problem of security from quite a different angle, he determined to press his advantage among the most valuable allies the British held in the southeast, the Indian tribes, led by the brilliant McGillivray and his colleagues.

He wisely did not offer them terms of peace, but summoned the heads of the clans at once to a great conference at which they would be offered all the advantages of friendship and trade. He consulted with his Indian advisers and made out a list of trade goods and supplies that might at once be put into the channels of the long-disrupted Indian trade. From the conference came a list of goods to be traded in, the price of each commodity being fixed by mutual agreement between the tribal chieftains and the Spanish Governor.[17] As a result of this wise policy, the Indians were almost at once brought to trade with the men against whom they had so long waged bitter war For the remainder of the time that Spain controlled the government of Louisiana and the frontier, the tribes never again took up arms against them. A bond of mutual respect had been formed which was to make for peace between Gálvez's young officers and officials and the Indians, lasting as long as the flag of Spain flew over the waters of the Gulf of Mexico and along the winding waters of the Mississippi.

King Carlos III gave extraordinary recognition of his pleasure over the manner in which his orders for the conduct of the war in America had been carried out. He decreed that Pensacola Bay be rechristened "Bahia de Sta. Maria de Gálvez," that the name of Fort Barrancas Coloradas be changed to "San Carlos," that Fort George be called "San Miguel." He promoted his victorious young commander to the rank of Lieutenant-General, commissioned him Governor of West Florida as well as Governor of Louisiana, specifying that his territory should be completely independent of the overall government of New Spain. Carlos further decreed that his personal salary be increased to 10,000 pesos during the war and conferred on him the title of Count.

The final and most poignant proof of the high place Bernardo de Gálvez had reached in the heart of the Spanish King and the Spanish people is best recorded in the royal order of Carlos III, forwarded to him by his uncle, José de Gálvez, on November 12, 1781:

> ". . . to perpetuate for posterity the memory of the heroic action in which you alone forced the entrance to the bay, you may place as the crest on your coat of arms the brig *Galveztown* with the motto Yo Solo."[18]

FOOTNOTES

[1]All references to the campaign will be found primarily in the Archivo del General Miranda, A.G.I., Cuba 2351 as follows: "Diario de Pensacola," 141-147; "Diario de le Occurido en la Escuadra," 150-179; "Journal of the Seige (sic) of Pensacola West Florida 1781," 179-191. Also, see A.G.S., Guerra Moderna, Legajo 7303, reservada, item no. 192; Carta 192, November 18, 1780; Carta 193, February 1781; Cartas nos. 293-312, reservadas; also Bernardo de Gálvez to Miguel Muzquiz, December, 1783 (a complete personal report from Havana on the Battle of Pensacola, disposition of troops and prisoners and including carta no. 296, reservada, a report from José Ezpeleta, Havana, March 28, 1782, on the victory celebration in Havana); Cartas nos. 299, 300; Cartas 301, 305, March 28, 1782 and May 17, 1782 (Reports of Gálvez from Guanico).

[2]"Diario de Pensacola," A.G.S., Guerra Moderna, Legajo 7303, Cartas 292-312, reservadas.

[3]*Ibid.*

[4]Bernardo de Gálvez to Miguel Muzquiz for José de Gálvez, *ibid.*

[5]Saavedra to José de Gálvez, April 7, 1781; A.G.I., 1578, no. 1; A.G.S., Guerra Moderna, Legajo 7303; also Cartas, reservadas, Legajo 7303, nos. 293-312.

[6]"Diario de Pensacola," A.G.S., Guerra Moderna, Cartas reservadas, nos. 293-312.

[7]"Diario de lo Ocurrido en la Escuadra," p. 151; A.G.S., Guerra Moderna, Legajo 7303.

[8]"Diario de Pensacola," Gálvez to Ezpeleta, March 1, 1781; A.G.S., Guerra Moderna, Legajo 6912.

[9]Gálvez to General Campbell, March, 1781; Ibid.

[10]Campbell's permit to leave Pensacola, March 23, 1781; A.G.S., Guerra Moderna,

Legajo 7303; also, A.G.I., Cuba, 188-3.

[11]Gálvez to Muzquiz from Havana, December 17, 1783 (Disposition of troops and battle plans); A.G.S., Guerra Moderna, Legajo 7303, Cartas 292-301; Saavedra to José de Gálvez, April 7, 1781; A.G.I., Legajo 1578, no. 12.

[12]Robert Farmar, "Journal of the Seige (sic) of Pensacola," pp. 23, 24, 59. Cited in Caughey, *Gálvez*, p. 207.

[13]Military affairs concerning the Pensacola expedition are the subject of *confidential letters and reports*, nos. 252-301 in A.G.S., Guerra Moderna, Legajo 7303. In Carta no. 193, February, 1781 is given the following information: the Regiments of Soria, Hibernia, Cataluna and Flandees, numbering 7704 men, sailed from Cadiz, April 28, 1780. Additional troops embarked at Campeche. After the campaign, 2944 troops were returned to Spain. In Carta no. 252 is the Report of a conference between Lt. General Cagigal and Col. Nicolas de Arrendondo and the commission of Don Josef de Ezpeleta as Brigadier and Colonel of the Regiment of Navarrato assigned to the expedition of Gálvez.

[14]A.G.S., Guerra Moderna, Legajo 7303, 252-301.

[15]Campbell to Gálvez, May 8, 1781; A.G.I., Cuba, 198; also A.G.S., Guerra Moderna, Legajo 7303.

[16]Articles of Capitulation, May 9, 1781; A.G.I., Cuba, 188-3.

[17]Miguel del Campillo, Archivo Historico Nacional, *Relaciones Diplomaticas entre España y los Estados Unidos del Norte de America*, I, Ch. 17, pp. 436-439; Legajo 3.885, exp. 22, no. 14.

[18]Royal Cedula, José de Gálvez to Bernardo de Gálvez, November 12, 1781; A.G.I., Cuba, 2359, certified copy.

Part Three

"POR LA VERDAD"

(FOR THE TRUTH)

CHAPTER XIX

1.

When the American Congress requested a report on the sum due for payment to Spain for the aid given during the war, even King Carlos III could not evaluate the amount since the aid had passed through so many hands before it reached its final destination. It was therefore to Gardoqui, who had been most intimately connected with the giving of direct help, that the Prime Minister, Floridablanca, turned for an accounting.

The request from the Prime Minister threw the conscientious Gardoqui into a state of consternation. No one in all Spain knew better than he the secret channels, the intricate maneuvering and the desperate expedients to which those who had the direction and management of grants had resorted, in times of urgency, in order to get supplies to the Americans with maximum speed. No one knew better than he what a vast amount of work would be necessary in order to coordinate the bills and evaluate the cost of such a huge outlay. He personally could vouch only for what he knew had taken place *within* Spain under his own supervision, but, knowing also the numerous ministries through which he would have to work in order to prepare an accurate report, and the secrecy under which all activities had been carried forward, he had no illusions as to the difficulties of this new task assigned him by his King and his Prime Minister. It is no wonder that the task loomed up as an almost insurmountable one. Gardoqui, far away from the official records of his own transactions, and without information concerning those sums given in the urgency of need from other points in the Spanish American dominions of Mexico, Cuba and New Orleans, meticulously set about the task of computing the total bill.

It was not until July, 1794, more than ten years after the close of the war, that Gardoqui wrote a despatch to Godoy, at that time elevated to the title of Duque de Alcúdia and Prime Minister for the new King, Carlos IV, on the subject of the debt of the United States:

"Excellency,
   On October 31st, 1792, your department asked me to give an account of the

241

indebtedness of the United States to Spain and I answered on November 2nd following, that I would order all departments under my authority [Gardoqui was then Minister de Hacienda] to give me all the data at their disposal. On the same date I addressed a private letter to you in which I stated that I presumed that there should be several documents connected with such debts in the files of the Ministry of Foreign Affairs, such papers recording a list of large amounts, either in money or in goods that had been lent by myself, and those reports will be found in the possession of that Ministry where I deposited them into the hands of the Marquis del Campo.

The amounts listed were given to the American Agents, Mr. Jay and Mr. Arthur Lee for the use of their government. Besides these I knew that the Count de Gálvez had lent them other sums and one amount, guaranteed by our own commissioners, amounted to 74,087 pesos fuertes.

Since receiving a reply to my request, in which I was informed that there were no documents relative to that debt to be found in our Treasury Secretary's office (as I feared, since all these transactions were made in the greatest secrecy), their Commissioner, Mr. William Short, has drawn several bills in my favor as repayment of the American debt to Spain; and although he has asked me for the original vouchers that his Government gave for the amount, he says, of 174,011 pesos fuertes, since I had no such document, and was waiting for the exact figures on these sums advanced by the Count de Gálvez, I have not been able to forward that document, nor even include the right and true indebtedness of his government.

But I have ordered the Exchequer to send back the corresponding receipts for the sums he has paid and these receipts will be the same as the original vouchers for which he asks, and sufficient testimony for him to prove to his Government that he has fulfilled his mission.

In this situation, as Your Excellency's letter of the 13th inst. shows clearly, it should be effectively demonstrated to them how great the benefits they have received from Spain and in order to reap all possible advantage in independent negotiation Your Excellency had expected me to be able to transfer to them the complete Memorial of their debt, as per your order to me of Oct. 31st., already mentioned. But, as I privately answered your request, the authenticated documents must be found in that Secretary's office, and I cannot add anything other than what I have answered and stated to you now.

In spite of this, for a better knowledge of these facts, and in order to afford you a clearer statement of our position in this matter, I must consider or divide into four classes, the amounts advanced to the United States:

1st. The sums given in Madrid to their Agent, Mr. Jay as they are shown in the documents I handed to the Marquis del Campo.

2nd. The sums I drew myself on Paris in favor of Commissioner Lee, and there will be justifying documents of my delivery of these to the Secretary del Campo in your own Ministry.

3rd. The cost of the many supplies sent by the firm of "Gardoqui" of Bilbao to the disposition of Congress and vouchers must be with the file of papers that surely were collected by that time concerning assistance being given.

4th. The sums anticipated in the list of the Count de Gálvez, of which I have neither sure nor accurate knowledge, but I know must by now be found in Your Excellency's Secretary's office, so I may not reasonably be expected to have sure or positive information about them.

It is quite certain that the United States gained powerful support and great advantages, since the shipments from Bilbao alone were very opportune and these advances were made in a time of high prices and great scarcity.

Although it is recognized that the corresponding payment of 5 percent interest will be a burden upon their people, we must also remember that we did them this most important service at the very same time that Spain herself was paying more than 7 percent interest on a loan that Holland had granted her.

But no one knows better than Your Excellency the enormous profits that the United States can derive from commercial intercourse with Spain because we have great demand for the products grown by these Provinces and we shall always pay for them in cash, and that is the greatest need in that Country at this time.

God preserve Your Exc long. . . .

San Ildefonso, July 21st, 1794.

Diego de Gardoqui - Duque de Alcúdia."[1]

It is all too easy to see why the great assistance given to the United States during the Revolution has long remained one of the best-kept secrets in diplomatic history when we read this painstakingly honest statement from Gardoqui to the new Prime Minister. Even the wise old merchant of Bilbao was forced to write that he could not, in all honesty, summarize the actual amount of the debt due Spain since he was unable to locate receipts for amounts of cash or goods with which he personally was familiar.

He wrote again to the Duque de Alcúdia on October 26th, 1794, relative to a debt long overdue, not due alone to Spain but to one of her tradesmen:

"United States Debit to Spain and Don Jose Toriño — credit.
Excellency,

Owing to the appeal of D. Jose Toriño, Tradesman, Madrid, explaining that Mr. Carmichael, former Agent of the United States still owes him 15,963 reales vellon from the credit against the United States, transferred by the Count de Espilly; as Mr. Carmichael is to leave Spain, Your Excellency will remember my official letter addressed to Your Secretary's office on October 31, 1792, including the said credit, and the certifying papers, in which I asked why Toriño had not yet been repaid.

As a consequence I must tell your Excellency that all my inquiries have been so far unsuccessful and Mr. Wm. Short, Commissioner of the United States has not paid any other sum than the 174,011 pesos fuertes, of which I spoke at length in my official letter of last July 21st.

However, Spain, having further legal credits due from the United States, it was impossible for me to give this money to Toriño because I had not got it.

Referring to Carmichael leaving our country, I think it would be better for him to return all the certification papers back so that Toriño will be able to negotiate the payment to himself.

As to the other point of Your Excellency's official letter in which Y. Ex. is not clear as to my report of last July 21st relating to the United States debt, and in which you made no mention of the communication sent to me by the Ministry on Nov. 7th, 1792, in reply to my private request of Nov. 2nd of that same month, for all pertinent documents that could be found there in dossiers dealing with the subjects I mentioned: I must admit that your remark is correct and I will state that my continued silence on the subject is due to the delay in my project of gathering together all possible documents about this matter in order to scrutinize them personally, as I have done with the greatest accuracy possible.

As a result of all this previous investigation, completing my report in my communication of last July 21st, I can assure Your Excellency that the Americans were given very important assistance from Spain by the Spanish Government during the years 1776, 1777 and 1778 to the enormous extent of 7,944,906 reales and 16 maravedies vellon besides 30,000 blankets sent to them when blankets were an absolute necessity, or their soldiers would have perished. In the sheet which I am enclosing with this official letter are these succors given in detail, and this is the final result of all documents sent me by Your Ministry on Nov. 7th mentioned above.

In addition to these are those supplied by the Count de Gálvez in America that were of vast importance; and that is natural since our assistance in those dominions has always been more generous.

As it is evident that the Congress has only repaid 174,011 pesos fuertes by means of Mr. Short, we must infer two consequences deserving attention:

1st. The services rendered to America by Spain have been of major importance and *perhaps they constituted the main sustainance toward the securing of the independence of the United States;* [authors italics]

2nd. These States have with us a debit of 7 millions of reales, including, as is natural, the interest. The certifying documents as to the American debt, including those showing what has been paid, are most important, and will remain with me, in case Your Excellency pleases to order me to settle that portion of the debt relating to the Spanish credit.

Referring to the debt in America, I told Your Excellency what it amounts to, as far as I know, and I am wondering if it be expedient to try and recover the 74,087 pesos fuertes guaranteed by our Agents there as well as a few other sums they owe us for other services.

I told you before that I think it only right to exact the interest due on the sums advanced because Congress is exacting them by taxes from their people toward that purpose, and if we receive interest it will be only an act of justice.

Nevertheless, as circumstances may suggest, remitting the whole debt, or a part of it, might be more valuable by way of bringing about greater advantages in other directions. Your Excellency, better than anyone else, will be able to decide that.

As for me, knowing well the American mood and system, it is necessary to be very cautious in allowing them such a concession. This is all I can say about this matter.

God preserve Your Exc. for long. . . .
San Lorenzo, October 26th, 1794.
Diego de Gardoqui - The Duque de Alcúdia"[2]

The United States paid Spain $248,098.00, in full payment of its debt.[3] This amount was based on the rate of exchange then prevailing, thirteen to seventeen years after the loans had been made. In the year 1780, within three or four years of the time the loans were made, one peso fuerte was exchangeable for forty continental paper-dollars. The banker or the mathematician will readily be able to estimate the substantial increase in the value of American currency during the twelve years which elapsed between the close of the Revolution and the final settlement in 1795. At the rate of 20 reales to one peso fuerte, the amount submitted by Gardoqui comes to something over 52,966 pesos.

If we bear in mind that Spain made these loans at a time when the peso was worth 40 continental dollars, then we arrive at a very different debt in terms of American currency, namely $2,118,640, truly an enormous sum when converted into the very stable Spanish peso. For a nation, whose only currency was in paper, that purchasing power may well have meant the difference between victory and defeat. It also puts quite a different complexion on Spanish aid when we look at the record expansion in trade and credit which permitted the United States currency to increase so vastly within twelve years.

Included with the report to Godoy on October 24th, 1794, was the following list of items gathered by Gardoqui:

"For the year 1776,

Assistance given to the United States of America through the Count of Aranda, Ambassador from Spain in Paris at that time.

Portfolio, No. 2: On June 27th the Marquis de Grimaldi remitted to him for the above purpose 1 million tournoises pounds

Idem, No. 3: On July 12th Aranda acknowledged receipt of this amount

Idem, No. 7: On September 17th report on the investment of this amount according to the plan agreed upon with the French Minister.

For the year 1777,

Idem, No. 1: On March 18th of that year Gardoqui acknowledged that in accordance with the directions he had received he had begun to remit *in goods* [author's italics] for the colonies on the vessel FABBY, commanded by Captain John Hoadge, a cargo valued at 3,000 pesos.

Idem, No. 6: On April 21st he was ordered by D. Bernardo del Campo to forward to the American Deputy of Congress, Arthur Lee, then residing in Paris. 50,000 pesos in bills of exchange.

Idem, No. 8: On the 24th of the same month he sent word to del Campo that that evening he was forwarding to Lee bills of exchange totaling 81,000 tournoises pounds.

Idem, No. 9: On the 27th of the same month he notified the Court that he was sending bills in the amount of 106,500 tournoises pounds, which, with the sum sent three days earlier, added up to 187,500 tournoises pounds.

Idem, No. 15: On May 10th and 12th Lee acknowledged receipt of these sums to Gardoqui who received the information on October 28th.

Idem, No. 12: On May 8th Gardoqui sent del Campo a list of all shipments of goods which had previously been made to the Colonies on six vessels, the FABBY mentioned above being one of these. All cargoes represented an expenditure of 946,906 reales and 16 maravides.

For the year 1778,

Portfolio, No. 1: On May 3rd del Campo ordered Gardoqui to remit again to the said Arthur Lee 50,000 pesos in bills drawn on Paris and 50,000 tournoises pounds for goods in kind, for the colonies.

Idem, No. 3: On the 11th of the same month he acknowledged having drawn bills in the sum of 22,500 tournoises pounds.

Idem, No. 5: On June 18th he reported that he had remitted bills amounting nearly to the 50,000 pesos.

Idem, No. 6: On the 20th he was advised that Lee had acknowledged receipt of bills of exchange representing 22,500 pounds.

Idem, No. 14: On August 11th Arthur Lee sent a letter from Paris dated July 30th in which he acknowledged receipt of the residue of the bills of exchange, completing payment of the 50,000 pesos.

Idem, No. 7: On June 25th Gardoqui sent to Bernardo del Campo a list of all bills he had drawn to the account of Lee, in carrying out the orders he [Gardoqui] had received.

Idem, No. 20: On October 3rd Gardoqui acknowledged having purchased goods to the value of 50,000 pesos and certified that they had been shipped to the Colonies.

Idem, No. 23: On November 6th he reported to del Campo that the American, Arthur Lee, had personally and privately ordered 30,000 blankets from him.

For the year 1779,

Portfolio, No. 1: On January 22nd and again on the 25th Gardoqui stated that Deputy Lee had asked the Court of Spain to pay for the 30,000 blankets, admitting that he had no money to pay for them.

Idem, On February 1st, del Campo answered the report above, ordering Gardoqui to inquire whether the Congress could pay for the purchase. Should the Congress declare payment was impossible, he, Gardoqui, was not to press them for this payment."

Gardoqui commented upon the foregoing data in these words:

"This is the truth concerning the American debt without a final settlement and payment for the 30,000 blankets; but, as I remember, these were paid for in good time. San Ildefonso, October 26th, 1794.

In order to be sure, Don Josef de Gardoqui and Sons, who were the shippers of all articles have been consulted as to whether the United States have paid for the said 30,000 blankets — Gardoqui." (the last note in Gardoqui's own handwriting is the notation which appears at the end of the document just quoted.)[4]

Further added to Gardoqui's report and to his detailed accounting for the aid given from Spain was the record, insofar as he knew it, which was supplied to the Congress by Spanish officials in America:

"List of assistances by way of loans or in money grants furnished at New Orleans and the Havanna to the American Colonists by order of their Governors, drawn from papers of the said Governors from the end of:

December 1776 - to June 1779

From New Orleans

On May 9th, 1778, to Mr. Oliver Pollock	6,294 pesos fuertes
On May 25th, 1778, to same	17,729 '' ''
On Aug. 5th and Sept. 12th, to same	15,948 '' ''

By letter of May, 1778 the Governor of Louisiana reported that goods sent by the Spanish to the Americans had amounted to 26,990 pesos fuertes, the goods consisting of clothing, armaments and cinchona [quinine].

From Havanna

An order was issued on March 27th, 1778, to lend up to 50,000 pesos fuertes; of this sum 14,424 pesos fuertes was to be given to D. Alexander Gillon, Rear Admiral of the South Carolina squadron of the American Fleet.

Bills were drawn upon D. Juan Miralles for this amount and he is known to have received it.

September 13th, 1780 - Gálvez.

(Although this list is dated September 13th, 1780 we [Gardoqui] insert it here because of its close connection with the preceding document in this report.)"[5]

Over a year after the foregoing information was supplied by Gardoqui, a short despatch was addressed to the "Principe de Paz," Prime Minister Godoy, Duque de Alcúdia, by William Short, the Deputy authorized by the Congress to act in the payment of the debt to Spain:

"September 13th 1795

Your Highness,

As the United States Government has ordered me to inform you of the amount of the debt due to Spain, as claimed by His Majesty's Agent, I inquired of the Finance Minister, with whom I have been treating, relative to the payment that has been made on the account of the United States.

As I failed to mention this to you in our conversation this morning I take the liberty of mentioning it now, thinking that possibly Your Highness would be pleased to get direct information from him concerning this matter. In order that you may clearly understand my Government's views in transmitting that order, I have sent to your Minister of Finance a copy of the letter, addressed to His Majesty's Agents in Philadelphia, by the Secretary of the Treasury of the United States of America on last May, 13th. [This was the first payment mentioned above by Gardoqui.]

I take this opportunity to reassure you of my highest and most sincere respect, as I have the honor. . . .

William Short to His Highness
Principe de Paz."[6]

William Short satisfactorily completed the mission he had undertaken at the behest of the Congress. Neither he, in Madrid, nor the Spanish agents, Jaudenes and Viar in Philadelphia, were the men to draw up a final treaty between the two countries. After Gardoqui returned to Spain in 1791, the United States decided to send an experienced diplomat directly to Madrid with a special mandate to draw up and sign such a treaty, acceptable to the Congress and to the Spanish Throne.

Accordingly, at Philadelphia on November the 24th, 1794, an order was drawn and sent to Thomas Pinckney, then Minister to Great Britain, detaching him from his present duties and directing him to go directly to Madrid. His credentials were authorized by Washington and Randolph, who was then Secretary of State. The result of this order was the departure of Pinckney on June 28, 1795, for Madrid, to relieve Short, who had been in Spain from February 1793.[7] On the 27th of October of the year 1795, the treaty was signed in San Lorenzo del Escorial and the long, laborious work toward the final recognition of the new nation of the United States was finished.

In this document, familiarly known to Americans as "Pinckney's Treaty," all the troublesome questions that had beset the representatives of the two countries for twelve years were finally and amicably settled. Gardoqui's original orders were partially consummated within the terms but such great concessions were made to the Americans, that one Spanish historian was to write more than a century and a half later:

> "What would they have thought? All those who had lived- from Aranda, Floridablanca, Campo . . . Count de Galvez, Miralles, Rondon, Gardoqui, Miro, Garondelet, Cespedes, Gayoso . . . and the hundreds more Spaniards of lesser destiny, who, all through the long years had fought and worked and who had through all the struggle and despair followed their vision, placing their entire strength at the service of Spain, many times without concrete orders and without means, had they seen all for which they had worked and dreamed annulled and made sterile by the flamboyant pen and the expert diplomacy of the Prince-of-Peace?"[8]

What tragic irony! The vain, arrogant, inexperienced Godoy was to pen the signature that marked the end of an era.

2.

The accounts are closed. The figures are written down in long columns listing the aid given in money or loans for the purchase of material things. They write their own, silent commentary, for behind these cold symbols is the warm reality of help freely poured out to fill a dire need.

If their story is incomplete, if it is only half-told, this is because it is not by statistics alone that a conclusion may be drawn, even though every gift were accurately recorded, every receipt vouched for, every loan paid in full. The account of Spanish aid would still remain but a half-truth because only partially told.

The archives of Seville, Madrid and Simancas are filled with thousands of documents that provide a more heart-warming tale of the ability and the personal sacrifice of such men as Gálvez in America, Aranda in Paris, and Gardoqui both in Spain and America. Therein are the evidences of deep friendships established in the heat of crisis. In these documents, we find the intangibles that form the warp and woof of the real story. When one remembers the blanket-weavers of Palencia and the wave of enthusiasm that swept that province when the news came to the pueblos of the need of Washington's freezing army, one can imagine these families, all too well acquainted with the cruel winters in northern Spain, murmuring as they wove, "Los Pobrecitos!"

We must consider the militiamen and "habitants" of Louisiana, their courage, their endurance and fortitude as they struggled through swamps, forests and raging rivers; the friendship of the Trader Vigo and of Commandant Leyba for Clark in the battle for the Illinois; the remarkable accomplishment of the people of Havana, in raising 1,500,000 pesos for Rochanbeau by public subscription in twenty-four hours, a feat of the 20th century that actually took place in the 18th. Let us remember also the close and affectionate bond between Bernardo de Gálvez and the American Oliver Pollock, which extended even to the doors of the prison in Havana when Pollock, in deepest degradation and despair, was forgotten by his own people; the quality of loyalty that could bring about the unostentatious gift of his private fortune to the American Cause by Juan de Miralles.

Let us recall that in focusing attention on Madrid, Burgos, and Paris, Philadelphia, New York, New Orleans and Havana, we should also bear in mind that other front, the sea. One of the most difficult of all intangibles to assess, the aid given by the fleet of Spain during the years 1776 to 1779, was most significant. As a deterrent to the ability of England to send troops and supplies to America almost at will, Spanish sea power enabled the revolting Colonies to gather their strength by presenting them the priceless gift of time. While forcing England to retain a sizeable part of her naval strength in home waters, it was successfully keeping German mercenaries idle in all the principal ports, where they piled up maintenance costs and created widespread bitterness among all classes of the English people. Spain's sea power also forced the English to alert and keep a substantial fleet of powerful ships in constant readiness to protect Gibraltar, if and when Spain should declare open war.

Should we need further evidence of the value of this intangible aid, we need only to remember the pledge of Franklin and Morris that, in the event that the Colonies became sunk in complete despair, there would be released the news that would give their people fresh courage and lift their hearts and minds; the news that Spain was an active though undeclared, ally. (Morale is neither bought nor sold, but it is a significant and potent force in action, whether individual or national.)

Many of the attitudes of a nation are founded upon the opinions of the few whose words become, for good or ill, the heritage of following generations. These attitudes are inevitably colored by the personality, the prejudices and the historic importance of a given writer. Whatever the reason, Spain has suffered a strange neglect and still remains, to many students of American history, our forgotten ally in the Revolution.

Over two hundred years have passed since Spain aligned herself with the Americans. It is time we should remember her help, both tangible and intangible. Let us add up the score. If we do only this we will erase from our escutcheon the blot of ingratitude toward a friend and ally.

FOOTNOTES

[1]Gardoqui to the Duke of Alcúdia, July 21, 1794; A.H.N.; Legajo 3898 bis.

[2]Gardoqui to the Duke of Alcúdia, October 26, 1794; *ibid.* despatch CLXXX (Original).

[3]Samuel Flagg Bemis, *The Diplomacy of the American Revolution*, (N.Y.), 1935, p. 92, footnote 27 and p. 93; also for detailed discussion of Spanish aid, see his *Pinckney's Treaty* (Baltimore, 1926) Appendix II. In the latter work the total amount paid is $342,120.62 ($174,011 borrowed by Jay, plus interest, paid by William Short in 1793 and $74,087, *including* interest, paid to Jaudenes and Viar in 1794).

[4]Gardoqui to the Duke of Alcúdia, October 26, 1794; A.H.N.; Legajo 3898 bis, despatch CLXXXI.

[5]Gardoqui to the Duke of Alcúdia, October 26, 1794, ibid., despatch CLXXXII, with enclosure of September 13, 1780 from Legajo 3884.

[6]William Short to the Duke of Alcúdia, September 13, 1795; *ibid.*, despatch CLXXXIII.

[7]Conrotte, *op. cit.*, p. 194 and footnote.

[8]Capillo, *op. cit.*, Nota Preliminar y Catálogo, p. C11.

Photograph of portrait of Don Bernardo de Gálvez, Governor General of Louisiana. Reproduced in Alcée Fortier, *A History of Louisiana,* Vol. II. Goupil & Co. of Paris, Manzi, Joyant & Co. Successors, 1904.

The Spanish Army in America

Julio Albi La Defensa de las Indias (1764-1799)
1987
Juan Marchena Fernandez Oficiales y Soldados
en el Ejercito de America 1983